THE HOWTH GUN-RUNNING AND
THE KILCOOLE GUN-RUNNING
1914

Originally published in 1964 by James Duffy & Co., Dublin

This edition published in 2014 by Merrion
an imprint of Irish Academic Press
8 Chapel Lane,
Sallins,
Co. Kildare,
Ireland

© This edition Merrion 2014
www.iap.ie

British Library Cataloguing in Publication Data
An entry can be found on request

ISBN 978-1-908928-65-8-(paper)
ISBN 978-1-908928-66-5 (PDF)
ISBN 978-1-908928-64-1 (EPUB)
ISBN 978-1-908928-88-7 (MOBI)

Library of Congress Cataloging-in-Publication Data
An entry can be found on request

Interior design by www.sinedesign.net
Printed in Ireland by SPRINT-print Ltd.

THE HOWTH GUN-RUNNING AND
THE KILCOOLE GUN-RUNNING
1914

RECOLLECTIONS & DOCUMENTS

EDITED BY F.X. MARTIN, O.S.A.

New Foreword by ÉAMON Ó CUÍV T.D.

New Introduction by Ruán O'Donnell
and Mícheál Ó hAodha, University of Limerick

MERRION

Contents

Part I

SOLDIERS WITHOUT ARMS

The Irish Volunteers in 1914   **1**

Part II

PLANNING THE GUN-RUNNING   17

Part III

GUNS ON THE HIGH SEAS   57

New Introduction

THE RUNNING of German guns and ammunition into Howth, County Dublin, on 26 July 1914 and Kilcoole, County Wicklow, on 1 August 1914, dramatically altered perceptions of the paramilitary threat posed by the Irish Volunteers. Founded in the Rotunda, Dublin, on 25 November 1913, the Irish Volunteers (Óglaigh na hÉireann) were conceived not simply as a counterweight to the existing and supremacist Ulster Volunteer Force but as a mass-based vehicle which the revolutionary Irish Republican Brotherhood hoped to steer into an uprising. Moderate Nationalists were on the cusp of achieving Home Rule in the autumn of 1914, although the prospect of a Dublin parliamentary forum elected on a narrow franchise did not appease the radical IRB and its Irish-American allies. However, as the UVF and right-wing elements of the British Conservative Party in opposition connived to undermine Westminster's promulgation of Home Rule, the prospect of internecine fighting in Ireland could not be ruled out in the north of the country.

Matters took a serious turn on 25 April 1914 when the UVF exploited the febrile political situation to import a substantial store of German weaponry and ammunition through the ports of Larne and Bangor. Unionism, a small minority of Irish public opinion, had localised grass roots strength in the north-east where the presence of an armed UVF element, tacitly supported by pro-Imperialist senior army officers, did not augur well for the smooth transition to devolved government. The 'conditional loyalty' observed by such persons could not countenance the principles of democracy and self-determination in Ireland.

Irish Volunteer leader Eoin MacNeill went to London on 7 May 1914 to meet John Redmond MP who was nervous that the new Nationalist force, already attracting members of his Irish Parliamentary Party, would jeopardize the enactment of the Home Rule Bill. MacNeill became convinced that Redmond would endeavour to either gain control of the Volunteers or render them inert on the political stage. A coterie of advanced Nationalists and Republicans, not least Alice Stopford Green, Roger Casement, Erskine Childers and Darrell Figgis held that Redmond, a constitutionalist in the tradition of Daniel O'Connell, would be less inclined to hijack the Volunteers if they possessed military potency.

A multi-faceted plan was then developed linking the financial resources of John Devoy and Joe McGarrity in the United States with arms-procuring missions undertaken by Darrell Figgis and The O'Rahilly in Europe. Ultimately, after several fruitless initiatives and tentative overtures, IRB leader Tom Clarke in Dublin endorsed O'Rahilly's application for Clan na Gael funding from America which netted $5,000 from Devoy. Bulmer Hobson, who straddled the secret world of Transatlantic 'Fenianism', played a central organizational role. Local funds were amassed in Britain and Ireland to enable the acquisition and shipment of German rifles and munitions. The inner circle of the grouping widened to include such diverse personalities as Mary Spring Rice, Conor O'Brien, Sir Thomas Myles and other patriotic-minded individuals united by the secular and progressive vision of Wolfe Tone.

The Westminster ban on private arms importation from 4 December 1913 complicated the situation, although various methodologies were devised in Dublin and London to maintain the absolute secrecy necessary for success. In Germany Figgis initially ordered 1,000 rifles with an option of 500 more and 45,000 rounds of ammunition; a deal which increased in scope as the circumstances of supply, transport and resources improved. After some shipping-related problems, Childers offered his 28-ton Norwegian-built yacht *Asgard* for the mission, an option not hitherto seriously considered owing to its insufficient capacity for the contraband and requisite crew of five. Support for the *Asgard* contingency was secured when Conor O'Brien undertook to bring his own *Kelpie*, a yacht of 20 tons, to embark whatever the *Asgard* could not accommodate. In what quickly became an exceptionally risk-laden plan, a further vessel, the motor-powered yacht *Chotah*, was added to the equation.

Reconnaissance identified one suitable suburban harbour, Howth, and one remote beach-landing site, Kilcoole, for the final phase of importation. Members of Na Fianna Éireann, Cumann na mBan, Irish Republican Brotherhood and Irish Volunteers acted in concert and with near complete success. Events in Dublin and Wicklow changed the course of Irish history. Possession of the weapons instantly enhanced the prestige of the Irish Volunteers and enabled the MacNeillites to withstand the potential death blow landed by Redmond's anticipated splitting of the organization in September 1914. Instead, a much reduced cadre of determined Irish Volunteers, under closer IRB control than most contemporaries realised, positioned themselves to mount the 1916 Rising.

Anti-civilian excesses by British troops in Dublin city on 26 July 1914 attained levels of violence rarely witnessed at that time and accelerated the process of alienation between the Imperial Parliament and the majority of persons they regarded as their Irish subjects. Further impelled by the catalytic Easter Rising in April 1916 in which the German weapons were utilized, the people of Ireland overwhelmingly opted for citizenship and sovereignty once the majority were first permitted to vote in December 1918. Denial of this national mandate resulted in the War of Independence which effectively emancipated twenty-six of the thirty-two counties from the Empire by 1922. Certain figures involved in the 1914 gun-running, including Liam Mellows, Sean MacDiarmada, Patrick

Pearse and Roger Casement were destined for early graves arising from their revolutionary commitment. Others, not least Éamon de Valera and Sean T. O'Ceallaigh, survived the Civil War of 1922-23 to play critical roles in national politics.

The incredible true story of missed rendezvous in the North Sea, dangerous transhipments, running repairs and capricious weather in the days preceding the outbreak of the Great War is contained in this fascinating book edited by Professor F.X. Martin, OSA. Subsequent efforts to receive, transport and conceal the precious cargoes are equally vividly and faithfully recorded. This volume, along with F.X. Martin's companion *The Irish Volunteers, 1913-1915, Recollections & Documents*, comprises a major and highly readable resource for the history of Ireland on the threshold of national rebirth.

Dr Ruan O'Donnell is a Senior Lecturer in the University of Limerick and a member of the National Union of Journalists. His research into the history of Irish republicanism has included the acclaimed *Special Category: The IRA in English Prisons*, published by Irish Academic Press.

F.X. Martin: A Life

F.X. (Francis Xavier) Martin O.S.A. (1922-2000) was an Irish cleric and historian who also came to wider public attention through his appearances on television and his role as social activist in attempts to preserve aspects of medieval Dublin during the 1970s. He was born in Ballylongford, County Kerry, one of a family of ten children (five sons and five daughters), although his family claimed descent from the well-known Martyn family from County Galway.

His father Conor Martin was a medical doctor while his mother, Katherine, was a Fitzmaurice and a native of County Kerry. Martin was raised in Dublin and educated at Belvedere College, after which he joined the Augustinian order of friars in 1941. He was ordained to the priesthood in 1952. He studied for his BA at UCD, where Aubrey Gwynn and R. Dudley Edwards were among his teachers. He wrote his MA thesis on the Capuchin friar Francis Lavalin Nugent, one of the driving forces for the counter-reformation in Ireland and earned a travelling studentship from the NUI (National University of Ireland) to Peterhouse, Cambridge. It was in this college that he completed his doctoral thesis on Giles of Viterbo, the prior-general of the Augustinian order during the era of Martin Luther. He completed his doctorate in 1959 and published it as the monograph *Giles of Viterbo 1469–1532* in the following year.

Martin then returned to Ireland where he joined the teaching staff of the Department of History in UCD and quickly earned a glowing reputation among the student body, both for the erudition and liveliness of his lecturing style and his warm and friendly nature as a person. He became the first Professor of Medieval History in University College Dublin on the retirement of Aubrey Gwynn in 1961 and soon set about building up one of the most highly regarded medieval history departments of any third-level college in Europe. His publications with respect to contributions to medieval and early modern history included: *Friar Nugent, Agent of the Counter-Reformation 1569–1635* (1962) and (with A. B. Scott) an edition of the *Expugnatio Hibernica by Gerald of Wales (Giraldus Cambrensis)* (1978). Martin was an unusual historian for his era since his interests extended across a number of historical periods and specialisms. Ironically, it was his research into the Easter Rising and the years immediately prior to the rebellion, rather than his work in relation to the Medieval era, that cemented his reputation in the eyes of Irish readers of history. Among his writings in this field were the current volume relating the experiences of the Irish Volunteers between 1913 and 1915 and a monograph relating to the Howth gun-running – *The Howth Gun-Running, 1914* (1964), an event, in the absence of which the Easter rebellion would have proved extremely unlikely. He had a particular interest in the revolutionary and political career of Eoin MacNeill and published *The Scholar Revolutionary: Eoin MacNeill 1867–1945 and the Making of the New Ireland* in 1973. Working in collaboration with T. W. Moody and F. J. Byrne, Martin worked on the nine-volume series *The Course of Irish History*, a book project which became a staple in most Irish households with an interest in history.

Martin was thrust into the public eye again in 1976 through his seminal role in the 'Save Wood Quay' campaign. An excellent communicator and orator, he was ideally suited to his new role as chairman of the Friends of Medieval Dublin, a group who campaigned to save this ancient Viking site from the ravages of developers intent on the erection of a series of buildings at the behest of Dublin Corporation. While this conservation campaign would ultimately end in failure – the civic offices were duly built on the site of these early Viking settlements – the campaign, as bravely-steered by Martin, did ensure valuable delays in the planning and building stages, thereby allowing important excavations on this site to be concluded. Not only did the Wood Quay campaign highlight Martin's talents as historian and social advocate but it was the first conservation campaign of its kind in Ireland to achieve national prominence. In 1994 his collaborative project (with Clare O'Reilly) with respect to the history of his own religious order – *The Irish Augustinians in Rome, 1656-1994 and Augustinian Missions throughout the World* – saw publication. A member of the Irish Manuscripts Commission from 1963 onwards, Martin was also elected to the RIA (Royal Irish Academy) in 1967. He died in Dublin in February 2000, and is buried in Glasnevin cemetery.

Dr Mícheál Ó hAodha has published many books in Irish and English, many of which relate to the history of the Irish diaspora and Irish Nationalism. His books have been published with Irish Academic Press, Palgrave/Manchester University Press, Mercier, Liffey Press, Coiscéim, Peter Lang and Rowman and Littlefield amongst others.

New Foreword

by Éamon Ó Cuív T.D.

It is a great honour to be asked to write a short foreword to this book and I welcome its timely republication a hundred years after these extraordinary events. The book itself is of particular importance as it relies on original material from the participants and other contemporaneous publications. The events outlined in many cases prove that fact can be stranger than fiction and show great enterprise, initiative and purpose on the part on the participants. Once the Irish Volunteers was set up it was inevitable that they would require arms for their purposes but the challenge following the Proclamation by the King in December 1913, banning the importation of arms, was how these would be procured. Not for the first time in the events of these years was the lead given by events in the North of Ireland where large quantities of arms were imported. This spurred the Irish Volunteers and their supporters in Nationalist Ireland to action. One of the interesting issues in the narrative is the wide variety of different personalities involved in the gun-running from the fishermen from Gola Island in Donegal to leaders of the Anglo-Irish community in Ireland and England, as well as a wide spectrum of opinion in the Irish Volunteers.

The important involvement of women in the enterprise is also very striking for its time. By its nature the gun-running which was hastily put together was a mixture of improvisation, good planning and luck. The diary by Mary Spring Rice is particularly interesting as it gives a detailed day by day account of the voyage to the rendezvous and back to Howth and to every major and minor incident that happened. The daring plan to land guns in Howth and to have a large contingent of Volunteers collect them is also of major importance in the development of the Irish Volunteers as an open military force and to the achievement of ultimate independence.

For all who wish to understand the events of a hundred years ago and to understand the issues of the time this book is a must. The motivations, aspirations and opinions of the participants are very informative as are the complex relationships between people of very different background and politics.

On the larger political front two issues stand out. One is the willingness of the British Conservatives of the time to step beyond the law to try and block even limited Home Rule and the other is the clear objection by the more radical forces in the Irish Volunteers to the use of the arms against Ulster Unionists.

I hope this book will reach a wide audience.

Guím gach rath orthu siúd a smaoinigh ar ath-fhoilsiú a dhéanamh ar an leabhar seo, céad bliain ón uair a tugadh faoi airm a thabhairt isteach d'Óglaigh na hÉireann. Tá ár mbuíochas tuillte acu agus go mba fada buan iad i mbun a gcuid oibre don náisiún.

Original Foreword

SPEECH DELIVERED at Howth 30 July 1961 at the ceremonial taking over by the Irish Government of the yacht *Asgard* as a training vessel for naval cadets.

A Thaoisigh, a Airí, a dhaoine uaisle,
  Tá scéala agam anois ó Oifigeach den Arm go bhfuil an luamh stairiúil sin, an Asgard, tugtha i dtír.
  Is méanar an scéala é agus is méanar an ócáid í seo.
  Seacht mbliana is dachad ó shoin, taca an lae seo, sheol an Asgard isteach an chéad uair i gcuan agus i gcaladh seo Bhinn Éadair. Bhí lastas luachmhar ar bord aici, gunnaí agus lón cogaidh chun ceart ár náisiúin a chosaint agus a saoirse a bhaint amach.
  Tá a lán daoine anseo inniu, bail ó Dhia orthu, a bhí anseo an lá éachtach úd, agus eolas aca ar eachtraí an lae sin.
  Inniu, tá ar bord an Asgard comhaltaí de Chabhlach na hÉireann— toradh bláfar ar a céad theacht.
  Gurab amhlaidh a bhéas choíche le gach gníomh cróga, ceart.

This is a glorious day—a joyful day for all of us. We are grateful to the Government for having secured the *Asgard* for the nation and made this day possible.

Many of you around this platform were privileged to have a part in the landing here forty-seven years ago. Your minds are now, I am sure, travelling back to the events of that day, and ranging forward again through the fateful years that followed— through Easter Week, the subsequent re-organization of the Volunteers, the establishment of Dáil Éireann, the declaration of Independence, and the ensuing struggle in which the Volunteers were the army of the Republic.

Today in the light of the freedom won, we salute all who, in any measure, helped to bring that freedom to us—in particular, those who brought to this quay the white yacht, the 'harbinger of Liberty', as The O'Rahilly called it. May it ever be for us a symbol of hope and confidence, and may the names of Erskine and Mrs Childers, Mary Spring Rice and their other companions of the *Asgard* never cease to be revered amongst us.

I feel that you would all wish to join with me in sending to Mrs Childers at Glendalough,[1] through her son, Erskine, here beside me, a message of our gratitude, our admiration and our love, with the assurance, that the great event of forty-seven years ago, in which she and her gallant husband took so memorable a part, will never be forgotten by the Irish people.

Beannacht Dé oraibh go léir.
ÉAMON DE VALERA

---

1 Mrs Childers died on 1 January 1964 at Glendalough House, Annamoe, Co. Wicklow.

List of Plates

1. German tug *Gladiator* out of Hamburg. *Gladiator* transported the arms to the rendezvous point at the Roetigen lightship where it met the *Asgard* and the *Kelpie*.
   (MS 7890/8/43 photo courtesy of Trinity College Dublin Library)

2. Returning from Howth: two Volunteers identified as Edward and John Bracken, 26 July 1914. (Photo courtesy of Kilmainham Gaol collection: 16PC-1A22-26)

3. Parchment of Inquest on Mary Duffy, shot by Scottish Borderers, Bachelors Walk, 26 July 1914. (Photo courtesy of Kilmainham Gaol collection: 16LG-1C35-11)

4. Sir Thomas Myles, captain of the *Chotah*, who delivered the arms consignment at Kilcoole, Co.Wicklow one week after the Howth landings. (Photo courtesy of James Langton)

5. Erskine Childers at the wheel with Gola Island fisherman, Pat McGinley. (MS 7890/8/23 photo courtesy of Trinity College Dublin Library)

6. Four of the crew: (L-R) Molly Childers, Mary Spring Rice, Gordon Shephard and Pat McGinley. (MS 7890/8/50 photo courtesy of Trinity College Dublin Library)

7. Childers at the wheel with Gordon Shephard. (MS 7890/8/49 photo courtesy of Trinity College Dublin Library)

8. Unloading of rifles: Erskine Childers and Mary Spring Rice on board the *Asgard.*

(Photo courtesy of NMI, Collins Barracks)

9. Volunteer Cycle Corps. Note the 'Mausers' strapped to bicycles. (Photo courtesy of James Langton)

10. Volunteers returning to Dublin after the landing. (Photo courtesy of Kilmainham Gaol collection: 16PO-1A23-07)

11. 30 July 1961: state commemoration in Howth (L-R) Éamon de Valera at microphone, Sean Lemass, Eamon Martin. (Photo courtesy of Eamon Murphy)

Introduction

By Rev. Professor F.X. Martin, O.S.A.

THE HOWTH gun-running was a dramatic Irish episode set against a bizarre English background. It was important in its immediate consequences, but more important still because it made the Rising of Easter Week 1916 possible.

The background to the gun-running was the struggle for power in the British Parliament between the Liberals and the Conservatives. The immediate issue at stake was whether the Liberal government under Asquith could succeed in enacting and enforcing a Home Rule Bill to give Ireland a measure of self-government. The campaign was not altogether a crusade on Asquith's part; he and the Liberals were being kept in power by the eighty-four Irish Nationalist M.P.s led by John Redmond and pledged to Home Rule. The alliance represented hard bargaining but not sharp practice. Asquith and Redmond were both gentlemen of the Old School, who believed in playing the parliamentary game of cards according to the rules. And on the run of the play, with a solid majority of Liberal-Labour and Irish M.P.s in the House of Commons, there seemed no doubt that the Home Rule prize was about to be carried off by Redmond and Asquith.

Then the unpardonable was committed. The Conservatives cheated. They first triumphantly produced 'the Orange card' as their trump, but when they found that their bluff was being challenged they produced the gun. The Orangemen in Ulster, led by 'King' Carson, raised the cry of 'Home Rule is Rome Rule' and prepared for civil war in Ireland and armed resistance to His Majesty's government. The Orangemen were encouraged by the Conservatives and by a substantial body of opinion in the British Army. It could be argued that English Conservative honour was still unsullied. Bonar Law, leader of the Conservative Party, was a Canadian of an Ulster Presbyterian father; Carson was an Irishman, and a Southern Irishman to boot; Sir Henry Wilson, in this affair as confirmed an intriguer as had ever worn the King's uniform, was also a Southern Irishman; two of his principal supporters, Field Marshal Roberts and Lord Kitchener, were also of Anglo-Irish Southern stock. But the sins of the Conservative Party could not be laid solely on these audacious scapegoats, nor were they mere cat's-paws.

Bonar Law and Carson were members of the English Privy Council; Wilson was Director of Military Intelligence in the War Office; Roberts and Kitchener were two of the leading British soldiers. All five spoke and acted with the weight, prestige and influence of the Conservative Party behind them. Bonar Law did not mince his words. He declared to an enthusiastic audience of Conservatives at Bristol in January 1914, 'We are drifting inevitably to civil war...It is the determination of the people of Ulster to resist by force if necessary the imposition of this [Home Rule] Bill... We have given a pledge that if Ulster resists we will support her in her resistance.'

For Asquith and the Liberal government, as for Redmond and the Nationalist M.P.s, it was an incredible situation. Asquith, now shaken from his serene optimism, described with pain and indignation the statements of the Conservatives and Orangemen as furnishing 'a complete grammar of anarchy', but only aroused chuckles of sardonic glee from his opponents. The Ulster Volunteers continued to drill and organize; by March 1914 their number had risen to 84,540; high-ranking British officers came to advise and train them; arms were being imported; a Provisional Government of Ulster—illegal, of course—was formed in September 1913. A chasm yawned at Asquith's feet when the 'Curragh Mutiny' of March 1914 showed that the government could not depend on the army to enforce its will in Ulster. Not since the 'Glorious Revolution' of 1688 had the army displayed this mutinous mood, and it was an ominous reminder that Ulster Protestants had played their part in overthrowing the English government of that time.

Ugly disorder showed itself even within the walls of parliament. Asquith tried unsuccessfully to deliver a speech for three-quarters of an hour under volleys of hoots, jeers, and cries of 'Traitor!' from the Conservative benches. Never before in the history of parliament had a prime minister been refused a hearing. On another occasion Winston Churchill, then a Liberal, and Sir John Seely, Secretary of State for War, were leaving the Chamber amid Conservative cries of 'Rats! Rats!' when Ronald McNeill, an Ulster Unionist M.P., was carried away in his fury and threw a volume of the Orders at Churchill, striking him on the forehead. Churchill started angrily towards McNeill but was restrained by two members. Meantime the supposedly turbulent Irish Nationalist M.P.s looked on with wry amusement at these displays of passion.

Ireland grew sceptical when it remembered Redmond's confident declaration at Dublin in March 1912, 'Trust the Old Party, and Home Rule next year'. The example of the Orangemen was infectious, and without Redmond's consent a new military organization, the Irish Volunteers, sprang into existence in Dublin on 25 November 1913. It was led by Professor Eoin MacNeill, a figure of national repute, supported by the bulk of the people, and backed by the secret oath-bound society, the Irish Republican Brotherhood (I.R.B.). The manifesto issued on 25 November made plain that the Volunteers were not founded in opposition to the Orangemen but 'to secure and maintain the rights and liberties common to all the people of Ireland.'

The Liberal government had let the Ulster Volunteer Force grow unchecked; now at the sight of the Irish Volunteers it took fright, and on 4 December 1913 issued a proclamation against the importation of arms and ammunition into Ireland. Still the Irish Volunteers grew and multiplied, and as they did their clamour for arms increased. Here was a national military force, drilling with wooden guns, pikes and broom handles. The implied insult could not be borne for long. Although the Ulster Volunteer Force had been importing and smuggling quantities of arms and ammunition they too felt the need for a full-scale arming of their soldiers.

Both the Ulster Volunteer Force and the Irish Volunteers saw there was one solution—gun-running. No major difficulty confronted the Orangemen; they already had a defence fund of £1,000,000, a highly efficient organization, and the connivance of public officials in England and northern Ireland. They proved they were in earnest. A cargo of 20,000 rifles and over 3,000,000 rounds of ammunition was sailed in to Larne on the night of 24 April 1914, with a flourish of secrecy. Police, coastguards and soldiers slept the sleep of the just while a cavalcade of 700 motor vehicles converged on Larne, the countryside made bright as day from the glare of their headlights.

The example of the Orangemen stimulated the Irish Volunteers. Their clamour for arms grew more insistent, but they were a poor man's organization, they were menaced by the proclamation prohibiting the importation of arms, and, outside of Ulster, Dublin Castle had a firm grip on the country through its civil servants, the R.I.C., and the Army. The I.R.B. fumed at its own inability to do more than buy guns singly, while MacNeill and his followers fared little better. Nor was any lead given by the Irish Nationalist M.P.s at Westminster; Redmond was an eagle caged in his eyrie under Big Ben.

Help came from an unexpected quarter, from a number of English and Anglo-Irish Liberals who were growing alarmed at Asquith's inability to reduce the Orangemen to order and to withstand the Conservative onslaught on the safeguards of the English Constitution. Sir Roger Casement, burning with indignation and energy, arrived in London, urging that talk cease and action be taken. An Anglo-Irish committee was privately formed in London, with Mrs Alice Stopford Green as chairman, and Mrs Erskine Childers as secretary. Mrs Green was Irish by birth, and widow of the distinguished English historian, E. R. Green. She was an engaging personality and an historian of considerable achievement in her own right. Mrs Childers was an American, one of the Osgoods of Boston. She was a woman of remarkable character; although a semi-invalid due to an accident in her early teens she overcame this disability sufficiently to lead an active life. Her husband, Erskine Childers, had served as a British officer in the Boer War, and attained some fame by his books on military affairs and his enlightening novel, *The Riddle of the Sands*. His Irish nationalist sympathies had become evident in 1911 with the publication of his *Framework of Home Rule*.

The committee was an informal circle of friends. On it, or associated with it, were Sir Roger Casement, Lord Ashbourne, Sir Alexander Lawrence, Lady Alice Young, Captain George Fitz Hardinge Berkeley, Min Ryan then in London and secretary of Cumann-na-mBan, the Honourable Mary Spring Rice, and her cousins, Conor and Hugh O'Brien.

A meeting of some of the committee was held in Mrs Green's house in Grosvenor Road, Westminster, on 8 May. Eoin MacNeill, head of the Irish Volunteers, was over in London to see John Redmond and attended the meeting. It was quickly agreed that guns was the one essential the Volunteers lacked, and there was spontaneous consent that the guns must be secured from the continent. But money was needed for guns, and equally important was how the guns were to be bought and put into the hands of the Volunteers despite the proclamation of 4 December 1913. These were the problems which still remained to be solved after the meeting.

Then Mary Spring Rice had her flash of inspiration. She went to her friends, the Childers, and suggested that guns be bought on the continent and smuggled to Ireland in a fishing smack, the *Santa Cruz,* which was then engaged in trade on the Lower Shannon and was based on Foynes, near her home, Mount Trenchard. She asked Erskine Childers to skipper the ship and he readily agreed, on condition that it was capable of the task. He travelled over to Ireland in mid-May 1914 and down to Foynes, where he inspected the smack with O'Brien and Mary Spring Rice. While these two believed that it should be bought, repaired and equipped for the gun-running he remained unconvinced that this was a practicable proposition. He went to Dublin and raised the question with MacNeill who gladly jumped at this opportunity of arming the Volunteers. The difficulty of transporting the guns to Ireland remained Childers's problem.

In Dublin the project was a secret between MacNeill, The O'Rahilly and Bulmer Hobson; Sir Roger Casement was chosen as their liaison officer with the committee in London. O'Rahilly, as Director of Arms for the Volunteers, travelled over to London several times to discuss plans with the committee. Childers finally decided that both his own yacht, *Asgard,* then laid up at Conway in Wales, and O'Brien's yacht, *Kelpie,* should be used for the gun-running.

Meantime, money was collected from the members of the committee, with Fitz Hardinge Berkeley and Mrs Green contributing the major share. Childers went to Conway in mid-June to inspect his yacht, and continued on to Dublin. A final plan was then agreed upon, known in its entirety only to Childers, MacNeill, Casement, and Hobson. It was set in three logical stages; the guns were to be bought as unobtrusively as possible on the continent; shipped secretly to the Irish coast; landed without hindrance in Ireland and distributed to the Volunteers.

The first part of the plan was entrusted principally to Darrell Figgis, an Anglo-Irishman of some literary repute who had become interested in the Volunteer movement. He was widely travelled, and spoke German and French. He accompanied Childers to Hamburg during the last week of May 1914, where they succeeded in purchasing 1,500 rifles and 45,000 rounds of ammunition from the firm of Moritz Magnus to which O'Rahilly had directed them. The guns were second-hand Mauser rifles, discarded by the German Army but effective nevertheless. Figgis had to arrange for the transport of the guns and ammunition by tug from Hamburg to the Roetigen lightship off the Belgian coast. This he did quite satisfactorily, with a typical measure of self-confidence and stage-play.

The second part of the plan devolved mainly on Childers and involved three yachts. The tug was to be met by the *Asgard* under Childers, and the *Kelpie* under Conor O'Brien. Childers would take 750 rifles and half of the ammunition. The other half of the cargo was to be shipped by O'Brien, but since he was well known as an Irish nationalist and a yachtsman, and in the suspicious atmosphere of the time might well be suspected of gun-running, he was to transfer his cargo at sea off the Welsh coast to Sir Thomas Myles's steam-yacht, *Chotah*.

The final stage of the plan, in so far as it concerned Howth, was daring in its concept. It had been proposed by Hobson to Childers, and it was left to Hobson to see it through. Myles was to land his cargo on an unfrequented beach at Kilcoole, county Wicklow, on the night of Saturday-Sunday, 25-26 July, where it would be met by a small contingent of Volunteers under the supervision of Seán Fitzgibbon, a Volunteer officer and a trusted friend of Hobson. Next day Volunteers would occupy Howth Harbour in time for Childers to sail in with his consignment of rifles and ammunition to the east pier. Other Volunteers and the Fianna under Pádraig Ó Riain would unload the arms, distribute them to the Volunteers and march back openly to Dublin. The Howth landing was intended to take Dublin Castle unawares, to give publicity and encouragement to the Volunteers, and to solve by a simple method the unloading and distribution of the arms. In the ultimate analysis it would make the Volunteers an effective military force.

The plan in its three stages was so finely balanced and neatly timed that any mishap at any point could have meant the failure of the whole scheme. *Asgard* and *Kelpie* were sailing boats, at the mercy of wind and wave. There was no direct wireless or telephonic communication between the principal figures in the drama, so that Figgis, Childers, O'Brien, Myles and Hobson had each to work his part of the scheme as best he could, but be prepared to improvise a radical change in case of a mishap. Threats dogged the scheme from the time Figgis had to cope with customs' clearance at Hamburg until the Volunteers returning from Howth with the rifles found their path barred by military and police. One of the most serious accidents to the Kilcoole consignment occurred when the mainsail of the *Chotah* split and made it impossible for the yacht to reach the Wicklow coast on Saturday night.

The *Asgard* had no easy voyage to Howth. On Friday night and Saturday morning the yacht was caught in one of the worst storms off Dublin since 1882 but Childers kept a masterful hand on the helm. Then the whole expedition was jeopardized, literally at the last hour. It had been agreed that the *Asgard* would lie off Lambay Island on Sunday morning, waiting for Figgis to appear in a motor boat at ten o'clock at the mouth of Howth Harbour as a sign that all was clear. If he did not make an appearance it was to be assumed that the British had discovered what was afoot. There would be no Volunteers at Howth and the Hobson plan was to be abandoned. Childers was to take to sea again, and make off around the southern coast to the mouth of the Shannon.

When that Sunday dawned and the forenoon wore on with no sign of Figgis the crew of the *Asgard* endured two hours of anxiety, doubt, then agony. It was a question of then or never. The *Asgard* had to get in to Howth and out on the one high tide in order to unload its cargo. Its arrival had also to coincide with the appearance of the Volunteer columns on the quayside. In these circumstances there was only one hour in one day in the year which would suit, since the *Asgard* needed a Spring tide, about midday, on a Sunday, in summertime. Childers, his face white with anxiety, made a snap decision and sailed in to Howth, arriving precisely at the agreed time, to find the first file of Volunteers led by Cathal Brugha marching down the pier to meet the yacht.

Erskine Childers was the hero of the Howth gun-running. In many qualities he bore a striking resemblance to a contemporary of his, Lawrence of Arabia, also of Anglo-Irish parentage. History may be studied as a pattern of 'movements', but the role of the individual remains of supreme importance for it is the individual who at a crucial moment deflects or thwarts a movement or carries it forward to victory. Childers, from the hour he accepted Mary Spring Rice's invitation to run the guns to Ireland until he warped the boat in beside the pier at Howth, showed a mastery of practical detail, persistent courage, and a visionary sense of the ultimate achievement. The guns from Hamburg were to be of greater importance than he could then foresee. The foundation of the Irish Volunteers in November 1913, the landing of the guns at Howth and Kilcoole, the Rising in 1916, were three steps which led logically but not inevitably one to the other. From the Easter Rising came the Declaration of Independence by Dáil Éireann on 21 January 1919 and the emergence of a separate Irish State in 1922.

The immediate effect of the Howth gun-running was the powerful fillip it gave to the Irish Volunteers. Their numbers increased rapidly; they now marched with a defiant step, confident that they were no longer playing at being soldiers. Lack of money had hitherto hamstrung all their efforts; funds were now sent with an open hand from all parts of Ireland, and even more generously from America. Since Redmond had nominally a major say in directing the Volunteers the gun-running strengthened his hand in dealing with Carson and Asquith, but paradoxically among Irish nationalists his control of affairs was weakened since they were aware that he had no part in the venture.

One central issue should not be overlooked. The gravest of crises had overtaken the Volunteers in June 1914 when Redmond, indignant that he had been excluded from control of this new national body, demanded that twenty-five of his nominees be co-opted on to the provisional committee of the Volunteers, to counter-balance the existing thirty who already included some of his followers. A minority group of nine, led by MacDiarmada and Pearse, refused Redmond's ultimatum and a split was threatened within the organization. The majority of the committee, led by Hobson, MacNeill and Casement, convinced that Redmond would shatter the Volunteer movement if he were not placated, were willing to accept his demand under duress, and eventually the minority group also accepted under protest. Had the committee split in June 1914 there would have been no Howth gun-running, as there would have been no united body of Volunteers to meet the *Asgard*. MacNeill was head of the Volunteers, and Hobson the organizer of the landing of the guns. Childers, at this stage, was a believer in Redmond and Home Rule, not in revolution and a republic. Without Howth and Kilcoole there could hardly have been a rising in 1916.

The guns arrived in the nick of time. Within a week of Howth and Kilcoole the European war broke out and any further gun-running by men such as Childers, O'Brien and Myles was out of the question. All three served with the British forces during the war.

A survey of the group who organized the gun-running reveals that on the whole they were Anglo-Irish, Liberal, Protestant, Home Rulers, and of the upper and professional classes. Their mutual bonds were as much social and personal as political. In many ways the gun-running had a family air about it. Mrs Stopford Green was chairman of the Anglo-Irish committee in London. She was a relative of Lady Alice Young, one of the eleven subscribers to the gun-running fund; Lady Alice was Irish, a Kennedy from Belgard, county Dublin, and widow of Sir Alexander Hutchinson Lawrence. His nephew, Sir Alexander Waldemar Lawrence, was also associated with the committee. Diarmuid Coffey, one of the crew of the *Kelpie*, was a cousin of the Lawrences and a friend of Conor O'Brien.

Mrs Green and Sir Roger Casement had become fast friends early in the century due to their mutual Irish nationalist interests, and he acted as the liaison between the Volunteers in Dublin and the committee in London. Childers was a friend of Sir George and Lady Alice Young, and Casement visited them on several occasions in their home at Cookham, Berkshire. Both Mrs Green and Casement were friends of Francis J. Bigger, the generous patron of the Irish cultural revival in Belfast. It was through Bigger that Patrick McGinley and Charles Duggan, two fishermen from Gola Island, county Donegal, were secured for the *Asgard*. Bulmer Hobson, who was given charge of the Irish end of the gun-running, was a personal friend of Casement since 1904.

Mary Spring Rice, who first suggested how the guns should be run to Ireland for the Volunteers, was daughter of Lord Monteagle, and like Casement and the Childers had come to know Mrs Green through Liberalism and the Irish cultural revival. She brought her cousins, Conor O'Brien and Hugh Vere O'Brien, in on the gun-running scheme. It was in the topsy-turvy nature of Anglo-Irish politics of this time that her first cousin, Sir Cecil Arthur Spring Rice, was then British ambassador at Washington and a member of the English Privy Council. Conor O'Brien's crew on the *Kelpie* consisted of his sister, Kitty, Diarmuid Coffey, and two sailors from Foynes, George Cahill and Thomas Fitzsimons.

The Childers, who played an essential part in the whole episode, had long been friends with Mrs Green, the O'Briens and the Spring Rices. Sir Thomas Myles, whose yacht *Chotah* carried the guns on the last stage of the journey to Kilcoole, was well-acquainted with Childers and Conor O'Brien. Yachting, Home Rule, and Liberalism were their common interests. Captain Gordon Shephard, who sailed on the *Asgard*, was a close friend of the Childers; he had been attracted to them through admiration for Erskine Childers as a yachtsman. Captain George Fitz Hardinge Berkeley, a generous subscriber to the gun-running fund, was Irish by birth, a friend of the Childers and a Liberal in politics. James Creed Meredith and Hervey de Montmorency, who saw the guns safely to Kilcoole on the *Chotah,* were Home Rulers and Liberals, friends of Conor O'Brien.

England at this time was convulsed by the suffragette movement. Women asserted themselves in Irish affairs by the prominent part they played in the gun-running. Mrs Stopford Green was chairman of the committee in London; Mary Spring Rice suggested a practical plan and sailed on the *Asgard;* Mrs Erskine Childers was secretary of the committee, and despite being a semi-invalid took a full part in the voyage of the *Asgard;* Kitty O'Brien was one of the crew of the *Kelpie;* Lady Alice Young and Min Ryan were among the eleven subscribers to the gun-running fund.

The I.R.B., which ultimately, in Easter Week 1916, was to gain most by the gun-running, played a subsidiary role in July 1914. Its connection with Howth and Kilcoole was through Bulmer Hobson. Many of the I.R.B. had no knowledge that a gun-running was planned; some of them, such as Con Colbert and Piaras Béaslaí, were at the Gaelic League Oireachtas in Killarney when the *Asgard* sailed into Howth. Hobson, as a controlling figure in the Irish Volunteers, was a natural agent to arrange for the landing of the guns. As a member of the Supreme Council of the I.R.B. and Chairman of its Dublin Centre's Board he secured the co-operation of Tom Clarke, Seán MacDiarmada, Cathal Brugha and the I.R.B. in general. As a principal founder of the Fianna scouts he was able to bring that disciplined organization into full use at Howth.

The gun-running at Howth taught Irish nationalists one bitter lesson—there was one law for Orangemen, another for the rest of Ireland. During the weeks previous to the Howth gun-running the

Orange Order in Dublin was discreetly importing rifles, revolvers and ammunition with the connivance of the government authorities and drilling its members in the Fowler Hall, Rutland Square, Dublin.[2] The largest consignment of arms, 600 rifles and 300 revolvers, was brought over on the mailboat from England with the knowledge of its captain, Burchill, and stored in Dublin. On Saturday, 25 July, 1914, five thousand members of the Ulster Volunteer Force paraded through Belfast, armed with rifles, and even accompanied by machine guns. They were neither challenged nor molested by the British authorities. The following day the Irish Volunteers returning with nine hundred rifles from Howth were confronted by police and soldiers. Worse still, an unarmed crowd which was jeering and pelting the soldiers at Bachelor's Walk was fired upon without warning, three civilians (one of them a woman) were killed and thirty-five wounded; five boys and six women were among the wounded; two of the victims, a man and a woman, were bayoneted not shot.

Years previously in the House of Commons when an Irish Nationalist M.P. made an ardent appeal for justice for Ireland he was dismissed by Balfour with the arrogant remark, "There isn't enough justice to go round.' On 31 August 1913 during the Great Lock-Out in Dublin the police savagely attacked and batoned an unarmed gathering of strikers and bystanders in Sackville Street; four hundred civilians were treated for injuries. Nothing similar had happened when an alarming series of strikes in England, Wales and Belfast threatened the economic stability of Great Britain during 1911 and 1912. Balfour's view was further confirmed in unforgettable terms when the King's Own Scottish Borderers fired on the crowd at Bachelor's Walk. These incidents, which Augustine Birrell was later to describe ruefully as 'the hoarded passions' of 1913 and Bachelor's Walk, festered in the people's memory. They help to explain why Easter Week 1916 saw the Irish Citizen Army and a section of the Irish

2 For information on this little-known aspect of the problem see the statements of Mr Knollys Stokes, Miss Ruby Stokes, Mr Patrick J. Coyne, Mr F. W. Gumley and Mr John Kerr, in *Irish Times*, 31 July 1964, p. 1; 5 August 1964, pp. 4, 7; 12 August 1964, p. 7; 25 August, 26 August 1964, p. 7.

Volunteers, with their Howth rifles, banded together in revolution, and why their bloody protest was made in the heart of Dublin, in Sackville Street and along Bachelor's Walk.

Balfour's remark is the epitaph of British rule in Ireland.

Acknowledgements

BETWEEN PUBLISHED and unpublished sources there is no dearth of material about the gun-running to Howth and Kilcoole, but this book is the first attempt to present a comprehensive view of the principal people and factors involved. The gun-running is near-contemporary history, a vivid memory for those who participated in the event; it has been thought well therefore to let the sources speak for themselves. Of necessity there has had to be a selection of material but it is hoped that a balanced picture emerges.

An important source of information but one too often neglected is the *Royal Commission into the circumstances connected with the landing of arms at Howth on July 26th 1914*, published in that same year. However, these findings are primarily concerned with the unauthorized intervention of the police at Clontarf and the shootings at Bachelor's Walk. The official British government papers concerning Ireland for these years are not available for historians and will not be released for examination until some future undefined date. On other Irish issues adequate compensation may be gained from the rich collection of documents in the Asquith Papers, in the Bodleian Library, Oxford. In so far as they concern the Howth gun-running, however, they deal almost entirely with the intervention of the police and the shootings at Bachelor's Walk. Within a week of the gun-running England declared war on Germany and Irish affairs became no more than a distraction for the British public and politicians.

I am deeply indebted to Mr D. S. Porter of the Bodleian Library for checking through the Asquith Papers.

The participants in and organizers of the gun-running have left detailed information on the affair—for example the letters of Mrs Childers and the diary of Mary Spring Rice, both written during the voyage of the *Asgard*; the letters of Eoin MacNeill, Roger Casement and Gordon Shephard; the published accounts by Bulmer Hobson and Hervey de Montmorency. Nor can it be argued that they present a one-sided picture; they were written by people who were agreed on the object of running guns to Ireland but who represented political opinions ranging from those of the British Tories to those of the Irish Republicans.

I am under a considerable debt to the many people and authorities who have helped me. Whenever possible I acknowledge my debt at the relevant points throughout the book, but there are some people who do not fit obviously into any one category or whose help extends to several sections of the book.

The papers of Erskine Childers and his wife, Molly, are an invaluable source of information. Childers had a meticulous mind and kept exact records; his son, Erskine, Minister for Transport and Power, kindly placed the papers concerning the gun-running at my disposal. My one regret is that space does not permit me to publish the papers in full; they are full of vivid detail. I was fortunate enough to have several discussions with Mrs Molly Childers about the gun-running; her memory of the voyage of the *Asgard* was vivid, and her comments illuminating. I have also to thank Robert C. Barton for facilitating my investigations.

Bulmer Hobson has published four accounts of the gun-running. The first, which is very valuable but often overlooked, was published in *The Irish Volunteer* on 24 July 1915; the second formed chapters 9 and 10 of his *A Short History of the Irish Volunteers*, Dublin 1918; the third appeared in *An tÓglach*, June 1931; the fourth, which embodied most of the material already published as well as further information, appeared in *The Irish Volunteers, 1913-1915,* ed. F. X. Martin, O.S.A. (Dublin: 1963). In addition, Bulmer Hobson has allowed me to publish without restriction from his papers in the National Library, and has answered my many queries.

Darrell Figgis relates in his *Recollections of the Irish War* (London: 1927), the part he played in the gun-running, but while his account reads easily it must be accepted with reservations because of the major role he casts for himself. I am grateful to Ernest Benn Ltd. of London for permission to re-publish from the book; thanks are also due to Allen Figgis of Dublin.

Conor O'Brien published two accounts of the voyage of the *Kelpie;* one in his *From Three Yachts* (London: 1928), and a shorter account in the *Irish Red Cross Junior Annual* (Dublin: 1947). These undoubtedly contribute to our knowledge of events, but O'Brien's memory did not always serve him accurately.

In order to appreciate the electric atmosphere created by Carson and the Orangemen one can hardly do better than read St. John Ervine's treatment of the Howth gun-running in his *Craigavon: Ulsterman* (London: 1949). There bigotry wears an unashamed face, and he spoils his own case by a crude insensitivity to opinions other than his own.

I have been able to draw on Eoin O'Mahony's encyclopaedic knowledge of Irish families; this was quite important for an understanding of the Anglo-Irish group who financed and partly organized the gun-running. District Justice Liam Price and Robert Stopford of Liss, Hants, gave me a free hand with the section of the Stopford Green papers in Mr Price's possession dealing with the Irish Volunteers. Dr Conor A. Maguire and Dr C. P. Curran went to some trouble to find me information on James Creed Meredith. Eamon Martin was present at both Howth and Kilcoole, and was able to advise me on several issues. Mrs Kitty O'Doherty was ready, as always, with encouragement and her memories of the summer months of 1914. Commander A. J. O'Brien Twohig enlightened me on the nautical problems involved in the voyage of the *Asgard*. Desmond Ryan and Cathal O'Shannon answered my many queries from their unrivalled knowledge of the period.

It is not generally realized that there are two survivors of the yachts which ran the guns to Ireland. Patrick McGinley who was on the *Asgard*, living since 1915 at Chicago, U.S.A.; Thomas Fitzsimons of Foynes Island who sailed on the *Kelpie*. Both replied fully to my queries. Sergeant J. K. Byrne of Bunbeg Garda Station went to considerable trouble in tracing the whereabouts of Patrick McGinley and in gathering information about Charles Duggan, who like McGinley came from Gola Island and sailed on the *Asgard*. Pádraig Ó Friel of Gola Island supplied information and a photograph of his uncle, Charles Duggan. Sergeant J. Hunt of Foynes Garda Station helped me to trace the whereabouts of Thomas Fitzsimons, now living at Ballycahane, Pallaskenry, County Limerick.

The Trustees of the National Library of Ireland gave permission to publish from the Bulmer Hobson and Stopford Green Papers. I wish to thank Dr Hayes, Director of the National Library, Mr Alf MacLochlainn, Keeper of Manuscripts, and the staff of the National Library for their patience with my many demands. Dr A. T. Lucas, Director of the National Museum, gave permission to re-publish the photographs taken by Captain Gordon Shephard during the voyage of the *Asgard* and at Howth. The War Office Records Centre, London, was helpful with my inquiries about Brigadier-General Gordon Shephard and Major Hervey de Montmorency. *The Sunday Press* and *Irish Press* have allowed me to use the maps, illustrations, and articles concerning the Howth gun-running which appeared in their pages.

Éamon de Valera, as a captain of the Irish Volunteers, was among those who gathered at the Scalp on 25 July 1914 in preparation for the expedition to meet the guns at Kilcoole. Later that evening word came that this consignment was delayed, but the following day, 26 July, he led his company of Volunteers to Howth and assisted in the landing of the guns. Forty-seven years later, on 30 July 1961, he was present at Howth, as head of the Irish Republic, when the *Asgard* was formally taken over by the Irish government as a training ship for cadets. He has allowed his moving speech on that occasion to appear as the foreword of this book.

It is a pleasure to acknowledge with gratitude the patience and whole-hearted co-operation of the publishers, Browne and Nolan Ltd.

F.X. MARTIN, O.S.A.

Part I
Soldiers Without Arms
The Irish Volunteers in 1914

1. By the King : A Proclamation for prohibiting the carriage coastwise of military arms and ammunition

GEORGE R.I.

WHEREAS by section eight of the Customs and Inland Revenue Act, 1879, it is (among other things) provided that arms, ammunition, and any articles which His Majesty shall judge capable of being converted into or made useful in increasing the quantity of military stores may by Proclamation be prohibited to be carried coastwise:

And whereas it is expedient that the goods hereinafter mentioned should be prohibited to be carried coastwise:

Now, therefore, We, by and with the advice of Our Privy Council, in pursuance of the said Act and of all other powers enabling Us in that behalf, do hereby proclaim, direct and order as follows: —

As from and after the date of this Proclamation, and subject as hereinafter provided, arms and ammunition, and the following goods, being articles which We judge capable of being converted into or made useful in increasing the quantity of military stores, that is to say, the component parts of any arms, empty cartridge cases, and explosives and combustibles for warlike purposes, shall be prohibited to be carried coastwise:

Provided always and it is hereby declared that nothing in this Proclamation shall apply to any arms or the component parts of any arms or any ammunition or any empty cartridge cases, which in the opinion of the Commissioners of Customs and Excise are adapted for use or intended to be used solely for sporting purposes, or to any explosives or combustibles which in the opinion of the said Commissioners are intended to be used solely for mining or any other unwarlike purposes.

Given at Our Court of *Saint James,* this *Fourth* day of *December,* in the year of Our Lord one thousand nine hundred and thirteen, and in the *Fourth* year of Our Reign.

GOD save the KING.

By the King
A Proclamation
for prohibiting the importation of
military arms and ammunition into Ireland

GEORGE R.I.

WHEREAS by section forty-three of the Customs Consolidation Act, 1876, it is provided that the importation of arms, ammunition, gunpowder, or any other goods may be prohibited by Proclamation:

And whereas it is expedient that the importation into Ireland of arms and ammunition and the other goods hereinafter mentioned should be prohibited:

Now, therefore, We, by and with the advice of Our Privy Council, in pursuance of the said Act and of all other powers enabling Us in that behalf, do hereby proclaim, direct and order as follows:

As from and after the date of this Proclamation, and subject as hereinafter provided, arms and ammunition, and the following goods, that is to say, the component parts of any arms, empty cartridge cases, and explosives and combustibles for warlike purposes, shall be prohibited to be imported into Ireland:

Provided always, and it is hereby declared, that nothing in this Proclamation shall apply to any arms or the component parts of any arms, or any ammunition, or any empty cartridge cases, which in the opinion of the Commissioners of Customs and Excise are adapted for use, or intended to be used, solely for sporting purposes, or to any explosives or combustibles which in the opinion of the said Commissioners are intended to be used solely for mining or any other unwarlike purposes. Given at Our Court of *Saint James*, this *Fourth* day of *December*, in the year of our Lord One thousand nine hundred and thirteen, and in the *Fourth* year of Our Reign.

GOD save the KING.

2. Conservatives and Orangemen defy the Government, 1913–1914
Sir Edward Carson at Newry, 7 September 1913[3]

I don't hesitate to tell you that you ought to set yourself against the constituted authority in the land ... I am told that the [Provisional] Government will be illegal. Of course, it will. Drilling is illegal. The Volunteers are illegal, and the Government know they are illegal, and the Government dare not interfere with what is illegal. And the reason the Government dare not interfere is because they know the moment they interfere with you, you would not brook their interference . . . Therefore, don't be afraid of illegalities. There are illegalities that are not crimes . . . They are illegalities taken to assert what is the right of every citizen—the protection of his freedom.

Bonar Law at Bristol, January 1914
We are drifting inevitably to civil war . . . It is the determination of the people of Ulster to resist by force if necessary the imposition of this Bill. The ground on which our American Colonies took up arms seems to me utterly trivial in comparison with the wrong with which Ulster is

---

3 For this and similar statements see *The Complete Grammar of Anarchy by Members of the War Cabinet and their Friends*, ed. John J. Korean (Dublin: 1918).

threatened. We have given a pledge that if Ulster resists we will support her in her resistance. We intend, with the help of the Almighty, to keep the pledge, and the keeping of it involves something more than the making of speeches.

Colonel Hickman, M.P. for Wolverhampton, November 1913
You may be quite certain that these [Orange] men are not going to fight with dummy muskets. They are going to use modern rifles and ammunition, and they are being taught to shoot. I know, because I buy the rifles myself. You can take it from me that they are the best, and if the men will only hold them straight there won't be many Nationalists to stand up against them.

3. Arms and Drill
by Ernest Blythe[4]

In *Irish Freedom*, December 1913, p. 3.[5]
There is no power in politics like the armed man. He is the final arbiter. When the poets have sung and the orators declaimed, when the politicians have planned and the kings taken counsel, the man with the bayonet shall make the law. Wealth can buy lands and servitors, but guards it must buy before all else; for the castle will go down before the cannon. The philosopher is a prince if he can persuade the soldiers; but the wisest head may be cut off by a sword, and the way to Paradise barred by a bayonet. There is no freedom or security, save for those who have arms in their hands or at their call.

---

4 Ernest Blythe, from near Lisburn, County Antrim, a member of the Church of Ireland. At an early age he became an ardent Gaelic Leaguer and a member of the I.R.B. He was appointed an organizer for the Irish Volunteers, and was deported to England by the British government in 1915. He was elected to the executive of Sinn Fein in October 1917, and was appointed Minister for Finance in the Free State government. He is now managing director of the Abbey Theatre, Dublin—*Ed.*

5 *Irish Freedom* was the monthly organ of the I.R.B. My thanks are due to Ernest Blythe for permission to re-publish this article—*Ed.*

And the rights and privileges of nations are equally dependent upon their control of military power. European civilization is spreading over the globe, not because of its intrinsic superiority, but because it produces mightier armies. If a nation were to establish a beautiful and healthy social system but had no military strength it would not lead the world by its wisdom. On the contrary, some half-barbarian people would ere long feel themselves called on to bestow upon it the advantages of civilization. And they would succeed.

It is a positive misfortune for a nation to have accumulated wealth if it be not strong in arms. At first it may buy off armies, but one will come who will refuse to be content with only part of the spoil he sees before him. It is not enough that a people should make themselves good soldiers, but that at least they must do if they are to avoid robbery, oppression, and enslavement. Freedom apart from military strength is an exotic which will never flourish and will not long survive. And for a nation which has been conquered the one way to regain freedom is to organize and increase its fighting power. The only thing that will loosen a conqueror's grip is the force or fear of the sword's edge. It is thus doubly incumbent upon every Irish Nationalist to arm and to drill, to buy a gun and to learn the use of it. It is his duty as a man that he may be amongst the guardians and rulers of society and not amongst the subjected and dependent. It is his duty, as a citizen of a country struggling for freedom and urgently in need of fighting men.

There is much effort today to belittle militarism; but the power of the soldier will survive the talk. The world in secular matters is ruled by force; but the one force which cannot be resisted or escaped is military force. The only guarantee of freedom is the ability of the ordinary citizen to resort to arms in preservation of his rights or for the destruction of tyranny. Franchises and constitutions are but means of using that to which the sword gives title. Rulers, whether they be kings, aristocrats, oligarchs, or elected persons with their never-ending audacity, are preserved from the temptations of their position only by fear of the people. They will say that they would save themselves from curses or adverse votes; but be sure they would care little for curses and votes if they did not know them to be the precursors of shots and blows. The man who has no gun and no heart to fight may be the equal of his neighbours when they discuss sea-serpents; but he counts for nothing when great public affairs are in the balance.

How valuable to a people or a section of a people are the most trumpery war preparations is shown by the present importance of Orange Ulster. The passing of the Home Rule Bill un-amended is a thing clearly to be desired in the interests of England, and still more in the interests of the Liberal Party. Yet we see English Ministers wavering towards a modification for the satisfaction of Ulster. Eighty thousand men with wooden guns and vaguest threats are of as much account as five times the number with resolutions of passionate aspiration. The lesson, however, is not that we should start rival battalions of bluff but that we consider whether, when one wooden gun will perturb a minister of the English Crown, five Mausers would not persuade him to keep to his own bounds. I know the Ulster Volunteers, and I am sorry that they are of no account. Nevertheless, advantage might be taken of the embarrassment which their existence causes the enemy, for Nationalists publicly to organize and drill. Whether the Home Rule Bill passes or peters out National Volunteer companies formed now will prove of great utility in the future. If it passes they will not be needed to fight our friends in Ulster; but they will give the Irish Parliament a backing in its dealings with the English Government better than logic or eloquence, than statecraft or wealth. If Home Rule falls through, the members of the Volunteers will have had a training which will enable a really formidable revolutionary movement to be set on foot. Those of us who were somewhat carried away by the 'Sinn Fein policy' when it was first expounded have had time to realise that it must be valueless except as the complement of military organization.

Prepare then, friends of Ireland, for the future; and doubt not that the future, like the past, is with the fighting man. Whatever comes, Ireland wants soldiers, and none is worthy of the name of Nationalist or citizen or man but the soldier. To become soldiers it is needful for each of us to do three things; first, to get guns; second, to learn to shoot with them; and third, to learn to act together and to obey and trust our officers, and so have confidence in ourselves and our comrades. The last is usually the most difficult for revolutionaries; for they cannot have the massed reviews and manoeuvres essential to it in time of peace. But a Volunteering movement such as is now possible would obviate the difficulty, and, therefore, it is clearly the duty of all who can to Volunteer.

4. Defence of Ireland Fund for Arms June-July 1914

From *The Irish Volunteer*, 4 July 1914, p. 4.[6]

Dear Sir,
The Defence of Ireland Fund will be opened in every district on Sunday, 28th June, and will be continued for four weeks following, and will conclude on Sunday, 26th July.

The money subscribed to this Fund will be directed solely to the PURCHASE OF ARMS AND AMMUNITION FOR THE VOLUNTEERS. (N.B.—The equipment so purchased will be distributed among the various Volunteer Companies in proportion to the amount they have collected or subscribed).

In order to give everyone an opportunity of subscribing, house-to-house collections are to be undertaken by the various Companies, and, with the permission of the local clergy, collections are to be organized at the church doors.

6 The acting editor of *The Irish Volunteer* at this time was Larry de Lacey of Enniscorthy, a journalist and a member of the I.R.B. After December 1914 the paper was published officially by the Irish Volunteers with Eoin MacNeill as editor—*Ed.*

The various Companies are, therefore, directed to take immediate steps to have this decision of the Provisional Committee put into effect. The members of your Company shall nominate five members of the Company (to be called the Company Collection Committee), whose duty shall be to arrange for the Company Collection and appoint (from amongst their number) a Company Treasurer, who shall receive all moneys collected by the Company, and who shall forthwith forward all moneys so received to the Treasurer of the District Collection Committees to be appointed as hereinafter mentioned. The local Companies, by arrangement amongst themselves, shall collect in any adjoining districts in which no Companies as yet exist.

The Companies in a district shall elect from their number a representative who, with similar representatives from other Companies shall form the District Collection Committee, which shall supervise generally the work of collection in the district, and shall appoint two Treasurers for each district to act jointly, and who shall undertake at their appointment to forward to Headquarters within one week of the closing of the Fund in the County, the moneys lodged with them, and a correct return thereof on the forms supplied from Headquarters.

Company Treasurers shall forward (with the moneys collected) to District Treasurers, returns on Official Forms.

Secretaries of Companies shall at once communicate to Headquarters particulars of the formation of District Collection Committees and names and addresses of Treasurers.

Individual Volunteers are to be encouraged, where they can afford it, to subscribe the price of their own rifles to the Company Rifle Funds.

The moneys collected for the Defence of Ireland Fund shall defray the expense of providing arms for those who cannot subscribe in full the price of their own equipment.

Arms and ammunition cannot be purchased on advantageous terms except in large quantities. A standard weapon can be procured only through a central authority.

That the collection in all districts may start at the same time, the Company Collection Committees shall be formed on or before 21st of June and the District Collection Committees on or before 28th of June.

By Order,
PROVISIONAL COMMITTEE.

5. No hostility to the Ulster Volunteer Force and the Unionists

In *The Irish Volunteer*, 11 July 1914, p. 4.

Every Irish Volunteer will recognize the duty, as binding on his own personal conduct, of endeavouring to secure the unity of all Ireland and of all Irishmen on the grounds of national liberty. Irish Volunteers, will, therefore, discountenance all manifestations of ill-will as between different sections of Irishmen, and will do their utmost to promote peace and goodwill throughout Ireland.

Several lying and sensational reports have been published, professing to relate acts of violence or hostility on the part of the Irish Volunteers towards the Ulster Volunteer Force and towards Irish Unionists. The authors of such reports hope and desire that their fictions may lead to actual occurrences such as they falsely describe and may raise difficulties in the way of national unity and national liberty. The conduct of the Irish Volunteers will be such as to defeat any malicious and unscrupulous designs of the kind.

By Order of the Provisional Committee of the Irish Volunteers
30th June 1914.

6. We must have rifles

In *The Irish Volunteer*, 4 July 1914, p. 1.

We must have rifles. Whether the Proclamation is torn up or not the rifles must come. There is not enough rifles in the country and thousands of trained men are ready for them. All the rest, uniform, equipment, standards, could be dispensed with, but the rifle is the soldier's arm. At the rate things are going it will take years to provide rifles for the men who could make efficient use of them, and the country is growing impatient at the delay. We are being taunted with our poverty in being unable to procure sufficient funds to make gun-running feasible, but it is not poverty that is in the way. Ireland is so loath to break the laws of the Constitution that the absolute necessity of breaking them and procuring arms is not yet realized, and when it is the arms will come. Therefore, every Volunteer should make it clear always and everywhere that now is the time for the rifle.

Where are the arms?

In *The Irish Volunteer*, 11 July 1914, p. 1.

It is true, lamentably true, that the number of rifles in the country is scandalously inadequate to the number of men qualified to use them; but there are some rifles, and the shotguns, or even weapons more easily improvised, would prevent the disarming of the national force, if it were contemplated. Meanwhile, we must have more rifles. They are coming in too slowly, thanks to the 'more effective methods' which the Government has adopted to bring about this result. A spirit of impatience for equipment is growing in the country, and if it does not find legitimate expression through the ordinary trade channels will translate itself into action that may be more undesirable from the point of view of all who wish for the ensured harmony of the future.

We must have rifles
The Proclamation Still

We have again and again preached the necessity of arms, appealing to the men of Ireland to get a rifle by any means in their power. We believed that the Government would have yielded to the serious representations made by traders, and that the panic of the moment having disappeared, the blundering and provocative proclamation would have been withdrawn; that a rudimentary idea of consistency would have shown how illogical and stupid it was to restrict the Irish people from the enjoyment of an elementary right of civilisation, while introducing an elaborate measure intended to endow them with a more complex citizenship. Perhaps some fantastic ideal of expediency has proved too attractive for realities of right and justice to prevail. But the expediency that dictates the retention, if not the original enactment, of the proclamation is as ruinous to the real interest of Ireland as the restriction of imports was in '48. And the justice of the one is on an exact equality with the other.

Drill for Freedom

It should be drill and drill and drill until every man in the battalion is fully qualified to take his place in a first class National army. And that it will be a first class army there is every reason to hope. The nation has gone into the soldiering business with a thoroughness that has scarcely ever been manifest in a patriotic movement in the past and the ultimate result can only be freedom, permanent and complete.

A chance for the fighting blood

It is up to the time when more attention should be devoted to the rifle. A good service rifle should be kept at the drill hall of every corps and explained to the recruits who should be trained to handle it, to take it asunder and re-assemble it, and above all to acquire a knowledge of the principles of musketry. When this is done, as it will be done, the demand for rifles will be so overwhelming that nothing can resist it. The fighting blood and the fighting instinct is in every Irishman and it only needs a little to arouse all the latent enthusiasm of our soldier race for the weapons with which freedom is won and kept.

Arms and the Proclamation

In *The Irish Volunteer*, 18 July 1914, p. 1.

Still the arms are coming into Ireland, slowly enough, but they will come quicker presently. It is a great pity from one point of view that they could not have been procured at once. If this were possible then the Volunteer Committees would have been able to see to their distribution, to see to it that only the best men were provided with arms, and that these arms were kept safely. Now the difficulty of getting rifles has whetted the thirst for them amongst some who, under normal circumstances would not have had so keen a desire to arm, and finding the difficulties in the way not insurmountable are arming themselves individually. This is not in the best interest of things, perhaps, but at all events until the proclamation is removed it will go on.

But the great danger from retaining the Proclamation in force is that it is a direct incentive to civil war. Those who are keen on arms—and who in Ireland just now is not?—will look with envious eyes upon those who have got them. There will, naturally, be a tendency to reason as follows: 'What rifles are in the country were got by breaking the law. Why should not we break another law, particularly against an assumed law-breaker, and arm too?'

Only the prudence and good sense of the Irish Volunteers has prevented the result of such logic up to the present, and will, doubtless, continue to do so; but the incentive is there—perhaps deliberately there.

Over the Ulster frontier

in *The Irish Volunteer,* 25 July 1914, p. 1.

Over the frontier rifles are being got ready too and the sinews of war prepared for Ireland. So we can afford to be joyous over it all. We were taught so much in adversity that it is due to us to set about putting our lesson in practice in prosperity. The clank of arms has brought back some of the old spirit that sang around the camp fires and roystered in the ballrooms before the battles of the Irish Brigade.

The future is ours. Nothing on earth can prevent the people of Ireland guiding the destinies of Ireland as long as the Volunteers exist as a permanent and equipped force. To attempt to restore the old order of things would be as idle as to bid the wind cease. A continental nationalist said somewhere that if over 50 per cent of a people thought nationally there would be no need for any patriotic movement; if 30 per cent thought nationally an armed movement would be necessary and successful, and if only a very small percentage realized their national duties terrorism might do something to loosen the chains of the slave. There was some truth in it. Anyhow there are enough armed men in Ireland to justify our faith in the future.

8. The Irish Volunteers demand arms

by *Eoin MacNeill* and *L. J. Kettle*
In *The Irish Volunteer*, 11 July 1914, p. 4,

Fellow-Countrymen,

It is close upon seven months since the Irish Volunteers were called into being by a manifesto issued on the 25th November, 1913, in the name of the Provisional Body who now make this further appeal to the courage and patriotism of Irishmen.

The time is not inopportune. To that first appeal a splendid response has been given by the youth and manhood of Ireland.

The call to Irishmen to form an army of national defence against aggression from whatever quarter it might come, and to take upon themselves the defence of those rights and liberties common to all the people of Ireland, has not fallen on deaf ears or cold hearts.

The right of a free people to carry arms in defence of their freedom is an elementary part of political liberty. The denial of that right is a denial of political liberty, and consistent only with a despotic form of government. They have rights who dare maintain them.

The demand of the people of Ireland is unmistakable. They demand this elementary right of freemen—the right to place arms in the hands of the organized and disciplined defenders of their liberty.

Ireland today possesses an army of men actuated by a common spirit of patriotism, daily acquiring and applying the habits of disciplined and concerted action and rapidly fitting themselves to bear arms.

We denounce as hostile to our liberty, civic as well as national, the denial of this right.

And further, since the action of the Government places in the way of Irishmen favourable to national autonomy obstacles which admittedly are inoperative in the case of those opposed to the policy of self-government, we urge the demand through every representative voice in Ireland for the immediate withdrawal of the proclamation prohibiting the import of arms into Ireland.

We are glad to recognise that the time has come when the Irish Parliamentary Party, with Mr John Redmond at its head has been able, owing to the development of the Irish Volunteer Organization on sound and well-defined national lines, to associate themselves by public declaration with a work which the nation has spontaneously taken in hands. Their accession is all the more welcome since, from the outset of the Irish Volunteer movement, we have made it our constant aim to bring about a whole and sincere unity of the Irish people on the grounds of national freedom.

In that spirit, too, we look forward with eager hope to the day when the minority of our fellow-countrymen, still apparently separated from us in affection, will be joined hand in hand with the majority in a Union, within which the rights and liberties common to all the people of Ireland will be sacred to all, and will be a trust to be defended by the arms and lives of all Irishmen.

Eoin MacNeill
L. J. Kettle
Hon. Sees. Provisional Committee

Part II
Planning
the Gun-Running

Acknowledgements:
Thanks are due to Miss Margaret Pearse for recommending that I publish in this book the relevant Pearse letters; to Mrs Dominic de Feo, Bala-Cynwyd, Philadelphia, U.S.A., for information about her father. Joseph McGarrity; to the Minister for Defence and the Marquess of Headfort for information on the *Asgard*; to Dr R. B. McDowell, Trinity College, Dublin, for easing my search among the Stopford Green Papers; to Professor Lennart Moberg, University of Uppsala, for tracing the meaning of the name *Asgard.*

9. Alice Stopford Green

by Máire Comerford

Mrs Alice Sophia Amelia Stopford Green, D.Litt, (1847-1929) spent the first twenty-five years of her life in Kells where her father, Rev. Edward Adderly Stopford, was Protestant archdeacon of Meath. She taught herself Greek so that she could help him in preparing his sermons. For seven years, from the age of seventeen to twenty-four, she was almost blind and was allowed to read for only fifteen minutes each day. J. P. Trevelyan remarks, in the *Dictionary of National Biography*, 'She emerged from her long ordeal with a mind well stored and a remarkably retentive memory.' Archdeacon Stopford died in 1874 and the family moved to London.

Three years later she married John Richard Green, and during the next six years, until he died, she underwent a period of education and a widening of horizons and sympathies in her husband's intellectual environment. He was, I think, the first author of a history of England for the people about the people, rather than about kings and battles.

Mrs Green, assisting him in his work, developed a devotion equal to his own in the story of people and places, and she learned to use his historical method. She told me many years later that it was in this way her interest in Ireland, her own country, was aroused.

When the Greens consulted original sources they found that Irish history, as written in English, was usually a misrepresentation of facts to suit imperialist propaganda. They were both too honest to be satisfied with anything but the truth, so far as it could be ascertained. She was to write

> 'There is no more pious duty to all of Irish birth than to help in recovering from centuries of obloquy the memory of noble men, Irish and Anglo-Irish, who built up the civilisation that once adorned their country. To them has been meted out the second death—the lot feared beyond all else by men of honour. They have been buried by the false hands of strangers in the deep pit of contempt, reproach, and forgetfulness—an unmerited grave of silence and of shame.'

Miss Máire Comerford was secretary to Mrs Green, 1919-1922—*Ed.*

Her first major book dealing with Ireland, *The Making of Ireland and its Undoing, 1200-1600,* was not published till 1908, twenty-five years after the death of John Richard Green, but I remember clearly her telling me that the origins of the book were in her husband's sick room, where she worked by the window in the intervals when concentration was possible for her, during his long illness. While acting as her husband's amanuensis, she was disabled by writer's cramp, and it was characteristic of her that she at once began to teach herself to write with her left hand. It is of course well known that her output of work was stupendous; that she revised and attended to sixteen re-printings of the *Short History of the English People* after the author's death—there were thirty-two printings up to 1920, the last four of them with Mrs Green's Epilogue covering the century, 1815-1914. Of her other published work the most notable is her two volume *Town Life in the Fifteenth Century* and her study of Henry II.

During the thirty-four years she continued to live in London her days from 5 a.m. to lunch time were divided between research, study and writing. Then the door opened to parties, and intellectual exchange with scholars, writers, politicians, social reformers. Mrs Sidney Webb in My Apprenticeship describes one of these parties as follows on 31 May 1896.

> 'We had a queer party at Alice Green's . . . five of the young Radicals—Asquith, Haldane, Grey, Buxton, and Acland—to meet five Fabians—Massingham, Clarke, Olivier, Shaw, and S.W., with Alice and myself. It was not successful; though not quite a failure, since all were pleasant and cordial. Asquith spoilt it. He was the ablest man of the lot, and determined that it should not go.'

Henry W. Nevinson, writing more from the Irish point of view, commented

> 'When I first began to know her she was living in Westminster, overlooking the river, and at her dinners and receptions I found gathered various persons of distinction—statesmen of both parties, like Mr Arthur Balfour, Sir Anthony MacDonnell, and Mr Augustine Birrell; champions of human freedom like E. D. Morel; writers, specially young Irish writers, like Padraic Colum and Robert Lynd. There she sat in our midst, queenly, Elizabethan, already white-

haired and ageing . . . dominating us all by knowledge, wit and courteous encouragement to shy people like myself.

All the greater honour was due to her when, in the middle of the Great War, she quietly left that scene of influence and authority and withdrew to her own land to watch events from St. Stephen's Green, giving her aid to the troubled course of Irish history, exposed to every danger, harried and raided by the Black and Tans, and the ex-officers and ex-gentlemen known as the "Auxiliaries," her house repeatedly searched, her books, documents, and historical manuscripts carted about in army lorries, lost, confused, or hurled back at her door with every discourtesy. But fine as she always was, she rose to an unimagined greatness when we sat together, with Gertrude Bannister and a few others on the night before the English Government hanged my friend Roger Casement . . . while he in his cell was watching for the dawn of his death, she continued to speak to us of life and of death with a courage and wisdom beyond all that I have ever known. It was as though we were listening to the discourse of Socrates in the hours before his own execution.'

When I first met Mrs Green on 29 June 1919 she was in company with Jack Yeats and his wife on holiday at Courtown Harbour, county Wexford.

When we, the local adherents of the Easter Week tradition, found an interesting or nationally important person in our midst we sometimes organized a picnic to which we invited, besides ourselves, one or two others, the nearest we could find to what we thought was the intellectual level of our principal guest.

We pounced on Mrs Green, and she charmingly concurred in our plan. I can remember her, sitting on the steps of Lord Mountnorris's ruined mansion, Camolin Park, county Wexford, participating in discussions about 1798, attentive to the tradition as expounded by the locals, allowing herself to be drawn to other topics, talking just at our level. Here was the perfect guest.

Later when I was her secretary I was present on dozens of occasions as a new circle of friends gathered round her at parties in St. Stephen's Green. I remember visits of George Russell, R. I. Best, Eoin MacNeill, Professor Bergin, James Douglas, Professor Edmund Curtis; others such as Erskine Childers, Mary Spring Rice, Robert Brennan, Frank Gallagher, Desmond Fitzgerald, made special appointments, or dropped in, for several of them were 'on the run.' I used recognize Mick Collins' tall bicycle if it was standing in the hall when I returned to the house, and I would wait on the alert in the office till I heard him leave.

When we were raided by the Auxiliaries after bedtime one night I recall Mrs Green as she stood, in contemptuous silence, outside her bedroom door, at the top of the stairs. She was wearing one of her stiffest silk brocade gowns which hung straight from the shoulders. Her head was high, and her hands low, slightly joining in front. Fortunately I was the only one to notice something not quite normal about her figure. A whole file of the banned Republican bulletin was inside the gown. She could not have moved without something slipping; but then nobody dared to ask her to move.

Two days later we were at 12 Bushy Park Road, home of Erskine and Molly Childers, at a meeting of the Dáil Éireann Lecture Committee, when the same party of Auxiliaries raided. The leader explained. 'I didn't have to knock. My uncle lived in this house once. I came in from the back.' Then he asked all present to give him their names. Mrs Childers smiled and said nothing; when he came to Mrs Green he said 'I know you.' She spoke across the room to me, 'This time he knows us even when we are dressed!' The questioning went no further.

She was appointed a senator under the Free State government, and died in Dublin on 28 May 1929, aged eighty-four.

10. Erskine Childers

Robert Erskine Childers (1870-1922) was born in London on 25 June 1870, second son of Robert Caesar Childers, a noted oriental scholar. From his father who died at the age of thirty-eight he inherited power of intense concentration, and from his mother, Anna Mary Henrietta Barton, of Glendalough House, county Wicklow, a love for Ireland. A close kinsman of his, H. C. E. Childers, was First Lord of the Admiralty, Secretary for War, and Chancellor of the Exchequer under Gladstone. He was chairman of the commission which made a momentous report, in Ireland's favour, on the financial relations between Great Britain and Ireland. Erskine Childers was educated at Haileybury and at Trinity College, Cambridge; his only home until his marriage was Glendalough House. He took his B.A. and the law tripos in 1893. Although quiet and reserved in manner he showed himself as a student to have a power of eloquence and a delicate sense of humour.

He volunteered for service against the Boers, and joined the City Imperial Volunteer battery of the Honourable Artillery Company. His *In the Ranks of the C.I.V.* (1900) was a vivid personal account of the war, and he also collaborated in the official volume, *The H.A.C. in South Africa* (1903). He wrote volume V of *The Times History of the War* in South Africa (1907), and in two further books, *War and the Arme Blanche* (1910), and *German Influence on British Cavalry* (1911), wrote vigorously against the antiquated uses of cavalry.

Ever since leaving Cambridge he had been devoted to sailing, and spent much of his spare time in a tiny yacht, navigating the North Sea, the Channel, or along the German and Baltic coasts. His *Riddle of the Sands* (1903) was an imaginary account of German preparations for a raid on England, but was based on his observations of the German coast, and won him immediate fame.

In September 1903 he went to Boston with the Honourable Artillery

Company, the first peaceful visit of an armed body of British soldiers to the United States since the American Revolution. On one occasion during the celebrations he happened to be sitting next to Miss Mary Alden Osgood of Boston, whose family can be traced back directly to an Osgood who went to America on the *Mayflower*. She and Childers fell in love at first sight, and were married at Boston on 5 January 1904. Years later Childers described his marriage as 'the most wonderful happiness that I know.' His letters to her, among the family papers, bear this out in a moving way. The Childers' returned to London, and established themselves in a Chelsea flat. Mrs Childers as a child had fractured both her hips in an accident, and for the rest of her life she was a semi-invalid. But she had an indomitable will to overcome her handicap, and she travelled widely with her husband in the *Asgard*.

Childers was a clerk in the House of Commons from 1895 until 1910, but his attitude towards Ireland was undergoing a steady evolution during those years. He came of Unionist stock and although he had returned from South Africa with a growing attraction to Liberalism, he could still write in 1902 'I am not a Home Ruler.' However, observation of Sir Horace Plunkett's co-operative movement in Ireland brought him to the point of commenting in a private letter in 1908, 'I have come back finally and immutably a convert to Home Rule.' Thereafter Ireland dominated his thoughts.

In 1910 he resigned from his post in the House of Commons, and spent some time in Liberal politics. The publication of his *Framework of Home Rule* in 1911 showed that he had already gone farther than many Liberals in advocating full dominion status for Ireland. This is an impressive work, precise in its detail and cogent in its logic. In May 1914 Childers and his wife, dismayed at the failure of the Liberal government to prevent the arming of the Ulster Volunteers, undertook to run a cargo of rifles to Ireland in the *Asgard* for the Irish Volunteers. The story of that adventure is told in some detail in this book.

Immediately after the Howth gun-running the European War broke out, and Childers was summoned for reconnaissance work on the seaplane carrier, *H.M.S. Engadine*. He was employed in intelligence work and in training officers in the Royal Naval Air Service. He was several times mentioned in dispatches, was promoted lieutenant-commander, and on amalgamation of the Naval Air Service with the Royal Air Force held the rank of major. He received the D.S.C. for his services in the War.

Childers had gladly joined in the 'War for Small Nations', and with his wife supported Redmond against MacNeill and the Volunteers, in the belief that Ireland was about to receive a substantial amount of self-government. In 1917 he was seconded to the secretariat of the ill-starred Irish Convention. The events in Ireland in 1917 and 1918 convinced him that nothing less than complete independence would satisfy its national aspirations. After demobilization in March 1919 he went to Dublin and offered his services to Griffith and the Sinn Féin Party.

He accompanied the Irish republican delegates who were sent to Paris in 1919 to place Ireland's case before the Versailles Conference. The following December he settled with his family at Bushy Park Road, Dublin, and became a principal publicist of the republican cause. He wrote continually in the Irish, English and foreign press, protesting against British government in Ireland and the methods it employed, such as the 'Black and Tans'.

In May 1921 he was elected a member of Dáil Éireann for county Wicklow, and was appointed Minister for Propaganda. After the Truce in July he went with de Valera on the first delegation to London, and was principal secretary to the later Irish delegation which concluded the Treaty with the British government in December 1921. He himself rejected the Treaty absolutely, and joined the Republican Army in opposition to the Free State government. While on service with mobile columns in Munster he edited the Republican newspaper, *Poblacht na hÉireann*.

He was captured by Free State soldiers on 10 November 1922 at his old home, Glendalough House, county Wicklow, court-martialled in Dublin on 17 November, and executed on 24 November at Beggar's Bush Barracks. When he was led out to be shot he shook hands with each member of the firing party.

11. Plans are laid in London

by Darrell Figgis[7]

From Recollections of the Irish War (London: 1927), pp. 11-20.

The chief Volunteer leaders with whom I came into contact early in 1914 were Eoin MacNeill, O'Rahilly, and Sir Roger Casement. Eoin MacNeill and O'Rahilly I had known well before. Roger Casement I never met till then; and of all the men I have ever met, in a wayfaring life, men of every sort and description, I have never met any man of so single and selfless a mind, or of so natural and noble a gesture of soul, as he.

At that time the thought in all our minds was how to equip the Volunteers with arms. If it were right to drill men it was essential to arm them. As to that everyone was agreed. The task was how to do it. As the work required secrecy, the Provisional Committee had constituted Eoin

7 Darrell Figgis (1882-1925), born in Dublin, was at first a tea-buyer at London and Calcutta, then turned to journalism and a literary life. Besides his flat in London he had a cottage on Achill Island. He joined the Irish Volunteers, and was chosen by the London committee, of which Mrs Green was chairman, to go with Childers to the continent and arrange about the purchase and transport of arms and ammunition for the Volunteers. He was arrested after the rising in 1916 and imprisoned in England. He was released, but re-arrested under the Coercion Act in February 1917 and deported to England. On return to Ireland he was once again arrested, in connection with the bogus 'German Plot', and again deported to England. He was Hon. Sec. of Sinn Fein from Oct. 1917 to May 1919, and editor of *The Republic*. He was acting secretary of the commission which drew up the constitution for the Irish Free State, and was a T.D. for county Dublin, 1923-5. He was involved in an unsavoury law-case in London, and while it was in progress he was found gassed in his room in a Bloomsbury boarding-house, on 27 October 1925. See the comments on him in R. Brennan, *Allegiance* (Dublin: 1950), pp. 163, 204-6 —*Ed.*

MacNeill and O'Rahilly a special Arms Sub-Committee, with powers to add to their number and to draw upon the Volunteer treasury without revealing their plans. Yet with an Arms Act in force, with British forces in possession of, and British gunboats guarding, the coast, with detectives watching every movement of the leaders, and with all letters examined in the post, the task was obviously one of extraordinary difficulty.

During the early months of 1914 I had frequently discussed this problem with these men. O'Rahilly was in charge of the actual inquiries with certain houses on the Continent, and as I lived in London, where mails (then) were not examined, we arranged that these inquiries should pass through my hands; all letters to Dublin being sent under cover. Yet what with one difficulty and another, one preoccupation and another, April came, and still nothing had been done beyond the gathering of information. In the meantime the men were becoming restive for the lack of arms—for there is nothing to which the Irishman is more sensitive than to ridicule—and to drill with wooden guns was to offer oneself as a target for ridicule.

Then the political situation compelled a rapid decision. For an attempt was made by the politicians to capture the movement; and the only way to save it, and keep it independent (to keep it in existence at all, in fact), seemed to be—arms.

During the early months of 1914 the Volunteers had spread too rapidly through the country for them to be looked upon with any favour by the older political leaders. Only slowly did they actually learn that the bonds of their control had been loosened. Preoccupied with the lobbies of Westminster, they had omitted to keep in touch with events in Ireland, where they had been trained to think their kingdom was secure. I had occasion to meet John Redmond fairly frequently during these months, and I remember what seemed to me the amazing incredulity with which he heard the news of the spread of the movement that to me had become a commonplace. His incredulity was as incredible to me as my commonplaces were incredible to him, and nothing more surely convinced me than those meetings of the wrong Irishmen did themselves, as well as did their country, by absenting themselves from home to attend a Parliament in London.

Yet one could perceive the political leaders were vaguely apprehensive. Their thoughts were concentrated on London lobbies, where a difficult battle had to be fought, but their instincts were alert and discomforted. Human nature will not be denied, and to the minds of these Master Builders (whose building seemed so near completion) there came the ancient, horrible fear of Youth knocking at the door. Therefore, while they disbelieved what they were told, they planned to capture and control the movement.

Moreover, there was another consideration in their minds. It must be remembered that at that time none doubted that within a few months Home Rule would begin to come into operation with the transfer of services. And John Redmond plainly said to me that he had no intention of forming a new government with so incommensurable an organization in the field in dispute of his authority.

In Ireland, therefore, the two chief political organizations, the United Irish League and the Ancient Order of Hibernians, were warned; and the new movement began to encounter suspicion and hostility where once all had gone well. Thus the problem matured that had been perceived from the beginning. With great wisdom and skill the leaders of the Volunteers had, during these early months, avoided all suspicion of opposing political organizations, and so had averted their hostility. The fruits of the political crop were, apparently, ripe to harvest, and the Volunteers had been presented as a drilled alternative should that harvest be threatened. Indeed, this was true political wisdom, spoken in all sincerity by the leaders of the revolutionary side of the movement, such as Eoin MacNeill and Roger Casement. It was not the faith of revolutionaries like Tom Clarke. But both were agreed that, however their ends might differ, the Volunteers, to be an effective body, must be kept as a separate organization, free from political control. Otherwise (it was argued) they would cease to be a drilled, disciplined force, and become a parade of political fustian, neither picturesque nor practical. And now this danger, long foreseen and adroitly averted, became a continual anxiety, with the alternative of a disastrous split.

In such passes the natural tendency is to play for time. Early in the year, therefore, I had been desired by Eoin MacNeill to get into contact with John Redmond, and to keep the issue in abeyance as long as possible. I would therefore be able to report what was passing in his mind, and at the same time the Volunteers would have time to strengthen themselves in the country. It is probable that, ultimately, some months of valuable time were gained in this way; but in April it became necessary that the actual leaders should themselves come to London to see the Parliamentary men.[8]

So on Thursday Eoin MacNeill and Roger Casement, who had been appointed for that purpose by the Provisional Committee, travelled to meet John Redmond, John Dillon, and Joseph Devlin at Westminster, and it was as a result of that meeting that the decision was taken to proceed without delay to the arming of the Volunteers.

This meeting was held the day following, and on Saturday I lunched with them at Mrs J. R. Green's house in Grosvenor Road, Westminster. After lunch we spoke of their meeting the previous day, and discussed the delicate difficulty that lay immediately before the Volunteers, for at the previous day's meeting John Redmond had suggested (what he later formulated as a demand) that he should nominate as his representatives as many members to the Provisional Committee as there were members already.

8 The events in London, particularly the important meeting in Mrs Green's house, which Figgis describes in the following pages as having taken place in April, almost certainly did not take place until the second week of May. See below, p. 33—Ed.

This then was the method to capture or split the movement: directly to attack the head while the political organizations were busy through the country seeking to envelop the body. If this suggestion were once made as a public demand it seemed impossible to refuse it, yet not to refuse it would be to alienate the Republican Brotherhood.

There seemed but one way to save the position. The Volunteers wanted arms. Those who provided arms would control the force, whoever was appointed to the Provisional Committee. Moreover, if the Republican Brotherhood knew that arms were actually on the way they might accept the immediate demand as inevitable, secure in the knowledge that there would be a further inevitable beyond it, when the existence of an armed force in Ireland would bring the practical control into their hands.

I therefore had asked how O'Rahilly stood in this matter. Eoin MacNeill, I well remember, illustrated the practical difficulties by producing from his pocket envelopes of letters, that had been opened for examination with no attempt to disguise the fact. He told also of the detectives who followed them everywhere. The movement stood in daily fear of proclamation, and with these constant nets about their feet how was it possible to proceed?

Then it was that I made the offer that was to change the entire course of my life, little though I would have believed it at the time. Eoin MacNeill was returning to Dublin that night, and I suggested that O'Rahilly should come over some day early the following week and bring with him all the information he had collected, all the addresses on the Continent, together with all the money on which they could possibly put their hands. The very night of his arrival, if necessary, I would leave for the Continent, while he returned to Ireland. I would use my best discretion and buy. 'Let us buy the rifles,' I said, urging my point, 'and so at least get into the problem. Having them on our hands, we will have to land them somewhere in Ireland.' But the first thing was to buy, and so to present our wits with a problem that they would have to answer. As I could move freely where they could not I offered myself for the making of a beginning.

Never while I live will my eyes forget the effect of my offer on one of the company present. The picture is indelibly written to the last detail.

It was a grey afternoon. The windows gave on to the Thames, and against the grey sky the warehouses on the southern bank were, through the gathering mist, lined in an outline of darker grey and black, the tall chimneys uplifted above them. The tide was out, and beside the distant quayside some coal-barges lay tilted on the sleek mud of the river-bottom, with their sides washed by the silver waters that raced seaward.

Against this picture, looking outward before the window-curtains, stood Roger Casement, a figure of perplexity, and the apparent dejection which he always wore so proudly, as though he had assumed the sorrows of the world. His face was in profile to me, his handsome head and noble outline cut out against the lattice-work of the curtain and the grey sky. His height seemed more than usually commanding, his black hair and beard longer than usual. His left leg was thrown forward, and the boot was torn in a great hole—for he gave his substance away always, and left himself thus in need, he who could so little afford to take these risks with his health. But as I spoke he left his place by the window and came forward towards me, his face alight with battle'. "That's talking" he said, throwing his hand on the table between us; and I remember the whimsical thought crossing my mind that language had wandered far from its meanings when one man could say to another that he was talking, when his appreciation and brevity betokened an end of talking.

All this, it must be remembered, was some weeks before the Larne gun-running, when, on the 24th of April, Carson and his friends ran rifles into Ireland past the blockade of the British Fleet. It has been thought that the Howth gun-running was a direct consequence of the success at Larne. Actually one was well in training when the other occurred,[9] and

9 Figgis' statement is most probably incorrect. Certainly nothing effective was undertaken by the committee until after the gun-running at Larne. Roger Casement, in an article in the *Evening Mail*,

when the news came from Larne we were delighted, and not only because it gave us an excellent protection for the task at which we were engaged.

Before we left Mrs Green's that evening it had been agreed that I should act on my offer. Eoin MacNeill was not at first quite clear as to beginning without seeing the end. His mind was naturally disinclined from this course of procedure, and wished to see beginning and end together; but he was thoroughly convinced of the necessity of immediate action, and before he left he formally committed the direction of the action into my hands, as, he explained, he was entitled to do under the powers given to him by the Provisional Committee.

In order to ensure absolute secrecy only he, Casement, and O'Rahilly were to know of my name in the matter until the rifles had actually been bought and landed. I was to make whatever arrangements I decided in London, and to communicate as little as possible with Ireland, even with Eoin MacNeill, about the matter. The action, in fact, was to be disengaged as completely as possible from Ireland, where MacNeill would assume general responsibility with the Provisional Committee. In case it were necessary for me to communicate with him he gave me a cover under which to write, and letters to me were also to come under cover. His name in the transaction was always to be John Nelson, and mine to be Edmund Farwell—a name suggested by Roger Casement, with some recondite meaning which he promised to expound, but which I forgot to ask and never got. Thus I would always have perfect cover under which to work while I made my arrangements in London and on the Continent. As for the arrangements in Ireland, these were to be in O'Rahilly's hands, and the two of us were to discuss the manner in which our respective plans were to interlock when he came to London the following week.

Then we left Grosvenor Road and walked to Casement's rooms in

---

of New York, 10 August 1916, (gives 8 May as the date of the meeting in London. This, and not Figgis' date, fits the sequence of events as we know them from contemporary sources such as the papers of Erskine Childers—*Ed.*

Knightsbridge as dusk was falling, still talking over the matter. We dined that night in some Italian restaurant opposite Victoria Tube Station, before going on to Euston, where MacNeill was to catch the Irish Mail. Just before the train left Tom Kettle joined us. He had come over to London in connection with the meeting the previous day, and MacNeill and he returned together.

Roger Casement was in walking mood, and the two of us walked to Shaftesbury Avenue, till I left him to return to Hampstead, where I then lived. It seems a momentous night in my years as I look back on it now, with all that was to flow out of the decision taken that day. None of us knew the future, a fortunate fact, no doubt. The action on which I had entered was to achieve world-publicity; and prominent statesmen, to mask their mature plans, were to attach to it responsibility for a world-war. But that night it seemed that it would be a quiet and secret affair. It would be an affair of some risks, to be sure, but it would be an honourable service, with a joy of adventure; and after it were over one would return to one's notebooks and literary projects. So my wife and I thought of it, as we discussed it that night—and so much for human prevision.

12. List of subscribers to the gun-running fund

This list is in the handwriting of Mrs Alice Stopford Green, and accompanies a letter of hers to Bulmer Hobson, dated 30 October 1914 from 30 Grosvenor Road, Westminster, London. Mrs Green was chairman of the private committee which financed the gun-running. In the letter she mentions that the total cost of the affair was £1,523-19-3d. She does not include her own name among the subscribers, although in fact she contributed generously.

The list is in the *Bulmer Hobson Papers*, N.L.I., MS 13174 (3).
Mrs Erskine Childers, 13 Embankment Gardens, S.W.
(Two friends of Mrs Childers subscribed through her anonymously.

Papers might be sent to her for these subscribers.)

Lord Ashbourne, Moorhurst, Holmwood, Surrey.[10]

Lady Young, Formosa Place, Cookham.[11]

The Hon. Mary Spring Rice, Mount Trenchard, Foynes.[12]

Conor O'Brien, c/o Hon. Mary Spring Rice.[13]

Hugh O'Brien, c/o Hon. Mary Spring Rice.[14]

G. F. H. Berkeley Esq., Hanwell Castle, near Banbury.[15]

Cumann-na-mBan Secretary, Miss M. Ryan, 18 Delamere Terrace, W.[16]

13. The boat at Foynes

Erskine Childers to his wife, 22 May 1914.
In the Childers Papers.

> On the train from Foynes to
> Dublin Friday 22 May 1914

Darling,

I reached Foynes about 1.30 yesterday in an unexpected fashion. It appears one has to change for Foynes on the way between Limerick and it but no one told me of this change at any point and I went past the junction till a ticket collector told me I was wrong. This was at Ardagh—a

---

10 For Lord Ashbourne see below, p. 117.

11 Lady Alice Eacy Young, daughter of Evory Kennedy, M.D., of Belgard, Co. Dublin. She first married Sir Alexander Hutchinson Lawrence, and after his death married secondly Sir George Young of Formosa Place, Cookham, Berkshire—see *Walford's County Families*, London 1919, p. 1474. For information on Lady Young I am indebted to John Lawrence, Chelsea, London; George Lawrence, Brockham End, Bath; Sir George Young, Cornwall Gardens, London—*Ed.*

12 For Mary Spring Rice see below, p. 68.

13 For Conor O' Brien see below, pp. 108-9.

14 Hugh Vere O'Brien, of Monare, Foynes, was a cousin of Conor.

15 For G. F. H. Berkeley see below, p. 185.

16 Now Mrs Richard Mulcahy—*Ed.*

little village—no cars—no train to Foynes for several hours. Distance 10 miles. So I sent my bag on by train, wired to Mary [Spring Rice] and walked. Half-way L. Knox[17] met me in a car and I arrived in time for lunch. The Lord [i.e., Monteagle] is still away—only Mary and Knox there and Conor [O'Brien] on his yacht. Afterwards we went to the *Santa Cruz* and found Conor, passing a Volunteer meeting in the village—the men having wooden guns. We spent some time examining the *S[anta] [Cruz]*. She is a fine powerful smack—very old but sound enough for sea with certain repairs—of course in an awful state of mess and confusion. We spent some time noting defects and considering plans —Conor had made a very good plan of proposed alterations. He is right, that the only way of fitting her up for us is to use the forward part exclusively—the stern is no good as the hold comes so far aft. A stateroom would be bulkheaded off for you and M[ary] on the starboard side. A w.c. on the port side and the rest would be the saloon and men's part in one. Water tank high up in the eyes of the boat. Light and air are difficulties. We decided it would be impossible to have skylights—would take too long to make, to say nothing of the cost, and we thought it best to have small dead-lights and ventilators over your 'stateroom' as well as a little square hatch for use in dry weather.

The saloon would have a big glass dead-light over part of the long fissure now open for the heel of the mast to rise through when mast is lowered. Also there would be the companion and door. Of course there's a lot of work even in the simplest fitting up on these lines and I fear it will be very uncomfortable for you at the best but that was inevitable.

Besides the boat has to be entirely re-rigged and numbers of repairs done. Mary wants to buy her outright from the Mill for £30 and recoup the heavy cost of outfit by letting her for trawling.

We roughly calculated that she will cost £70 to fit out i.e. for carpentry, blacksmith, rigging etc. and not counting things which are needed in any case for the *Sibella*—such as w.c., and all the 1000 and one small

---

17 The Knoxes were cousins of the Spring Rices—*Ed.*

fittings that are down in your list. I too am very sceptical about the time. They say she will be ready for sea in a month, say June 20th. Not myself knowing the local workers, I cannot of course check this but I have grave doubts. (The sails seem to be all-right).

> We have had long talks and I have thought much and doubtfully over it and decided to go on and do it. The thing is that there seems no alternative. M[ary] dead against Conor having command, and says is useless at a crisis and that rules out *Kelpie* which is anyway too small for the purpose, except in the last resort.
>
> Erskine.

14. Childers and Figgis in quest of guns May 1914

Expense sheet, written by Erskine Childers, in the Childers Papers.
May Erskine Childers spent: Marks pfn frs cents £ s. d.

	Marks pfn frs cents	£ s. d.
27 2 Tickets to Liege		3 3 0
@ £1-11-6d. each cab to Charing X		2 0
28 lunch at Liege		8 65
Hotel Liege and breakfast		3 50
coffee		2 00
2 Tickets Liege to Hamburg	14 15= 11 1	
conductor train to Hamburg		1 00
coffee etc. at Koln		1 50
2 sleeping tickets		16 00
tips		1 00
29 dinner 2 at Hamburg		6 50
30 Hotel bill		13 00
2 sample revolvers		11 00

2 Tickets to London via Flushing	95 40	
dinner for 2 on train	3 65	
	138 05	6 18 0
31 2 breakfasts Folkestone	10	
cab home E.G.	10	
sundries	10	

15. Buying the guns at Hamburg

by Darrell Figgis

From *Recollections of the Irish War,* pp. 21-34.[18]

The supreme difficulty that confronted us at every turn was that ours was a poor man's movement. The rich did not smile on us, nor were the wealthy kind. Even while one began to put together the separate pieces of one's plan, Sir Edward Carson, unknown to us, was maturing (or others acting for him were maturing) his own scheme for just such a project, but where he was clad in soft raiment we were lean and naked, and where rich men filled his coffers we had to fare by our wits. It made a woeful difference—a difference that antiquity has not robbed of its sting.

I was faced with the difficulty in London, and O'Rahilly was faced with it in Ireland. He did not, indeed, come to London for a further fortnight for just this very reason. Only a few hundred pounds could be collected at so short a notice, and the inadequacy of this sum laughed at us. In the meantime he sent me the address of a firm in Hamburg, and I arranged with them to send samples of two rifles, one of an ancient pattern, the other of a pattern downright antique, to a firm in Hounsditch for inspection.

While he delayed I rehearsed all possible plans, that they might

18 Throughout this and subsequent chapters Figgis presents himself as the principal figure in the gun-running. This does not square with the facts as we know them from other contemporary reliable sources.—*Ed.*

be made to fit to the plans he would bring, and it was always at that point of juncture they failed. It was clear that whatever money could be gathered together would barely suffice for a presentable purchase of arms. Assuming that problem answered, and the rifles bought and ready to ship, how were they to be brought to Ireland for delivery where O'Rahilly arranged to have them? To charter a vessel was out of the question. Our more fortunate, if a little uneasy, comrades in Ulster were at that very moment devising just so splendid a gesture; but gestures of this sort were not for our humbler, though not less determined, folk.

Always in our conversations, therefore, Roger Casement and I returned to this problem. That it was always present in his mind I knew by the fact that during the first week a number of persons came from him with plans to discuss. Then he himself said that the daughter of an Irish peer had offered to contrive the use of her father's yacht, but she herself frankly indicated the difficulties to its use.[19]

The boat itself was not suitable, and it lay in a river creek near a police barracks. Its removal would certainly be noted and the boat marked. It was therefore decided that Casement and I should continue our inquiries.

Then on the eve of his leaving for Ireland he wrote saying he had discovered the very boat. It belonged to Mr Erskine Childers, the English publicist who had written a book on Ireland, and who was ready to help. He gave me his address, and urged me to see him without delay.

On receipt of this letter I went at once to see Mr Childers at his flat in Chelsea. He told me that Casement had spoken to him fully concerning our project, and that he was willing to help in every way possible, recognizing the risks that were involved, and the necessity for absolute secrecy. He described his yacht, and said that he had laid it at the end of the previous summer at (if I remember aright) Criccieth,[20] in North Wales, but that it could easily be put into seaworthy condition at very

19 For an accurate account of Mary Spring Rice's proposal see above, pp. 36-7, and below, p. 50
20 The yacht was at Conway, not at nearby Criccieth—*Ed.*

short notice. And while he spoke of his yacht, which was clearly the very thing for which we had been looking, I weighed in my mind a number of balances that had nothing whatever to do with yachts at all.

For I had, then and there, either to invite him or not; for though Casement had, it seemed, practically invited him, Casement had also invited others who had come to me, and I had found it necessary, for one reason or another, to set them to work that was not intended to come to anything. Childers was a different case. He had either to be swallowed whole or rejected whole. And the balances, as I weighed them, always inclined towards him, quite apart from the matter of the yacht, which was the chief cause of his assistance being sought.

It then seemed to me strange, for example, that an Englishman[21] should desire to bear these risks in our service; but on the other hand, his position in England, his social connections, his influence with a section of the Liberal Party, then in power, were safeguards not to be thrown lightly aside. I knew it would be said (as it very quickly was) that an Englishman, though his worth were gold, should not be told of our plans against his country; but then Roger Casement had already told him fully of them, and a man of his tradition would be bound by adding responsibility to knowledge, where he might not regard himself bound if that addition were not made. Besides, if he helped, he would help only at sea, where he was a yachtsman of known skill, and where his services for Great Britain had been such that he would hardly be suspected of trafficking with those who wished to run guns to her peril.

So, while he spoke, I weighed these things. O'Rahilly was expecting to come any day now, and I was still unable to join my plans to his where the sea stretched between us. That threw the last consideration in the scale, and when Mr Childers had finished I told him my plans.

---

21 Figgis adds in a note about Childers, 'In later years he maintained his right as an Irishman, but at that time none of us thought of him as other than a well-known English publicist who had eloquently and learnedly espoused our cause.' Childers wrote of himself 'I am by birth, domicile and deliberate choice, an Irishman.'

My proposal was to distribute my responsibility to a selected London committee, each member of which would take charge of one part of the whole action. Mrs Green should be invited to give her great name and large capacity to the care of its treasury, to collect, receive and account all moneys. Mr Childers would take charge of all arrangements for the shipment of our little armoury. And I would, while generally responsible for their delivery (a responsibility of which I could not rid myself), take charge of their purchase and of their delivery on to Mr Childers' yacht wherever we should arrange for this to occur. To this he added a suggestion that Mrs Childers should be added to our committee, as the channel of communication when we would be at the separate ends of our common action.

Without delay we went then to Mrs Green, who agreed to act as treasurer. Without her it is improbable that we could have brought our enterprise to an end. It was she who in great part covered the liabilities incurred, until they should be met by donations, promises, and the sale of the guns when landed. It was under her direction that a number of wage-earners were banded together, each one of whom, out of her or his poverty, covered a limited share of that liability until the final sale to the Volunteers, risking that much of absolute loss if the enterprise failed. At every hour of the day and night she was always ready to lend herself and her resources to our hazardous enterprise.

Within a few days O'Rahilly came. I met him in the porch of the Victoria Hotel in Northumberland Avenue. There he told me that he had been followed from Ireland, and that Dublin detectives were even at that moment waiting outside the hotel for him. But London is not Dublin in the matter of following a sleuth, and that night he slept at Hampstead unknown and unguarded. His first and chief anxiety was concerning Childers. When he had been satisfied in that regard, he unfolded his part of the plan while I unfolded ours. Briefly, his plan consisted of a number of secret dumps around the southern and western Irish coast. He explained that at each of these dumps the yacht would, during June, as though cruising for pleasure, deliver agreed lots of rifles on agreed dates. In this way the difficulty of distribution from one centre in Ireland would be avoided, and the dumps would be chosen (several of them, he said, had already been arranged) for speedy delivery to districts where it was known that companies were ready to buy.

I was not happy about the plan, and, when we discussed it at a meeting of our committee the following morning, neither was Childers. The risks of delivery at ten centres seemed a hundred times greater than delivery at one centre. But the plan had been approved in Ireland, and we had no alternative but to proceed with our part of the enterprise. The rest of our discussion turned on matters of finance, since it was imperative that we should know to what extent we could commit ourselves.

Casement was now back in London, and he took Childers and myself to see a friend of his at St. Mary Axe who was agent for a Belgian armoury firm. In the meantime the samples had arrived from Hamburg, and one of them, an old 9 mm. bore Mauser rifle, seemed the thing for our purpose, cheap and undeniably effective—as was afterwards proved. Rifles are one of the infernal inventions of man's wit—the prehistoric caveman's hunger and battle for life surviving as a slayer's lust in the finished craftsmanship of machinery. But if they are to be used it is right that they be effective, and our strange love (I have the original sample yet) would, we decided, be effective— patiently and weightily effective.

Thus, with O'Rahilly's information and our own separate inquiries, I was now ready to proceed to the Continent. Childers came with me. We went first to Liege, to the armoury firm of which Roger Casement's friend was agent. While day dawned we sped through flat Belgian fields, where roads went straight into the distance, flanked by slender poplars, where every acre was alive with green cultivation, chill with dew, and clothed with the golden warmth of May, but where, presently, armies were to march and slaughter reign, in memory, for that cockpit of Europe, of a hundred other armies and a hundred other reigns of slaughter. And we, too, as we sped, went to buy instruments of slaughter in a city that was not only itself an ancient cockpit of war, but the armoury of the obsolete and obsolescent weapons of Europe, where poor nations came to buy discarded toys of their wealthy brethren.

Liege merchants, however, could not help us. Their toys were pretty but too expensive. We were not so foolish as to refuse them. Baffled sellers have other means of profit in such forbidden gear; but we left Liege that night knowing well that its merchandise was not for our purses.

We went to Hamburg, a city beautiful and modernly ancient, like a comely matron who can keep her place with the liveliest of youth. We lodged at a pleasant little hotel opposite the railway station, and after our morning coffee we went a few hundred yards down the same Strasse to O'Rahilly's firm of Michael Magnus, Junior.[22]

It was a wonderful firm. It moved my admiration then, and has never ceased to move it since. It was conducted by two brothers—Michael, masterful and calm, and his elder brother Moritz, expressive and expostulant. In an adventurous life I had not suspected the existence of such persons. A few months later Europe was to be loud with claimants for the honour of being considered the Friend of Small Nationalities. I did not hear my good friends Michael and Moritz then, but I thought of them. For here they were, the genuine Friends of Small Nationalities, professing nothing large, but practicing their faith and friendship consistently, neglecting fine speeches and directing their attention to good deeds. They were not politicians looking to fill their sails with favourable winds. Practical men, rather, after the manner of their compatriot St. Peter, who held that faith without works is dead. Therefore, after every war, they bought armaments of all sorts from neglected battlefields, and established an armoury to which small nations might repair for the

---

22 The shipper's receipt from Hamburg, in the Childers Papers and dated 10 July 1914, describes the firm as Morite Magnus Jnr.—*Ed.*

righting of their wrongs, and where they plied their faith, through good repute and bad, in the brief hope of immediate reward.

The tokens of their faith, from large shell-cases to small pistols, were about us as we sat in their upholstered room; but something had occurred to weaken that faith. That was evident to both Childers and myself. They had the article we needed; we had the small tribute they so reasonably required; yet the two brothers constantly retired to consult how they might make clear to us that they would not help. As a matter of fact they both spoke excellent English, but we found a curious inability to understand them when they came to rehearsals of that critical sentence. Oddly enough, we even sometimes understood them in a completely opposite sense, and so, baffled, they withdrew again. When they withdrew, Childers expostulated that we were wasting our time, since it was clear they would not sell, whatever the cause might be. It was not easy to make clear to him that, since we had found the article we wanted, if we were patient enough, and bland enough, and imperturbable enough, nothing could prevent us getting it. The great thing was to husband our energy so as not to be the first to be fatigued.

Later I learned the cause of their reluctance. I little thought when I learned it how strangely I should afterwards remember it, when the whole world was at war. For, a few weeks before this, Carson had run his cargo of rifles at Larne, and these rifles had been bought in Hamburg. Germany, I was told, believed that Britain was looking for a cause of war, and the German Government had therefore warned all firms that they must under no circumstances sell arms to Ireland. Another affair such as Larne, with its noise and alarm, might bring serious consequences that Germany was anxious to avert. This, be it remembered, was told me before our affair at Howth, and two months before the European war. I thought it fantastic then, though I soon had cause to know that the fear was genuine.

However, at the time I knew nothing of this. We were puzzled but bland, immovably fixed in their capacious upholstery, and astonishingly unintelligent. Then, more by chance than through good wit, I let drop that we desired these rifles for Mexico. Mexico? The two brothers looked quickly at one another and withdrew for another consultation. Childers complained that no one in their senses would mistake us for Mexicans, and I had barely answered that lies like this were not told for belief, but merely to give the other side a reasonable excuse for agreement, when the two brothers returned. They were very cautious, and they expressed their interest in the case of Mexico; but it was obvious that they were now in quite another mood. Their caution was now not reluctance, but a wary tread towards a business deal.

We entered the office of Magnus at 9.20 in the morning, and it was after 12.30 before we had bought our rifles. It had proved an unexpectedly and unreasonably stubborn battle, and we had no knowledge of the cause of the difficulty beyond what we could infer from the catching at the Mexican straw. It was therefore necessary to have the matter in writing. I drew out then the chief heads of a memorandum of agreement. After lunch, when Michael Magnus was our admirable host, we continued to work at that agreement till nearly seven that night, when we exchanged signed copies, subject to its revision by consent on the morrow, Whit-Saturday, when we were to return home. The rifles, we were told, were warehoused at Liege, and Magnus was to wire me within one month to come for them— first to inspect them in detail and then to bear them away.

That night Childers stayed to examine the agreement while I went to the opera. No amount of banter could dissuade him from an examination word by word of that agreement. Yet actually it was worthless as a legal document. I had signed it as Edmund Farwell, and he had signed it also under his assumed name. Its only value was for its effect on Magnus, and that did not require every comma to be in its right place. Our true safeguard was in our banking arrangements, by which no money would be released till a mate's receipt had been given for the cargo. Yet when I came down to coffee the next morning Childers was still worrying over that agreement, seeking for verbal perfection where we had the substance of what we wanted.

The following day we returned home. Before we did so, however, we went with Magnus to the Direktor of the Deutsche Bank to complete our banking arrangements, and to a shipping-house to charter a tug. Here we met another difficulty. We had already purchased a thousand rifles, with the option of another five hundred to be taken with them, and this committed us to moneys which it was doubtful if we could gather in the time. But now an extortionate sum of £300 was demanded for a tug down the river, and by no means could we get the price lowered.

Therefore we left this an open question, and the following week we went to Antwerp to see if we could better the price. We tried three houses there, and at each the price was £300. Clearly we were on another's trail, and that trail, as clearly, was Carson's. So at Antwerp, seeing that we were not to do business there, we were simple and ingenuous and frank. A fleet of Irish trawlers, we said, were to meet the tug we wanted, and we would send them fuller details later. I have been told, in such a way as to believe it, that all Irish trawlers were watched and carefully searched for some time after this. Yachts escaped attention.

In the meantime Mrs Green had her organization at work for the collection of money, and on OUT return from Antwerp, while I awaited the telegram from Magnus, Childers and I gave our attention to arrangements for shipment and landing. He was doubtful if his yacht would conveniently carry 1,500 rifles, if we found ourselves able to take the other 500, and he therefore proposed that he should ask Conor O'Brien, whose yacht was only slightly smaller than his own, to take a share of our cargo. We agreed upon this; but this meant that Childers, when on his way to Criccieth, would need to continue on to Dublin, and, while there, see O'Rahilly. Then Casement wrote saying that he gravely doubted the wisdom of continuing with O'Rahilly, who was being too closely followed by detectives. Knowing the trouble O'Rahilly had taken in the matter since the beginning of the year, I was averse to breaking with him. Moreover, if we broke with him, this would have to be done unknown to him in order to leave the detectives to follow a false clue. The success of our enterprise would require this; but no one could have taken such a course with a man so loyal and loveable as O'Rahilly without mean thoughts of himself. Childers did not know O'Rahilly and did not share my feelings in the matter; but for some time I would not consent until Roger Casement crossed to London and explained that a change would have to be made. At that time I was waiting for the telegram from Magnus while struggling with arrears of my own work. Moreover, about this time Casement was completing his arrangements to cross to America, and was due to leave within a week. We therefore agreed that Childers should leave for Dublin as soon as possible, taking letters of introduction with him from Casement.

Before he returned (perhaps before he left) Casement had gone, as I remember the unpleasant circumstances that followed. On the morning of his return I met Childers at his flat, where we all were to lunch. To my extreme surprise Childers would say nothing, but that he met a man who was to be known as 'Dolan', with whom he had made other plans which he was not at liberty to divulge. I asked who 'Dolan' was, and he claimed confidence there, too. The situation was awkward, for I was a guest in his house, yet with a responsibility of which I could not rid myself. I rose to leave, protesting another appointment and asked him to dine with me at my club. He countered me by the offer of his club. So we arranged an independent meeting for that evening.

I was greatly distressed. The situation was as unpleasant as it could be. There had been small earlier causes for discontent, but our common responsibilities did not allow of their entertainment. This, however, was a different matter. It affected not one's personal feelings so much as one's responsibilities. So, as we sat in a tavern in Whitehall, I spoke frankly, and said that whereas until that moment we had been two good comrades together, I had now to remember that he held his trust from me, whereas I held it from those who were in turn my chiefs. I had no intention of delivering any rifles into his yacht until I knew what he proposed to do with them. In the first place, I wished to know who 'Dolan' was; in the second, what the new plan was.

Then I learned that 'Dolan' was Bulmer Hobson, a member of the Provisional Committee; and that the plan was to hold up the port of Howth, near Dublin, and land the rifles in the port openly in broad day, avoiding all the dangers and difficulties of manoeuvres at night. Where the difficulty had been I could not perceive, for the name carried its own guarantee, and the plan was clearly the right one. It had the simple boldness that attunes and tempers the blood. Besides, audacity has always been its own best protection, since it is never expected and robs one's foeman of the initiative—a quality beyond price in manoeuvre.

16. Final plans at Dublin

Erskine Childers to his wife, 21 June 1914
In the *Childers Papers*. Dublin Sunday night, 21 June 1914

Darling,

I got to Conway about 2.15 and stayed till a 5.15 train which took me to Holyhead and caught the evening boat so I got to Dublin at 10.30 and had a good night's rest. The condition of the yacht was rather dispiriting—very behind-hand and everything done rather slackly. All the gear in different places so that I could not properly check it but there seems to be much missing and I suspect Nowell's carelessness. Sails not ready yet. However he says he will be ready by the end of the week and I shall probably send over the two men as soon as possible to help. The vixen compass (not its binnacle which is there) is not in store, and appears not to be on the inventory. Is it at the flat—do you remember? The clock and barometer are on the inventory but Crossfield seems to know nothing of them.

8.30 p.m.

I wrote so far after breakfast and then people began coming. I ought to say that last night on arrival I found Casement staying here and also Colonel Moore, the latter a rather embarrassing factor as he knows nothing. I took a private sitting-room but he came in this morning and found Mary [Spring Rice] here much to her disgust! I had had a long talk already with Casement in his bedroom as to our view of their recent action and communicated what Mrs G[reen] said. I think all is fairly well in that quarter. They are going to go on working as hard as ever and the first bitterness is passing but they were terribly bitter.[23]

I told them all we felt. I tried to cheer them. Ultimately I did tell Casement that I had seen Redmond. I found that concealing it made such a mystery and I think it did no harm. They fear Dillon and T. P. [O'Connor] far more than Redmond. Devlin made a very bad anti-Ulster speech yesterday, I see,—just the very thing the Volunteers were out to stop. Casement looks ill —bad cold—He is burning himself up, I think. He told me a lot about the negotiations which was new to me.

Mary came at 10.30. Smiling and cheerful as usual. We talked over plans for the cruise and its destination. It is settled that C[onnor] is to take his, unless I find the two men can't come with us, possibly. We are to meet down south and if Gordon S[hephard] can't come he might be able to spare a friend for us, from there on. C[onnor] came later and we talked over this.

---

23 The 'recent action' and 'bitterness' concerned the crisis over Redmond's demand for the addition of twenty-five of his nominees on the Provisional Committee of the Volunteers. For this crisis see *The Irish Volunteers, 1913-1915*, ed. F. X. Martin, O.S.A., Dublin 1963, pp. 43-53, 141-155.

Arrival plans many but all very vague. F[iggis'] as sent through his wife the other day is really the most specific we have (barring Dolan's) but it is a distant desolate place.[24]

Dolan[25] came later and we had long talks. He is pessimistic about all the ordinary sort of plans and produced a very daring one of his own which took my breath away. It has points of difficulty however, concerned with that old defect I have been worrying over. On the other hand he says he cannot guarantee good arrangements on the west or elsewhere as organization is so bad that he could not lay his hand on the men: though in certain limited districts he can do so but other conditions are bad. He lunched with me and went on talking afterwards till nearly 5 when I went off to see MacNeill. It is all right about the money— his [£]200 was Committee money from a fund in his charge. O'R[ahilly]'s is private which he promised and always intended to give. I explained our doubts but there was really nothing to explain—they seemed perfectly happy.—I saw O'Rahilly himself later and came away about 8. I am now awaiting a second visit from M[ary] and C[onnor]. But I must stop this first.

17. Everything completed

Figgis to Childers
In the *Childers Papers*
Lloyd Hotel Hamburg7/vii/1914
Dear C,

I hope to be able to get back by 12 o'clock on Sat. That is what I am at present trying to arrange. Failing which, and if better for you, I could manage 12 on Sunday; but, frankly, I much prefer the earlier day. I think I shall have everything completed and ready by then.

By the way, what do you think of 'Gladiator' for the name of that boat? It sounds good, don't you think? It struck me at once when I saw it

---

24 Figgis is likely to have suggested Achill Island, since he had a cottage there and knew the area well—*Ed.*

25 The *nom de guerre* for Bulmer Hobson—*Ed.*

on a tug on the river here.

I had hoped to hear from you; but it occurs to me that you may have written to the Poste Restante. I have not been there yet; but will do so.

Salutations to you and to your party.

Go raibh an t-ádh ort agus ar an obair.

Mise do chara fíor

Darrell Figgis

18. Now or Never!

Pádraig Pearse to Joe McGarrity, 17 July 1914.[26]
Authenticated copy in *Bulmer Hobson Papers*, N.L.I., MS 13162.

St. Enda's College,

Rathfarnham,

17th July 1914

A Chara Chroidhe,

I am writing on behalf of the large and important element in the Irish Volunteers represented by the nine dissentients on the Provisional Committee—in other words, on behalf of the men who are still determined to keep the movement straight and to lend it, if they can, to a genuine national purpose. Our appeal is this: we want the American Committee to make arrangements, if possible, to send us at once at least as much arms and ammunition as will arm our men in Dublin,—say

26 Joseph McGarrity (1874-1940), was born at Carrickmore, Co. Tyrone. He emigrated to the U.S.A. at the age of sixteen and made a fortune at Philadelphia in the liquor distilling business. Much of his money was spent on the cause of Ireland. He was a leader of Clann-na-Gael, and a staunch supporter of the Irish Volunteers, St. Enda's School, and the 1916 Rising. He was host to Hobson, Pearse, Terence MacSwiney, Dr P. McCartan, Eamon de Valera, and other Irish leaders who came to the U.S.A. He founded the Irish Press at Philadelphia, and managed the bond drive which brought in $5,500,000 for the Irish Republic. He was an uncompromising believer in an Irish republic to embrace thirty-two counties. He died on 5 August 1940—*Ed.*

1000 rifles with a fair amount of ammunition for each. We want this request to take precedence of any other request that may have been made by MacNeill or by anyone else. A friend of mine will be in America before this reaches you, and, though he was not one of the nine dissentients, his *bona fides* is above suspicion and he will, I think, give you further reasons showing the necessity of doing what I suggest, if the situation is to be saved. The men with whom I am acting more immediately in this are Sean MacDiarmada, Kent, and Fitzgibbon. Let me, at the risk of writing an unduly long letter, give the facts of the situation as they exist at the present moment.

I give my colleagues who voted for the surrender to Redmond credit for doing what seemed to them absolutely the best thing in the interests of the movement. Most of them expressed distrust of Redmond, but said that a split must be avoided at all hazards at this stage. Hobson made a strong Separatist speech, saying that Redmond was out to smash the movement, and that the best way to prevent him was to accept his terms for the present and to remain in the movement to meet and best him should he try treachery later on. (I think they have been too hard on Hobson on your side, and regret very much to hear that he has been dropped as Dublin correspondent of the *Gaelic American*. He has lost the acting editorship of *Freedom*, too, and is left without income of any sort. He may have to leave Dublin, which would be an incalculable loss. (Weigh all this.) To resume—I admit that the temptation to vote for unity in Ireland was very great (no one foresaw the American difficulty) but I and the eight others resisted mainly on these grounds:

(1) that we were bound to keep faith with those who had come into the movement on our assurance that it was open to all parties; and (2) that we could not be sure that Redmond, so closely allied with Asquith, could or would co-operate with us in arming the Volunteers.

Now, it appears that in the second thing we were wrong; and the danger to be feared from Redmond is of a different and a graver sort. He does want to arm the Volunteers, or a portion of them; but he wants *to arm them, not against England, but against the Orangemen.* The Volunteers are to be used to force Home Rule on Ulster, and possibly to enforce the *dismemberment of Ireland.* Some semblance of Home Rule must, at all costs, be placed on the statute books: the Volunteers have been captured in- order to secure this, no matter how humiliating the terms. All this has been made plain to us within the last few days. When Gore and Walsh went to London from the Provisional Committee to see Redmond, Redmond told them he had bought 4000 rifles with ammunition at a cost of £10,000, of which he had paid down a portion so as to secure the rifles,—the balance to be paid when or before delivery could be effected.[27] He looked to the enlarged Volunteer Committee to 'run' the guns for him, and hinted (so I understand from Gore) that the Government might relax the precautions so as to convenience us. On Tuesday night last, at the first meeting of the enlarged Committee, Devlin stated that he had just 'run' enough guns into Belfast to arm his men; and he added afterwards to one of the members that his lot included two machine guns. All this would be excellent if the men were genuine nationalists. But they are only Home Rulers—at—any—price.

Man after man of Redmond's nominees stood up at the meeting and made clear that it is against Ulster the guns are to be used. They spoke of the 'massacre' which might break out in the north any minute. They said that all arms reaching us for the present must go to Ulster. It was even suggested that those of us in the south and west who have guns (and guns have just reached Co. Wexford, I know for a fact, and, according to the newspapers, Co. Tipperary) should send them north for use by the Catholics there to defend themselves when the 'massacre' breaks out. The whole tone of the movement has changed, judging at least from the talk at the Provisional Committee. The men whom Redmond has nominated

---

27 George Walsh, who went to London with Gore, was a prominent member of the A.O.H. and of the Irish Volunteers. Though a Redmondite in 1914, he became a member of Sinn Féin in 1918, and was on active service with the Volunteers, 1920-1921. His son, Kevin, kindly allowed me to examine his father's papers which include material on the 1914 negotiations with Redmond in London. See the notice on Walsh by Colonel Dan Bryan in *University Review*, vol. 2, no. 11, p. 52.

clearly regard it as a Pro-Asquith and Anti-Carson movement. They speak of the 'friendly English government' whose efforts we are to 'second'.

Now, here is the situation. The Unionists are armed. The Redmondites are rapidly arming. The Nationalists (Sinn Féiners and Separatists) remain unarmed. It will be an irony of ironies if this movement comes and goes and leaves MS—the physical force men!—the only unarmed group in the country. And this is the intention of those at the head of affairs. *Arms are to be prevented from reaching those whom Redmond cannot control.* On Tuesday night, (without notice) they carried a resolution appointing a Standing Committee which is practically to take charge of the movement—the full Provisional Committee is to meet only once a month. The following are the members of the Standing Committee: Burke, Donovan, Fitzgibbon, Hobson, Judge, Meredith, Nugent, Fr. O'Hare, Walsh, MacNeill, L. Kettle, Gore, O'Rahilly. Of these 13, only Hobson and Fitzgibbon can be absolutely relied on; Judge (tho' a Hibernian) I believe sound and courageous; MacNeill and O'Rahilly are honest, but weak, and frightfully subject to panic. The rest will do exactly as Redmond tells them. At most we can count on only 5 out of the 13 who now rule the Volunteers; but possibly only 2 or 3.

I think you will see the necessity of our not allowing a crash to come until our men at least are armed. *Dublin is with us almost to a man; Cork City and Co.; Limerick City; Waterford City; Galway City; Co. Kerry;* and a large minority everywhere including all the best men—the young, active men. We owe it to these men to arm them; we shall be stultified forever if we allow the chance to go by. We propose to commence in Dublin, which is the soundest, and where we have most influence.

Now, is it in your power to get 1000 rifles and ammunition for us?— more, if possible, but at least 1000 to start with. Springfields would do, but better perhaps Mausers, 7 millimetres, which is the pattern most easy to get. The great point is to have rifles for which we shall be able to get ammunition easily. Your plan should be, I think, to send someone to Europe to make a purchase and then to come on to Dublin to make arrangements with us. Of course you would not land guns until we had completed all arrangements for receiving and distributing them. If need be, we will stand some of the cost, for, if we know guns are coming, we will see that our companies retain their Defence of Ireland funds in their own hands instead of forwarding the money to the suspected Provisional Committee or its precious Standing Committee. Now, please act on this at once: disregard other appeals for the present and co-operate with McDermott, Kent, Fitzgibbon, and me in seeing that the sound men are armed at the earliest possible instant. Let us at least reap that much good out of the movement before it degenerates.

You can communicate with me confidentially on this or other matters as follows. All letters addressed to 'Miss O'Hara, c/o Miss Byrne, Cullenswood House, Oakley Road, Rathmines, Dublin' will be handed unopened to me. Use plain envelopes. Cables may go to same address.

Please regard all inside information in this letter as for your *private ear* or those of colleagues, but not to be used in *Gaelic American* or elsewhere in public. I should not like things said at Provisional Committee to get into the press through me.

I am sending Devoy a letter almost identical with this.

The cause is in your hands now. We are here to do our part.

God bless you and prosper whatever effort you may make. It is up to us and you to *accomplish* something now.

Kindest regards to your family and all Philadelphia friends.

Sincerely and fraternally yours, P. H. Pearse.

19. The Asgard

The yacht was a wedding present from Dr and Mrs Hamilton Osgood of Boston to Erskine Childers and their daughter, Molly. It was built at Laurvig, Norway, in 1905, with Colin Archer as designer and builder. It is a 28 ton, 49 foot, ketch, with a 13' beam and 7' 9" draft, designed on the lines of, but smaller than, the *Fram* which carried Nansen on his Polar expeditions. Childers and his wife travelled widely in the yacht, especially through Baltic and Scandinavian waters. The name of the yacht is from the Old Norse word, *Ásgardr*, meaning 'Home of the Gods'.

Gordon Shephard, a close friend of the Childers' wrote in 1913, The *Asgard* is a fine sea-boat; and besides being weatherly she rides the sea with a very easy motion, a quality which many good sea-boats, especially yachts, do not possess.' In the autumn of 1913 Shephard sailed it from Christiania in Norway via Bergen and the Shetland Islands to Holyhead, covering 1,253 miles in stormy weather. For this feat he was awarded the Challenge Cup of the Royal Cruising Club.

After the Howth gun-running the yacht was laid up at Bangor, North Wales, and in 1926 was disposed of by Mrs Childers to a couple of young sea-lovers. By 1960 it was in the hands of Colonel E. Mullock of Falmouth, who had had it modernized, installing electric fittings and Diesel engines. In January 1961 it was bought for £3,500 by Captain C. Hughes of Ontario, a former officer of the Royal Engineers, who intended to sail it to Canada. However, within a short time he abandoned the project and offered the yacht for sale.

Early in 1961 the young Marquis of Headfort heard of the offer, and with a typical act of impulsive generosity crossed over from Ireland on his own initiative in order to inspect the yacht at Southampton and to see Colonel Mullock at Truro, Cornwall. He was prepared, if necessary, to buy the *Asgard* and organize a public appeal in order to ensure its return to Ireland. While he was engaged in negotiations with Captain Hughes through Colonel Mullock and the Southampton agents (Camper and Nicholson) the Irish government became interested. Mr Gerald Boland, Minister for Justice, as a Volunteer veteran, raised the matter with the Taoiseach, Mr Lemass, and eventually through the Board of Works the yacht was bought for the nation for £4,500.

On 30 July 1961 the *Asgard* sailed back into Howth Harbour, escorted by naval corvettes, saluted by guns, with Air Corps planes flying overhead. There it was formally handed over to the government, as a training vessel for naval cadets. It carried a number of 'Howth' rifles which were ceremoniously handed up from the *Asgard* to some of the former Volunteers and Fianna who had been there forty-seven years previously to receive them. The President, Eamon de Valera, welcomed the *Asgard* in a speech which appears as the foreword of this book.

Part III
Guns on the High Seas

Thanks are due to The Lord Monteagle of Brandon for permission to publish the diary of Mary Spring Rice; to Mr Erskine H. Childers for providing me with an authenticated copy of the diary from his mother's papers; to Sir Shane Leslie for permission to quote two of the letters which he published in Gordon Shephard's *Memoirs*; to Mrs Margaret O'Brien, literary executor of Conor O'Brien, and to the Irish Red Cross for permission to re-publish O'Brien's article from *Irish Red Cross Junior Annual*, 1947; to Mrs Elinor Wiltshire, for information about her uncle, Conor O Brien; to Dr Brendan O'Brien for permission to reproduce the portrait of Conor O'Brien by Kitty Clausen.

Information on Sir Thomas Myles was readily supplied by his relatives Dr Alice Dwyer-Joyce, Histon, Cambridge, England; Mrs Louise Hill Shaw, New Maiden, Surrey; Mr R. Shaw, Surbiton, Surrey; Mrs Isobel Palmer, Dunlaoghaire, Co. Dublin. Mr E, Hannan, Secretary, St Laurence's Hospital (Richmond), Dublin, was most helpful on a number of points and supplied me with a copy of the painting of Sir Thomas Myles in the Students Library of the Hospital.

Diarmuid Coffey kindly sent me the text of his broadcast some months before his death (9 July 1964), and gave me permission to publish it. I am grateful to Mrs Sheela Coffey for information about her husbands career, and to the Radio Eireann authorities for their consent to publish the text.

20. Rendezvous at the Roetigen Lightship

by Darrell Figgis

From *Recollections of the Irish War*, pp. 34-43.

Childers left for Criccieth, and I left shortly afterwards for Liege to complete the last part of our enterprise. As nearly as I can remember I left for Liege on the last day of June, and as I was to take delivery of the further 500 rifles, and to purchase 45,000 rounds of ammunition, for none of which had we made banking arrangements, I took a considerable sum of money with me. My appointment was to meet Erskine Childers and Conor O'Brien at 12 noon at the Roetigen lightship at the mouth of the Scheldt on Sunday, the 12th of July. This would leave them a fortnight to get to Ireland, lest they fell becalmed in July weather. Childers was to bring 1,000 rifles into Howth Harbour punctually at 12.45 on Sunday the 26th, and Conor O'Brien was to land 500 at Kilcoole, Co. Wicklow,[28] the night before to distract attention southward. My wife was to hold the line of communication, and before Childers left Cowes on his way outward we were to exchange telegrams through my wife that all was well on each side.

At Liege my troubles began. There Moritz Magnus was in charge, and though he was the kindest-hearted of men, the most expressive, and the most expostulant, he was not the most efficient. The rifles were all ready, and had each to be inspected, lock, stock, and barrel, but no arrangements had been made for packing them ready on rail for Hamburg. A friend of mine was on holiday in Bruges, and I wired him to help me with the inspection while I installed myself as foreman of works, and negotiated with trade-union officials for a staff. The result was the oddest collection of old women and men that I have ever been blest to see. The days were blistered with heat, and they all worked stripped to the waist. They were homely people, but the example was one I quickly followed, and, while

28 The original understanding was that each yacht would take half of the cargo; see below, pp. 79, 101—*Ed.*

we made a cheery and emphatically jocose party together, we got the work done. As the guns came from inspection we wrapped them in straw and tied them in canvas, twenty apiece. And so, by working early and late, we managed to have the whole consignment put on rail for Hamburg by Saturday evening, the 4th of July, and I was able to spend Sunday peacefully in Cologne and hear Beethoven's Mass in D major in the Cathedral.

At Hamburg our original difficulty took a new and anxious form. On returning to the hotel the first evening I was informed that a police official had been making inquiries. This did not of itself mean anything, but the next morning Michael Magnus told me that they had been warned. Both he and his brother consulted together gravely. It was, they said to me, a serious matter for them, for they could not act against their Government, though they could not think how their Government came by knowledge of our deal. I was being watched, and should be very careful of my movements. Fortunately, it did not appear that their Government suspected that business had already been transacted. They impressed on me that it was for Mexico I wished the rifles. I must always, they said, keep that to the front. England had no interest in Mexico.

These were anxious days. By Wednesday evening I had received no wire from Cowes; my wife had wired (in code) that she had no news, the bundles of rifles had not arrived from Liege, no ammunition had appeared, and I was being followed. Yet the tug had been chartered to leave at eight o'clock on Friday evening.

Lastly, to put the crown on trouble, the shippers informed Magnus that the port regulations required that all outgoing cargoes be examined and certified by a Customs Officer. This was a problem that none of us had suspected, and it seemed insurmountable, for the shippers were a firm of repute and could not afford evasion. But a careful examination of the regulations revealed that a pilot could act as Customs Officer. We decided therefore to engage a pilot, and the shippers undertook to discover a pilot who could (failing Mexican) speak English, and who would have other suitable qualities. As for the skipper and his crew, these had already been provided for in advance. On Thursday I received my wire from Cowes. On Thursday the 'machine-parts' arrived from Liege. But the boxes ammunition did not arrive in Hamburg till within three hours of our time for casting-off from the quayside, and did not reach the quayside till nearly seven o'clock. Neither anger on earth nor prayer to heaven hastened their delivery till the last point of exasperation. And when they were at last got into the hold, and a case here and there opened for examination, to my horror I found they were all dum-dum.[29]

No matter. I would have taken explosive bullets then, I believe, with considerable relish.

All was now ready for the pilot. On him, and on the handling of him, depended everything. I do not believe I have ever scanned any man's face so anxiously, yet so guardedly, for signs either of beneficence or of corruptibility. Either would have been equally suitable. But he was a grave and stern man, with a face like a mask, out of the mouth of which dropped a very big pipe.

I was introduced to him by the skipper as a distinguished Mexican, and I realized with a shock that I had for the first time met someone who believed that I was a Mexican. For the two had spoken in German together. Speaking in English I asked him if he spoke Mexican. No, he did not; but he spoke English. Excellent, that would do as well. He smoked a cigar? He stowed his pipe in his pocket and lit my cigar. He liked it? He did, and said twice, emphatically, that the brand was good. It was the only emphasis I had as yet got out of him, and he was right, the cigar was good. It had been chosen for him. I was glad to have found a man of taste; I hoped he would honour me by accepting the box from which it came. He took the box, stowed it under his arm, and shook my hand.

So he smoked in the cool of a July evening, and walked the deck of the tug as we lay amid the shipping of the port of Hamburg. Then I told

---

29 The bullets were neither dum-dum nor explosive; see below p. 190, n.

him that unhappily I was not very well. He noted the fact without letting the unfortunate occurrence disturb his enjoyment of his cigar. What time would we reach the river mouth? At about 2.30 a.m., he said. At that hour, unfortunately, I hoped to be sleeping soundly and would deny myself the courtesy of his taking leave. He would permit me, therefore, to pay his fee now as I wished at once to turn in.

So we went into the chart-room, where I paid him his fee, and he gave me his receipt. When this was done I quietly passed him three English bank-notes. His blue eyes looked at me with simple wonderment. This was not customary, he said. We had come to the critical moment. Had it been customary, I said, it would not be the courtesy I intended. It was thus we liked to conduct affairs in my country. I hoped he would give me this pleasure. He put the notes carefully and reflectively in his wallet.

We took a few further turns on the deck before he went down to examine the cargo. I walked the deck awaiting his return in an anxiety I could scarcely contain. I found it even difficult to breathe, and only by steady pacing could I control myself, for it would never do to let my anxiety reveal itself. Then I heard him coming up the ladder from the hold. He walked past me, and only as he passed me did he turn for one quick moment and look at me. The light of understanding was in his eye.

He went up on the bridge and spoke to the skipper. The skipper called to the crew, the hawsers were cast off, and the tug began to make a way down the river. All was well. They had chosen a good pilot, who was also a Customs Officer.

Sunday, the 12th of July, 1914, in the North Sea was heavy with ochreous-golden mist. Our world was narrowed to within a few cables' length of the tug, a distance across which heavy surgeless rollers swept, leaving the tug rocking in their wake. These rollers emerged from the mist, smooth and burnished, as from some distant world, lifted the tug upon them, and, while she slid down their sides, they rolled away into the mist, their flanks gleaming in the dull, golden light that fell through the curtain that had enveloped us. Not a breath of wind did they bring with them, not a breath did they draw after them. The day was sultry and close, and not a stir of air visited our faces. From the moment when we cleared the river we had made only half-speed, and about ten on Sunday morning we lay idly rocking among the rollers, lest we should make the lightship too early. It was important that we should not draw the attention of those on the lightship, and for that reason the heavy mist suited us well, though it gave us and our yachts a greater difficulty in picking up one another. Towards noon we drifted nearer, till the lightship hove in sight, and then we lay out of sight to the westward, across the line on which the yachts should come.

It was not till 2.30 that a yacht was called. As she bore up out of the mist I examined her through my glasses, but though she was painted white like Childers' (O'Brien's being, as I had been advised, black), she was many times too large, and carried two masts. She bore down close upon us, and examined us so carefully as she passed that she left us greatly wondering who she might be when she had gone. Then we waited again, rocking in the waves, unnecessarily anxious as the hours passed.

Later in the afternoon the mist lifted a little, widening our world, and putting silver in the place of dull gold. At 5.30 another yacht was called. She was like what O'Brien's should have been, and she was evidently bearing towards us; but I had never met Conor O'Brien and was concerned to know how I should recognize him. He himself quickly settled this, however, by passing us close, and hailing: 'Is that the boat with the rifles for the Irish Volunteers?' or some words of the like sort equally embarrassing to me, beside whom the skipper stood. So I called back in poor Irish asking him to speak in that language, and I was greatly relieved to hear the skipper's low voice asking if this were Mexican.

The hint was evidently taken, for as the yacht bore round again another man standing beside the first hailed me, this time in Irish. This was, I discovered when I made my way on board the yacht, Dermot Coffey, and I marvelled at the odd occurrence, for my last act before leaving London had been to send a review of an historical book of his to a London journal. Now I met the author for the first time in this fashion in the North Sea.

Conor O'Brien's sister and the two men comprised the whole crew, and without delay we shipped his share of rifles on board his yacht, stowing them in the hold he had prepared for their reception. It was very nearly eight o'clock before we finished, and hardly had we finished, and were trimming his cargo, when another yacht was called.

This was Erskine Childers'. One yacht succeeded to the other with singular punctuality, for Childers hardly had time to greet O'Brien before the black yacht cast clear and lurched into the gathering dusk, and the white yacht took its place. The new yacht, however, was larger, and it had a greater burden to carry, though I wondered, as I looked on it after the difficulty we had had with the other, where the cargo was to be put. It was manned by a larger crew. In addition to Childers, there were Mrs Childers, Miss Mary Spring Rice, two Donegal fishermen, and a young friend of Childers who was introduced to me as a clerk from the War Office.

With a crew so large (and so various) it was a hard task to stow the cargo and leave room for passengers. There were the boxes of ammunition as well as the rifles. Conor O'Brien's lot was to be landed at night at Kilcoole in motor-boats, and, therefore, we had stowed it in the original canvas parcels. Childers' had to be landed on to Howth pier, and the tug's crew therefore slit the bags while we stowed the rifles. We began the work at about 8.30 and we did not finish until about 1.30, through a hot and sultry night. By the time we had finished we could not but pity the voyagers on the yacht, for there was no place to eat or to sleep except on rifles or on cartridge-boxes.

When the task was finished, and while the yacht's crew trimmed cargo, we took her in tow to the Straits of Dover, where we cast loose about seven in the morning. She went on then down the Channel, while we made for Dover, where I was to be landed. She had a fortnight before her, and she had, we afterwards learned, the quiet satisfaction of bearing our forbidden cargo through the British fleet as it lay in review at Spithead, none suspecting what she bore beneath their guns.

21. The first stage of the journey

Gordon Shephard to his mother, Lady Agnes Shephard.[30]

From *Memoirs of Brigadier-General Gordon Shephard,* ed. Shane Leslie London 1924, pp. 173-4.

(Cowes) 9 July, 1914.

I arrived at Degonway [near Conway] at 9.30 on Friday and at 10 a.m. we started. They have this year two fishermen from Connaught for crew[31] so we consisted of Childers and Mrs Childers, Miss Spring Rice,

---

30 Gordon Shephard, born at Madras on 9 July 1885, son of Horatio Hale Shephard, then advocate-general of the presidency of Madras. Gordon passed into Sandhurst in June 1903, and was commissioned in January 1905. His first boat was the *Laural,* which he bought for £25 in 1905. In August 1909 he wrote, 'I dined yesterday with a great yachtsman, a clerk in the House of Lords, but nevertheless a good Radical. He strongly recommended me to go to Texel and work south to Flushing or only to The Hook and then back. His name is Childers.' Afterwards he sailed frequently with the Childers'. In 1911 Shephard undertook a daring voyage from Ramsgate to St. Petersburg in a 12 ton yawl, and in consequence was awarded the Challenge Cup of the Royal Cruising Club; he was again awarded the Challenge Cup in 1913. He began flying in May 1911, and in the same year was moved with his regiment to Dublin; in July 1912 he joined the Flying Corps at Farnborough. Within a week of the Howth gun-running, on the eve of the First Great War, he was mobilised for service and on 13 August 1914 flew to France in command of a flight of the Royal Flying Corps. In Feb. 1917 he was promoted Brigadier-General, then the youngest in the British Army. He was mentioned in dispatches six times, was awarded the Military Cross, the D.S.O., and was made a Chevalier of the Legion of Honour. On 19 Jan. 1918 he was killed when his plane crashed near Bailleul. Two days later Erskine Childers wrote to Lady Agnes Shephard, Gordon's mother, 'He was one of my heroes and will always be so. Molly and I loved him.' See *Memoirs of Brigadier-General Gordon Shephard,* ed. Shane Leslie London: 1924.

31 The two fishermen, Patrick McGinley and Charles Duggan were from Gola Island, Co. Donegal. C. Duggan died on 25 June 1958, aged 80; P. McGinley lives at Chicago, U.S.A.—*Ed.*

two hands, and self. Miss S. R. is a wonder. She has never been far to sea before, yet she was hardly ill at all and looks and is most useful. We came round without stopping and arrived early this morning. Good weather on the whole, but head winds as far as the Land's End, and then a fine fair wind up the Channel. The Childers' had an appointment here with some Irish people[32] on another yacht.

They have not yet decided where to go to, but do not expect to hear from me till my leave is up . . .

22. Diary of the Asgard 1–26 July 1914
by Mary Spring Rice[33]

WED. 1ST. A long, hot and anxious journey over to Conway to join the yacht, starting with breakfast at 6.15 a.m. motoring to Limerick for the 8.15, and crossing over by the 1.15 boat. I was full of apprehensions that even now at the eleventh hour something might have upset all our carefully laid schemes. Erskine met me at the station looking fearfully worried and tired. As we sat at dinner at the hotel before going on board he explained to me the various contretemps that had arisen; how badly the people at Conway had fitted out the yacht, how only one of the Donegal fishermen [Pat McGinley] hired by Mr Bigger as crew had come, and he had had to get a boy out of the I[rish] V[olunteer] Office as a stop-gap.[34]

32 Conor O'Brien and his crew on the *Kelpie*—*Ed.*

33 Mary Ellen Spring Rice was only daughter of Thomas, second Baron Monteagle of Mount Brandon, Mount Trenchard, Foynes, Co. Limerick. She was a close friend of the Childers', a strong supporter of Home Rule and later of Sinn Féin. She died on 1 December 1924 in the Vale of Clwydd Sanatorium, North Wales, aged 44, after two years' illness. When her funeral took place at Foynes on 4 December she was given a guard of honour by the local I.R.A., the Gaelic League, and the Trade Unionists —*Ed.*

34 Mrs Childers in a note describes him as 'Mr John Dolan of Seamount Road, Malahide, who worked splendidly at every kind of hard task.' Mention should be made of an account of the Howth gun-running, as told by Mrs Childers and published by Maire Mhac an tSaoi, 'Gunnaí Bheann Éadair' in *Comhar*, Deireadh Fómhair, 1945, pp. 2-3.

He was still hoping for the other fisherman to turn up and also expected the friend whose name I had not been told but of whom I heard so much from Molly to join him at Holyhead; and they were to start at 4 a.m. next morning, hoping to get to Holyhead that evening.

It was an exciting moment when I saw *Asgard* for the first time. Her white paint showing up in the evening light. I had not expected anything nearly so smart, but she looked fine and solid too and much broader in the beam than the *Kelpie*. Down below I was warmly greeted by poor Molly who was trying to cope with a fearful scene of confusion. In the midst of ropes, tinned foods, marline, and clothes just unpacked, we laboured to get things straightened out before our early start. I wearily pulled my clothes out of canvas bags and holdalls and stowed them as best I could, there was a fearsome thunderstorm going on and it was breathlessly hot: however, I got to sleep at last and only half woke at the 4 a.m. start.

THURS. 2ND. There was too much noise on deck to sleep long, and Molly and I struggled into our clothes pretty early. The glass had dropped very low and a thick mist had come on, in fact it looked like dirty weather outside, and Erskine hesitated about going on. Dolan, the I.V. Office boy, though full of silent Sinn Fein enthusiasm, did not know one end of a rope from another. However he was very obliging about washing up and getting food ready. Erskine and Molly were both dead tired and I longed for the advent of the friend and the second fisherman. Finally as the weather grew thicker and worse we settled to turn back and wait for the tide next morning to get over the bar, and wire to the friend to come to Deganwy (close to which we were now lying), instead of to Holyhead. I was aching to be really off, but it was rather a mercy to be in harbour for a day to get things straightened up a bit, and I persuaded Molly to let me take a hand in the cooking. One bright spot in the day was that the second fisherman turned up— Duggan by name—and proved to be very nice.

FRIDAY 3RD. Up early for I was to go ashore to bring Mr Gordon [Shephard], the friend, whose name was at last disclosed, off to the *Asgard* as soon as possible, going up to the Junction to meet him, for fear he should go on to Llandudno by mistake, and not change for Deganwy. His train was due there at 9.17 and we were due to sail at 9.30 to get over the bar. I got to the Junction and looked anxiously along the train from Holyhead, it was full of depressed holiday-makers (it was still pouring), and dull old men who looked up indignantly from their papers, as I looked into carriage after carriage in vain. I went back drearily to Deganwy, thinking we were stuck again, and was just going off in the dinghy when Mr Gordon suddenly appeared. He had apparently spent a somewhat depressing night in a railway waiting room, however, there he was, and in an extraordinarily short time we threw his luggage on board and were off. Just over the bar in time, thank Heaven, but it was a near thing. Really started! I could hardly believe it. I only regretted not having written to Conor to tell him of our starting so late. How he would ramp round at Cowes! I thought of him storming round and talking to the Lord knows who, with de Montmorency arriving as an additional danger.

It was a head wind and it fell very light so we spent most of the afternoon beating about the bay. I, however, was so pleased to be actually started and not to be ill, (it was like a mill pond), that I felt fairly indifferent as to the rate or direction in which we were travelling.

SAT. 4TH. It was distinctly a fresh breeze when I woke up; and got, what I thought was very rough indeed as the day went on. Cooking buttered eggs in the fo'castle seemed impossible but was not so bad when it came to the point.

Pat has got to be rather good at cherishing the Primus, so I leave that to him. All the same I was glad to escape from the fo'castle on to the deck, where I stayed most of the day, my lunch and tea alike consisting of small pieces of captain biscuits munched in the cockpit. Erskine, Molly and I all felt (and some of us were) extremely ill. Poor Molly had to lie down in her cabin, so was much the worst off. I felt just able to survive while I stayed on deck, and all the afternoon the wind rose; it was S.E. and there was lots of it, and a very choppy short sea into which the *Asgard* drove her bows.

I curled up in an unhappy heap on the cockpit floor, cold and miserable, in a leaky oilskin (oh, uncle, it was Dunhills), feeling dimly that Mr Gordon, who was steering, would much have preferred me out of the way, also that the *Asgard* now looked extremely small, a mere cockleshell on the waves; and I wondered how long it would go on like this. Mr Gordon every now and again assured me it was not really rough. However, late in the evening he and Erskine determined to make a board in towards Fishguard, and put in there if it got very bad, and my drooping spirits revived though it was still horribly rough when I crept into my bunk.

SUN. 5TH. Much calmer, thank Heaven, but I still felt fairly ill though I managed to get to the fo'castle for a few minutes and started Pat to boil the eggs—timing them. We all felt on the mend this morning, and it was a comfort to see Erskine able to eat something again, and Molly able to come on deck. E. and Mr Gordon lamented all day and indeed for many days to come, over that board in towards Fishguard and the time lost thereby. E. regarded it as a neglect of duty for the sake of comfort.

All day the wind headed us and we spent the afternoon trying to get round Strumble Head against a strong wind and tide, and racing a Brixham trawler which eventually walked right away from us, to our disgust, we having been ahead for ages. It was a perfect afternoon and one began to feel like settling down. Erskine lost the look of tense anxiety which he had when we started, though still greatly pre-occupied with the problems ahead—times and seasons, transhipping, etc.—and that afternoon we assembled in the cockpit, the men being safely below, while he unfolded to us the landing scheme.

I had, of course, been aching to know it for weeks, and was half appalled at the daringness of it, and half delighted at the coup if it really came off. But there seemed many a slip— Howth so near Dublin, trams, telephone, soldiers, coast-guards, and cruisers; how we discussed all these possibilities as we sat round after supper that evening and many evenings to come! Molly and I decided it was altogether too hot to sleep with the cabin door shut and as it opened straight into the hatch and companion, it meant rather sleeping in public. The theory was that one put out the light and then no one could see in, but as it got light about 4 a.m. that rather broke down; however I don't really mind, compared to sleeping in a tug—I can hear Elizabeth saying how like me!

MON. 6TH. Got up to find us still struggling to get past the Smalls Lighthouse; no wind and a great swell, but I felt much better than yesterday, although dressing was an exhausting business, and I recruited for half an hour on deck before descending into the fo'castle to see to breakfast. All efforts to rouse Mr Gordon proved in vain until a tin of Golden Syrup was got out; on hearing this he shut the saloon door, (he had the passage bunk) and appeared in a surprisingly short time. One of my chief duties, I found, was keeping the food hot for the late-comers, and as I sat close to the fo'castle door and the stove was just inside, it was quite handy.

Erskine and Molly went up on deck when Mr Gordon, lured by the Golden Syrup, came in to his breakfast. I was amused to see how thoroughly comfortable he made himself, quite a la Leonard curled up on the seat with the Golden Syrup tin propped up beside him. I went up on deck and shortly afterwards heard a shriek from Molly—'He's pouring all the Golden Syrup on to the bunk.' I peered down. Evidently he had gone to sleep with it propped up beside him, and it had overflowed. However there were three more tins on board.

We mopped up the bunk, and went up to study the wind, which had fallen very light; there was a great swell, we rolled about desperately and still were not past the Smalls. We all felt rather despairing, and Mr Gordon, who is a sort of cold water douche, in case any of us did get too optimistic, made an elaborate calculation to prove that we should certainly get to the rendezvous at the Ruytigen too late.

We only seemed to have averaged about 2 knots since we left Conway. At last we got up nearer to the Smalls, and Erskine decided to go inside through the passage with a bubbling tide race and horrible looking rocks. Altogether it looked a wicked place, however of course one felt a sublime confidence in Erskine's steering, and we got through alright. Then the wind got up and we were soon humming along. In fact by tea-time it was a problem to keep anything on the table.

We had now left the Welsh coast and thankful we were to see the last of it. I never knew Wales went on so long—we were making for Cornwall along the mouth of the Bristol Channel with a big Atlantic swell rolling in and still beating with a wind about sou' sou' west. To bed with the prospect of a very rough night; Mr Gordon having assured me that when we went about I should certainly be shot out of my bunk, so I moved the water-can out of the way, thinking how painful it would be to fall on. Undressing was a slow and painful process, but once in, I slept the sleep of the just, and awoke to find a glorious morning with the sun shining on the purple coast and white cliffs of Cornwall.

TUES. 7TH. The half-hour on deck before breakfast is very joyful after the stuffiness of dressing with the cabin door shut. I do as much dressing as possible with it open, but there were moments when it had to be shut and then the fog. When I came up on deck this morning, and felt the fresh sunshine and delicious morning air, I felt life was really very good; and there was Cornwall quite near—it seemed only just round the corner to Cowes. I found Erskine steering and poring over a chart, —'we are just off St. Agnes' Head', he said. He has given himself rather a nasty finger by running something into it. All that day we beat along the coast of Cornwall; we had some thought of putting into St. Ives, which looked most attractive in the sunlight, and waiting for the afternoon tide, but this was sternly discouraged by Erskine—firmly resolved that not a moment of time that he could help should be wasted on the way to the rendezvous. I believe he was quite right, though Mr Gordon had got as far as planning out his lunch ashore, and I was just meditating if it would take the shine out of my Cowes shore clothes to wear them, when Erskine had appeared and said firmly we should push on even if we only made a few yards against the tide.

Later on Pat got a hit on the head from a block which gave him a horrible cut just over his eye. Molly dressed it in the saloon, while I held the things for her; it was an awful job, for there was a good sea on round Land's End and everything was falling about in all directions.

It was a great moment when we rounded the Longships still beating against a stiff southerly wind, and very misty—still this was the moment we had prayed for, when we thought of the fair wind up-channel, through all our long weary beat down the Welsh coast. And now it was NOT a fair wind till we got past the Lizard. We had one (to me) rather awful moment, when, as we scudded along through the misty twilight, we suddenly heard a deep fog-bell booming on the port side. 'Damn it' said Mr Gordon at the wheel (and he never uses language as a rule) 'the Runnelstone Buoy'. It was hard to make out the position of the Buoy in the mist, and it sounded alarmingly near, however we went about, and presently Molly's quick eyes discovered it. I had contemplated for a few moments how long the *Asgard* would live on the Runnelstone Rocks, and what it would feel like when she broke up, and then was relieved to hear the fog-bell growing fainter in the distance.

At long last round the Lizard and a fair wind up-channel. I was much absorbed in getting supper ready, as when I went below I found it was a quarter to 8, and Pat being ill I had to do all the work myself; there were tins to be hunted for in the lockers, potatoes to be cooked, everything to be found, and the table set—with the boat rolling about in a big swell all the time.

Poor Pat must have had a chastened time pitching about in his small stuffy bunk with his cut-open head. I stopped my cooking operations to put a wet bandage round his head, one of the parents' handkerchiefs just came in handy—mine would never have gone round. As I fell about the fo'castle searching for everything, I made up my mind I would know where things were myself in future.

Molly took a watch with Mr Gordon to-night as Pat was *hors de combat*, and I got up at two and made them hot drinks for the change of the watch. I found I went to sleep again quite easily and slept on shamefully late on Wednesday morning, and actually felt hungry for breakfast.

WED. 8TH. Mr Gordon wasn't satisfied until we had set every stitch of canvas on the boat—just like Leonard and Conor— however we had to take down the spinnaker going through Portland Race, and I should, personally, have felt happier without the topsail, however we were going against time as usual and had to push on. Erskine steered her wonderfully through the choppy sea though it was rather hard on his injured hand. Now at 7 p.m. we are scudding along with the wind dead aft, doing about 7 or 8 knots with a blue sky and a stiff breeze, hoping to make the Needles to-night. I frankly confess I am looking forward immensely to being in harbour again, in fact we have talked of the joys of Cowes, and of the meals we are going to eat ashore, for the last 3 days.

All the same I was rather afraid to face Conor, who had been there for days, and was probably in a state of wild impatience. I hadn't liked to write from Conway that we were starting till we were actually off and then there was not time. But I had many misgivings as we approached Cowes.

We got in at 1 a.m. It was quite beautiful passing through the searchlights with the water all gleaming and rippling under a sort of unearthly glow. While the men stowed the sails and settled things up generally, I went down hastily to make hot drinks, and so to bed at 2 a.m.

THURS. 9TH. We had the best intentions of getting up early, but when I turned over in my bunk it was already 8.30. I struggled hastily into more or less clean clothes, and managed to get breakfast about 9 o'clock. There was a lot to do—repairs to sails, etc., for some of the gear had gone in that rough weather off the Welsh coast—besides we had the Hamburg business to settle. Hardly had we finished our last mouthful, when a loud 'Asgard ahoy' was heard, and I dashed up on deck to be received with a torrent of abuse from Conor. Why were we so late? Why had we never written? He had spent all his money waiting for us and de Montmorency had gone back to Dublin.[35] I found to my horror that Conor had been sending a series of wild telegrams to Mrs Green via de Montmorency asking her where we were. If all Cowes, and Dublin, not to say the Castle, do not know of our expedition, it is a miracle. The only hope is the Government are fairly stupid. I tried my best to calm Conor down and finally he departed somewhat soothed. Meanwhile Mr Gordon had been struggling into his shore clothes in the saloon, and finally appeared resplendent in blue serge (I should hardly have known him) and we went ashore. I found I could hardly stand so I tottered to a lamp post and clung to it regardless of Molly's protests. It might be quite true as she said that people would think I was drunk, but if I stopped clinging to it I should certainly fall down which would be worse. So I clung till I felt a little more secure, but all that day I felt rather dizzy and fairly reeled along the streets of Cowes. We spent rather a harassing morning, getting our letters and sending telegrams to Figgis at Hamburg with final directions about our rendezvous and transhipment. We must have looked a quaint party, Molly and Erskine and I driving around Cowes whispering to each other, sending prepaid wires, and anxiously

---

35 For Hervey de Montmorency's eventful career see his autobiography, *Sword and Stirrup*, London: 1936; see also below, pp. 76, 119—*Ed.*

returning to the post-office for the answers. I was rather worried at not having heard from father and did not know where to tell him to write, our ports of call were so uncertain, and I was afraid he would worry if he didn't know our movements. Lunch at the Royal Marine Hotel, that meal which we had greedily discussed for days beforehand, was very large and excellent. I had made up my mind three days ago to have an iced lemon squash, and had thought of it ever since. After lunch more shopping till I could hardly drag one leg after another. Finally I managed to get my Cowes yachting cap just before the shops shut, and we all met for dinner; another large meal, at the hotel. I have over-eaten shockingly to-day, and spent all my money, not on meals, which Erskine insisted on paying for, but on the yachting cap, and on various luxuries in the way of extra pots and pans for the fo'castle. I got a friendly grocer to cash a cheque, spent all that, then I met Mr Gordon and borrowed two shillings from him, and finally landed up without one penny at the hotel.

As we sat at dinner we espied through the window Conor, Dermod Coffey, and Kitty landing. This must be the olive branch, we thought, and so it was. They had coffee at the hotel with us, and then took us on board to see the beauties of the *Kelpie.*

It was a perfect evening, and all was peace and quietness, Conor having quite calmed down. Details about transhipment were settled, each boat was to take half the cargo, and Conor was to sail in the morning tide, we could not get off till the afternoon as the sail-maker didn't finish on board the *Asgard.* We were to try and meet at Dover, but not wait there beyond 8 p.m. Saturday. While the others were talking plans, I gathered from Kitty something of the course of events before we arrived at Cowes. It was a great blow after the pictures we had been drawing of de Montmorency as the bold buccaneer, to find that he had left the *Kelpie* because the cabin clock ticked too loud and after a night at the hotel had gone back to Dublin. It was probably fortunate he went back in view of the discomforts he would have come in for later on, but it was a sad blow to all our romantic theories about him.

Kitty explained Conor's financial difficulties by their having bought such a lot of cream which was apparently very dear at Cowes. At any rate we parted in a much more friendly way than we had met in the morning and that was something.

FRIDAY 10th. Up early and breakfast before 8, to get ashore and do a couple more things as we may not have time to put in at Dover. Great calculations all the time as to space. How I hope Molly and I won't have to leave in the tug. The space certainly does look very small for all we shall have to put in but she and I don't take much room to sleep. We spent the rest of the morning clearing the lockers in the bunks to make room for guns, storing a lot of the provisions under the fo'castle floor, a plan which had its drawbacks when you wanted to get out something on a very rough day. I had a field day in the fo'castle so as to try and use the space to the best advantage.

At slack water in the afternoon we got up the anchor and were off again, beating up the Solent against a head wind and as usual against time. The wind got up a good bit and cooking supper was not an easy job, or going to bed. Mr Gordon insisted on setting the topsail, much to Molly's disgust, and she went to bed protesting how much more comfortable we should have been without it. I rather agreed with her at the time as I struggled into my bunk, and sighed that all men were alike about setting topsails on all possible occasions, but we sped along, so perhaps it was as well.

SAT. 11TH. Much calmer, which made getting up and cooking more pleasant, but it was a bad look-out for getting to Dover. All day long we had light head-winds, and 8 p.m. found us still struggling to get round Beachy Head. A roasting hot day, even on the sea, and my pink sunbonnet was my one joy. We had laid in a lot of fruit and vegetables at Cowes, and were living much more luxuriously than before. Mr Gordon had great ideas of being as comfortable as possible, and he and Molly had bought lavishly. But it was a depressing day, full of doubts and anxieties.

SUNDAY 12TH. The day of the meeting, should we ever get there? It certainly didn't look like it, when I came up on deck to find Erskine steering in a calm sea with a light breeze ruffling the water and the fog just lifting and letting the sun through,—a heavenly summer morning— if one had no gun-running appointments at the Ruytigen Lightship, 45 miles away, at 12 noon to make one pray for a wind. I had slept like a top, thanks to the calm night and was really hungry for breakfast.

But we all felt rather anxious, and made calculations about the fair tide after Dover, and speculated as to how long the tug would wait if we were late and as to what directions there might be in Figgis's letter to Dover which we had not time to call for. Then we all fell to work doing the final cleaning of the saloon and cabin for the guns. This meant cutting up the two saloon bunks and Molly, Pat and Mr Gordon were soon hard at work chopping and sawing. We were keeping right in shore as the tide was still against us, and when I came on deck after looking through the store of eggs (a very important part of the supplies) I saw Folkestone beach within a stone's throw, full of the 'smart set' parading their best clothes in the brilliant sunshine, while on the starboard side lay 4 or 5 warships with their bells ringing for church. The *Asgard* slipped along between the shore and the ships, her crew making an awful noise chopping and sawing, which they devoutly hoped was not heard on either side. Then it fell a flat calm; however the tide had turned now and we drifted along.

We were discussing whether we should take the saloon table to pieces, which Molly inclined to, Mr Gordon being strongly for keeping it as it was and packing guns under it, when suddenly there was a joyful shout from Duggan at the wheel, 'A west wind', and sure enough a breeze had sprung up. Hastily the spinnaker was set on the bowsprit, then the wind shifted and it was set on the boom, and it was 2.30 by the time we sat down to lunch. Meanwhile the fog had come on fairly thick, and it was becoming a difficult question how we should make out the Ruytigen. Erskine had told the men our objective, and Duggan, at any rate, was as excited as we were.

We heard the East Goodwin fog signal booming away on our port side and then we listened and listened for the Sandettie fog signal which was pretty well on the course for the Ruytigen, and Erskine and Mr Gordon disputed about how much to allow for the tide sweeping us north. It was an anxious afternoon, even Mr Gordon gave up his after-lunch sleep, and we all stayed on deck, straining through the sultry summer air to hear the faint boom of the signal—past the line of the Sandettie now and still no sound—it was a question now if we should find the Ruytigen before the tide turned.

At last Molly's quick eyes sighted a buoy—then a lightship— the Ruytigen at last. We had come just right, certainly a triumph of navigation; but no sign of the *Kelpie* or the tug. I thought gloomily of all the possibilities—some change of plan in the letter for which we had not called at Dover; Conor having gone off somewhere in the tug in despair at our being late, or Conor still at Dover and cursing us for not calling there. Then a sail on the horizon—'Conor' cried everyone anxiously, and we all strained to see. I, of course, could not distinguish the boat, so I kept watching Molly's face, which at last fell dismally; it was only a fishing smack, and despair settled down on us fearing we should not find him or the tug before night. A cry from Molly revived our drooping spirits. 'Conor and the tug. Do you see? A steamer and a yacht mixed up—lying close to one another— now the tug is coming towards us.'

A few moments of breathless excitement, then there was no doubt, the tug was bearing straight down on us. I rushed down to the cabin to shove away my last remains of clothes and get the place clear. I had felt it was unlucky to do this till we were sure of the tug, superstitious as always. We hastily hauled bags of clothes and mattresses and stowed them aft of the mizzen. As the tug came up Darrell Figgis called from her deck that

Conor had taken 600 rifles and 20,000 rounds of ammunition. 'He's left you 900 and 29,000 rounds,' he shouted. We looked at each other. Could we ever take them? We had only counted on 750, and they looked enormous, each thickly done up in straw.

However, before we could say 'knife' we were all at work unloading. It was a perfect night, quite calm, the tug looked black and huge alongside us. Her deck was full of German sailors who jabbered away and looked curiously at us, as they passed down the big canvas bales to Pat and Duggan on our deck. I found myself in the saloon with Mr Gordon, Pat passing us down rifles through the skylight, and we packing them in, butts at the end and barrels in the centre, as fast as we could. They came in bales of ten, and we counted them as we stowed them— '8, 9, 10, steady a minute, Pat, till I stow this one.' Inside the cabin Erskine and Molly were doing the same thing. 40 went into the port bunk in the saloon, should we ever get them all in? 'We'll have to take the straw off and pack them singly if we're ever to take 900,' said Mr Gordon, so we shouted up to take the straw off. It was fearfully hot work; they were fairly heavy and thick with grease which made them horrible to handle. Gradually, however, the pile grew and presently the saloon was half full, level with the table; and we went up on deck to help strip straw off, as they could hardly hand them down fast enough. Then when we had undone a certain number—below again to pack them in. So it went on through the night—still bale after bale of rifles were passed down from the tug, and every now and again we shouted to the German crew to know how many more were still to come, and the saloon got full, and the cabin and the passage, and then we began to put on another layer, and to pile them at the foot of the companion hatch. Meanwhile, the ammunition had been coming down in fearfully heavy boxes, which were stowed with infinite labour aft under the cockpit, a very difficult place to get at, at the foot of the companion, in the sail lockers, and a couple in the fo'castle. Erskine was very keen to take all the ammunition we possibly could, and certainly it seemed rather a sin to leave it to be put overboard by the tug, and aboard it all came somehow; several boxes were left on the deck till we could make room to stow them. Personally, I felt rather nervous as to the effect this tremendous extra weight would have on the yacht in bad weather, but Erskine's one thought was to take everything. As we toiled away I heard them saying we had drifted right down near the Ruytigen, the people there must have wondered what on earth we were doing, but there was no time to alter our position, only try to finish it before it got light, and a faint glimmer of dawn was beginning to show as we stowed away feverishly to get them in. Molly put pieces of chocolate literally into our mouths as we worked and that kept us going, till, about 2 a.m. the last box was heaved on to the deck and the last rifle shoved down the companion, and the captain of the tug came on board to have a drink and consult where he would tow us to. While Mr Gordon entertained him in his best German in what was left of the saloon I collected the letters I had been accumulating to post since Cowes, and gave them to Darrell Figgis, charging him to post them at Dover or some port so as not to arouse suspicion, as even father might have thought it odd if I had posted him a letter in London. I found out afterwards that Figgis had posted them at Hendon, of all unlikely places for a person in a yacht to call at.

Oh, how tired we all were! I tumbled into the fo'castle, crawling over the guns in the saloon to get to it, and got the kettle on for hot drinks while the men were fixing the tow ropes. Down they came then and we all drank cocoa and beef-tea and then shifted down the mattresses and bags of clothes, which had been stowed aft of the mizzen, and lumped them down on the guns anyhow—we were too tired to settle them properly— and lay down on them just as the grey light of the dawn was breaking. I remember thinking how absurd it was to go to bed in daylight and then went off into a dead sleep.

MONDAY 13TH. Shouts from the tug roused me and for a minute I lay and wondered what had happened, we were going so unnaturally fast; then I remembered we were being towed and roused myself to go on deck. We were going about 10 knots through a fortunately calm sea in a thick fog, very low in the water, the deck covered with boxes labelled 'Patronen für Handfeuerwaffen: Hamburg', littered with straw, and generally looking about as disreputable as we could. The whole thing seemed like a dream of the night. Had I really spent the night handing down and stowing rifles? However, down below there was the solid reality—saloon cabin and passage were all built up 2/2 feet high with guns, and there was no illusion about the bruises one got as one crawled about on them. The tug was to cast us off at Dover, and by the time that operation was finished and the men free to come down, I had breakfast ready. The sun was beginning to clear away the fog into a lovely summer day, and as we squatted cross-legged at breakfast, trying to be used to the camp attitude (the guns now being built up level with the table) we all felt a tremendous sense of relief. At any rate, we had kept the appointment, had got the guns on board, and were started on the return journey, though the risks of discovery were now increased tenfold, and the excitement proportionately greater.

There was still a good deal to be done stowing properly some of the guns that had just been shoved in anyhow by the companion in the haste to be off before dawn, and then they had all to be covered with sailcloths and mattresses, and the clothes and rugs sorted out again to their rightful owners. Even working all the morning we hadn't got things really straight by lunch time, but we were all tired and very dirty again; our hands covered with gun grease and filth. A stiff breeze sprang up and Erskine decided to throw over the three boxes of ammunition left on deck as she was so low in the water and there seemed no more space below, every corner was filled and several boxes had gone into the fo'castle, which was already crowded with stores. I specially hated them there, having a vague fear if the oil stove flared up, the ammunition might blow up and burn us all. Over the three went, and Erskine bitterly repented it next day as things got straightened out, and he thought he might have managed to stow them, but it was too much of a give away to leave them lying on the deck, besides the drawback of having them weigh so high up in the boat, and really below it was a case of 'no room to live'. So Molly and I were both rather relieved when they disappeared into the water.

The rest of the day was slack; we got a good breeze in the afternoon and lay about on the deck half asleep except for one alarm passing a lot of warships near Folkestone when one of them began to fire a number of shots as we came up, our guilty consciences thinking it might be a signal to stop.

We passed quite close to our friend the *Gladiator* (the tug) during the afternoon, which caused a momentary excitement. A beautiful night with a calm sea and a glorious moon, and I should have been tempted to stay on deck, but, literally, I could not keep my eyes open and found my bed on top of the guns extraordinarily comfortable.

TUESDAY 14TH. I suppose one will get used to moving about on one's hands and knees, and the saloon is quite comfortable to squat in with a cushion at one's back. But if it is rough I wonder what it will be like trying to get about it. More work this morning, shifting some of the guns and hauling up the mattresses that cover them to dry on deck. Molly produced two splendid waterproof sheets which were tucked over those most likely to get wet at the foot of the companion. Also we sorted provisions, etc. in those lockers which were still getatable, and now things really looked ship-shape, but it is terribly easy to lose one's possessions in the cabin; they drop between the mattresses into the rifles and disappear. There will be a lot of hairpins found among them when they are unloaded.

Off Beachy Head about 7 a.m. and a fair wind, which, alas, shifted to the beam, and then to a head wind by lunch time and dropped very light. Some of the paint on the yacht's side, which had been scraped off by the tug, was made good this morning, and, outwardly, she looks quite like a yacht again now. How Erskine's sore finger has survived Sunday night I can't think, but it really does look a bit better to-day, though it was very sore-looking yesterday. It is a great job for Molly dressing it in rough weather, but she managed to accomplish it. I though she would be half dead after Sunday, but her spirit carries her through, though the difficulties of getting about for her now are, of course, enormous. The odd thing about this sort of life is that one spends such a lot of time cleaning up, and yet one is always dirty. Crawling is not good for the clothes, or gun grease for the hands, and doing one's hair squatting like a Red Indian is rather a job. One has to turn the mattress right back off the guns in our cabin to be able to turn down the basin, so that one only does it when one really does feel too dirty to eat before washing. The cabin door had to be fixed permanently open so we had an arrangement of a dishcloth which could be hung across as a curtain when one was dressing, but it was too stuffy to keep it hung up at night and shut out the precious air that came down the companion. The worst was on a wet night when Molly insisted on shutting the companion hatch, not so much for herself as to keep the guns dry, and then the stuffiness was awful.

WEDNESDAY 15TH. A good breeze this morning and cooking the breakfast was difficult. Everyone has now come to the conclusion that fried bacon is the best thing for breakfast, so, unless it is almost impossible to keep the pan on the Primus, fried bacon it is. Also, the eggs which got wet in the fo'castle, are beginning to get a bit musty for boiling. Fried eggs are very hard on rough days; they fly about the pan and get disintegrated. Awfully late at breakfast, and Mr Gordon was shaving in the saloon, while I, propped up against the ammunition box in the doorway, was shoving in the breakfast things and trying to prevent them getting all mixed up with the shaving apparatus, as everything was shooting about the table. We have got into a sort of routine now and it is surprising how fast the day passes. I generally crawl into my clothes between 7.30 and 8 with sleepy remonstrances from Molly for disturbing her so early, and calls from Erskine as to when breakfast will be ready. He usually takes the second watch and is very hungry by 8 o'clock. So, washing is reserved for later, and I crawl to the fo'castle—Pat generally has the Primus going and if one has not to tie the pans on with string, and hold on with one hand while you do everything, breakfast doesn't take very long. I manage to get a sort of wash with Monkey soap out of a mug—better than nothing. Then portions have to be kept hot for late comers, Molly—for whom dressing is such an effort—or Erskine, who has something to do on deck, just as everything is on the table, and Mr Gordon, whose food has almost always to be kept hot; he generally sleeps till the rest are well settled at breakfast.

After breakfast I do a little washing behind the dishcloth in the cabin; then, if fine, the mattresses and blankets are given an airing on deck, and probably Molly wants the things collected— hot water, etc.—for dressing Erskine's hand. Then peace till lunch-time, and I sit in the cockpit and sew or read, or learn Irish from Duggan, or study where we are going on the chart. Lunch is cold and only has to be laid out, and my labours don't really begin again till after the tea when I start to get ready supper. Of course on wet wild days one is kept busy trying to keep the guns tucked up and dry.

We had passed St. Catherine's in the night, the place full of steamers and sailing vessels and one of the latter all but ran us down last night.

I shivered in the cabin below wondering what was going to happen. It seems to be quite amazing how anyone can steer clear of boats in a crowded place at night, it must be so hard to judge their distance and pace. I feel pretty happy when Erskine and Mr Gordon are steering, but not at all with Duggan or Pat. We spent a long time to-day making Portland Head, beating all the time with a stiff breeze and a choppy sea. I steered part of the morning and found it quite hard work the wheel was so stiff. Through Portland Race in the evening, just as I was cooking the dinner, and awfully rough. One didn't venture to leave a pot on the stove without holding it; it was almost impossible to keep on one's feet, as the floor was as usual covered with oil, and the boat pitching in all directions. As it was, part of the stew upset but I got such unmerited praise for having managed to cook at all that it was well worth the trouble. Pat was a great help, he will be quite a ship's cook at the end. A beautiful night with the moon, but still rather a choppy sea and one couldn't get to sleep early.

THURSDAY 16TH. Again woke to find ourselves beating along West Bay. A nice calm sea after yesterday was a great boon, and we kept close in to the Devonshire coast which was lovely, the colouring very like Ireland, only warmer with more red showing in the rocks. Off Dartmouth we had an exciting race with a Brixham trawler and beat her handsomely. We were in among a whole fleet of them and they looked very picturesque with their red-brown sails showing up against the brilliant coastline. Mr Gordon had a brilliant idea of hailing a small fisher-boat as we passed and for two shillings we got a fine lot of pollock, bream and mackerel, and are all looking forward to fresh fish tonight after a course of sardines and tinned meat. Six days at sea now and the bread locker is beginning to run very low and we are fearfully economical of water. Molly protests if I wash more than once a day, but with grease from cooking, black from washing potatoes, and oil from the fo'castle, it becomes necessary sometimes. The cargo below has curtailed the air space considerably, and one spent as much time as possible on deck. Mr Gordon says his bunk is too stuffy to sleep in, and has taken to sleeping in the passage, and it is almost a gymnastic feat to get by without walking on him. How Molly manages to get about with her leg is a constant wonder to me. I find it quite hard enough. The wind which had been lively all the afternoon fell very light about tea-time (it was still dead ahead), and by dinner time we were rolling about in a wet misty calm with a horrid swell which just upset a

1. German tug *Gladiator* out of Hamburg. *Gladiator* transported the arms to the rendezvous point at the Roetigen lightship where it met the *Asgard* and the *Kelpie*. (MS 7890/8/43 photo courtesy of Trinity College Dublin Library)

2. Returning from Howth: two Volunteers identified as Edward and John Bracken, 26 July 1914. (Photo courtesy of Kilmainham Gaol collection: 16PC-1A22-26)

3. Parchment of Inquest on Mary Duffy, shot by Scottish Borderers, Bachelors Walk, 26 July 1914. (Photo courtesy of Kilmainham Gaol collection: 16LG-1C35-11)

4. Sir Thomas Myles, captain of the *Chotah*, who delivered the arms consignment at Kilcoole, Co. Wicklow one week after the Howth landings. (Photo courtesy of James Langton)

5. Erskine Childers at the wheel with Gola Island fisherman Pat McGinley. (MS 7890/8/23 photo courtesy of Trinity College Dublin Library)

6. Four of the crew: (L-R) Molly Childers, Mary Spring Rice, Gordon Shephard and Pat McGinley. (MS 7890/8/50 photo courtesy of Trinity College Dublin Library)

7. Childers at the wheel with Gordon Shephard. (MS 7890/8/49 photo courtesy of Trinity College Dublin Library)

8. Unloading of rifles: Erskine Childers and Mary Spring Rice on board the *Asgard*. (Photo courtesy of NMI, Collins Barracks)

9. Volunteer Cycle Corps. Note the 'Mausers' strapped to bicycles.
(Photo courtesy of James Langton)

10. Volunteers returning to Dublin after the landing. (Photo courtesy of Kilmainham Gaol
collection: 16PO-1A23-07)

11. 30 July 1961: state commemoration in Howth (L-R) Éamon de Valera at microphone, Sean Lemass, Eamon Martin. (Photo courtesy of Eamon Murphy)

whole dish of fried pollock, which I had cooked, on to the floor. Everyone had been looking forward to the fish for dinner so it was rather a disaster. I hastily cooked some more but it was rather short commons, and the bread which I made did not bake well, as the stove got cold mysteriously while it was in the oven. So, altogether the cookery tonight was not much of a success though the company was very tolerant about it.

After dinner a fresh breeze sprang up and we beat along past Devonport, and, to my horror, got in among the fleet. They seemed to be executing some night manoeuvres and were all round us with their great lights towering up; it would have been very picturesque if one had been looking on from a safe position on shore. There was one awful moment when a destroyer came very near. I stood holding up the stern light on the starboard side watching her getting nearer and nearer, with my heart in my mouth, then mercifully at the last moment she changed her course and passed us by. Then the big jib had to be shifted and the jib sheet got lost under the dinghy and Molly and I had to fish for it lying flat on the deck and wriggling under the dinghy. By the time we were clear of the fleet, and all the alarms and excursions over, it was 1 a.m. and I was glad to get to bed.

FRIDAY 17TH. Horribly choppy this morning, but the wind fell and it was nearly calm by midday. I had a bath before lunch, the first I have had, which was heavenly. I did envy the men their morning bathe. I never seemed to have had time for it with cooking the breakfast. We stood right to sea this morning and are now heading for the land in the Bay, past the Lizard, we hope, and then it will be a dead beat up to the Longships.

A grey, gloomy-looking day, but a calm sea for which mercy I am very duly thankful. But, alas, the wind is falling very light and heading up. If we don't get round the Longships by midnight we probably can't make Milford Haven Sunday morning to land Mr Gordon, who is due back to London that day. We might land him on the north Cornish coast, if we are too late to make Milford, but we still hope, and make every inch we can against the everlasting head winds. It's a great pity he has to go, as if we get bad weather we shall be rather shorthanded without him.

It was a grey misty night, and I sat on deck straining to see the lights of the Wolf and Longships looming out of the darkness, and thinking that at any rate we felt more hopeful than when we rounded them on the outward journey. We had the stuff on board and a good margin of time for Howth. Mr Gordon said he would cook the supper tonight, and produced a wonderful dish, which he called a sweet omelette; it was really buttered eggs cooked with golden syrup, but it tasted better than it sounds.

SATURDAY 18TH. Round the Longships at last and a fair wind and a lovely morning. But the wind was very light and there was a most abominable swell which upset everything, including our tempers. The question now was, should we put Mr Gordon ashore at St. Ives or chance getting to Milford in time, and we finally decided to run straight for Milford. All day there were alternate calms and light breezes with a lot of swell and the sails flapping and blocks banging in a distracting way. However, we averaged about ten knots, quite one of the most unpleasant days we have had with a thick mist a good part of the time. Molly spent the morning mending a great rent in the foresail, and I trying to make a blouse—stuff and needles being soaking wet and we sitting in oilskins in the cockpit.

No dinner thrown on the floor tonight, but a cup of coffee spilt, to Molly's grief. 'Gordon' she said, 'You're ruining the guns with that coffee.' However, no doubt, Erskine will put carbolated vaseline on them tomorrow. He always does that after they have had doses of tea, coffee and fruit juice spilt on them.

Every stitch of canvas was being set and re-set throughout the night to catch all the wind there was which was constantly shifting, and everyone but me was up from 2 a.m. I, having been up two nights, slept the sleep of the just, and only heard through my dreams the shifting and setting of the spinnaker, etc., though my guns are not so comfortable for sleeping on as they were, especially on the starboard tack.

SUNDAY 19TH. I woke up fairly early to find everyone in great agitation as to whether we should be in time for Mr Gordon to catch his early train; we were coming up the long reach of Milford Haven, and Molly was trying to help Mr Gordon to pack and collect his clothes from the various bunks in which they were shoved. I looked hastily for some shore clothes and at last discovered some; not absolutely rolled into a longing to go on shore, I had suggested that Erskine had better stay on board rather than me in case any coastguards came to see the yacht's papers, and that I would buy the provisions we needed—bread, potatoes, butter, onions and see what we could do about getting water. At last Mr Gordon's lost hat and boots were found and shoved in, the dinghy was lowered and Duggan put us ashore. Of course, he had landed at the end furthest from the railway station, and, stumbling up the steep streets, we started to walk there. It was an endless way and, having had no breakfast, I was not feeling very energetic, but we got to a hotel at last and found that there was no train till 6.30 p.m. The early train only went from a station several miles away. 'Do you think we ought to go back and have breakfast on the yacht and spend the morning tidying up?' I said, and then I saw through the open door of the coffee room someone else's breakfast laid out and it was so tempting. We ordered it in the hotel forthwith and very good it was. I had what Molly calls her 'shore appetite' and ate a vast meal. A fellow traveller breakfasting at the hotel was most anxious to know how we fared on the yacht, what sort of a cook we had? 'Oh, we've quite a good cook; we really manage very well,' said Mr Gordon, looking at me over the marmalade, convulsed with suppressed laughter.

After breakfast we went in search of provisions. I was afraid the Welsh might have tiresome Sabbatarian principles against Sunday trading, but not at all. They were ready to sell anything. I spent a £1 before I knew where I was and then a small boy— Arthur by name—was awakened from his Sunday sleep and appeared with a handcart on which two large baskets laden with bread, butter, bacon, onions, etc. were fastened, and we started off for the quay. The streets of Milford are very steep and the handcart fairly raced down—Arthur acting as a kind of brake— and Mr Gordon and I, helpless with laughter, running behind. As we panted down the streets after the handcart we crossed the track of the church-goers very prim and proper in their Sunday best.

But, alas! At the quay nothing could attract the attention of the yacht's crew. We waved first the *Daily Mail*, then my white coat in vain; Mr Gordon, with secret joy, said the only thing to do was to go back to the hotel, sleep and have lunch.

Having had only an hour's sleep in the night, and being a person like Leonard who sleeps at any odd moment, he was overjoyed at the prospect of bed, and no effort of the hotel chambermaid could wake him till nearly 3 p.m. I wrote letters, read the magazines and day-dreamed; not to mention a scrumptious hot bath; but I felt rather mean at leaving Molly to do all the tidying up on board. Our meal turned into tea instead of lunch, and by the time it was over it was 4 o'clock.

I felt very guilty. Not so Mr Gordon. He was quite satisfied, he had had a much better sleep than he would have had in the yacht. 'I don't mind rowing back to say goodbye' he remarked, and we set off in the rain to walk to the further quay where we finally did manage to attract *Asgard's* attention. Molly received me somewhat coldly and evidently did not believe we had made any serious efforts to attract their attention. She had spent all the morning up and down looking out for us, she said, and would like to have come ashore herself. No wonder the thought of my two shore meals and hot bath was too much for her. I felt all I could do to atone for my misdeeds was to try and cook an extra good supper.

Mr Gordon finally departed in a downpour of rain, with many promises of coming to Howth on the eventful Sunday. Such rain and half a gale of wind! I was thankful to be safe in Milford Haven instead of rolling about in the Bristol Channel.

MONDAY 20TH. Gleams of sunshine between the showers when we woke and it cleared out into a brilliantly fine day with a tearing east wind. We put off sending ashore for water till the afternoon and had decided to spend another night at Milford, when, just as we were going down to lunch at 2 o'clock, the anchor began to drag. Visions of drifting ashore with half the population coming to salvage us came to our minds. However, Erskine hoisted the mizzen and jib and managed to get the anchor in and we sailed away down the harbour, thinking of looking for another anchorage to spend the night. But Erskine, once we were under way, could not bear to lose a fair wind and thought we had much better go on. Molly was for staying another night in Milford Haven, but as he was so obviously anxious to go, she gave in, and we were soon skimming past St. Anne's Head and turning northward towards the Bishop's Lighthouse. Then, alas, the wind dropped and we drifted most of the night.

A great argument this evening as to what we should feel if Asquith in his statement today announced the repeal of the Arms Proclamation. Molly said she would be quite glad, but Erskine confessed to some feelings of disappointment if the Proclamation was withdrawn within 5 days before we were to land the guns, and I frankly confessed I should be horribly disappointed.

TUESDAY 21ST. Still a flat calm, but a heavenly summer morning, and after breakfast a little breeze sprang up. Erskine tried the ammunition this morning and was much relieved to find it did fit. An alarm occurred after lunch when we heard a steamer approaching through the mist (it was very thick with a bright sun overhead) and Molly thought it was a warship, it sounded so large, and what she could be doing in Cardigan Bay we couldn't imagine. 'Let's cover up the ammunition,' said Erskine, hastily putting two cushions on the two boxes in the cockpit. It turned out to be only the Fishguard steamer going at a great rate, so we must be much further south than we thought.

WEDNESDAY 22ND. Half a gale arose in the night. I was dimly conscious of a great bucketing about, of Molly crawling over me to relieve Erskine at the wheel, and of my continually rolling across the cabin. Painfully and gradually I got into some clothes and, feeling rather green, staggered on deck where the fresh air soon put some heart into me to cook breakfast. We were steering straight for Holyhead, having been almost over to the Irish coast during the night, and there was a good sea on, the ammunition boxes sitting in water in the cockpit showed it had been pretty rough. I managed to produce bacon (of a sort) for breakfast. Erskine, who had had a strenuous night, was very glad of his breakfast, though he had charged me not to try to cook anything. He is the most appreciative person to cook for, but he has the habit common to everyone on board, of starting to do something else just as the food is hot and ready. Molly generally begins to do some elaborate cleaning—Erskine disappears on deck, or, worse still, gets out the charts over the breakfast table and takes bearing of the course, and back has to go the food into the oven again. Mr Gordon never attempted to get up till everyone else 'was at breakfast, except on the rare occasions when he shaved, and his food was kept hot as a matter of course. Molly had a horrid accident this morning, the companion ladder fell on her head and gave her a horrid knock, and she lay down till we were almost in Holyhead. The race was not so bad as it might have been, though pretty choppy, but it was rather touch and go that we were not swept down past the stack by a furious tide. Holyhead, 'harbour of refuge', was indeed well named, I thought, as we rounded the break-water and came up into its calm water after the choppy angry sea outside. It was nearly lunch time when we anchored, and Erskine lay down to get half an hour's sleep before lunch. Molly was in the cabin and I in the saloon sewing the collar of my blouse, when I heard Pat's voice on deck saying 'Yacht *Asgard*,' evidently answering someone. It flashed across me it might be the coastguards. 'Erskine,' I shouted, 'wake up, you're wanted; they're asking her name.' But Erskine is very hard to wake and I was just meditating shaking him when he turned over and said sleepily, 'What?' 'Come on deck', and I dashed up, he after me. There were the coastguards in a boat close by, calling out questions 'Last port — destination — registered tonnage — owner's name.' Erskine, now thoroughly awake, shouted prompt answers, some of them truth and some of them fiction, and, to our immense relief, they rowed away and we breathed again. Luckily someone had had the presence of mind to throw a sail over the ammunition boxes in the cockpit. Molly kept watch on deck all that afternoon while Erskine had a sleep and I went on shore for shopping. I felt rather weary and weak about the legs after the bucketing we had had last night and dragged myself from one shop to another. Molly, as usual wanting to save me all trouble, had told me to get a cab, but they didn't seem to grow in Holyhead. I tore open the newspaper and breathed again when I saw the Arms Proclamation was not withdrawn. I also got an Irish paper and found they had been searching all round for gun-runners, some in the Shannon, which was very disquieting, in case we had to go round there. It seemed so odd to find Holyhead was a real town with shops and streets, and not just a station with a very long train and a very bright light.

THURSDAY 23RD. I slept till about 8.30 a.m. and was only roused by Erskine calling out to ask when we were going to have breakfast. Almost every morning this happened, though rather earlier, and then Molly would tell me to lie still and that it was much too early to get up. I spent a peaceful morning finishing my blouse as we had settled to spend another night in Holyhead.

The weather was not looking too good; it was raining with a lot of wind from the s.w. Erskine came ashore with me after lunch chiefly to have his hair cut. Meanwhile, I did some more shopping, for we were laying in provisions in case the Howth scheme didn't come off and we had to go round to the Shannon.

Tea at the hotel was a glorious meal with a wash beforehand that really cleaned my hands which were ruined by a course of gun-grease, potato washing, paraffin and, worst of all, binnacle oil. As we sat devouring hot, buttered toast, marmalade and strawberry jam, I said to Erskine: 'That was a heavenly looking bath in the bathroom here; I was almost tempted to have a bath.' 'Why don't you?' he said. 'I've had quite a bath quite recently, you know—Sunday.' 'Yes' said Erskine, 'of course you had.' 'And it's only Thursday' I said, and then we looked at each other and laughed at the thought of what our standard of washing had sunk to. To bed tonight with the usual howling wind through the rigging, and rather dismal forebodings of the morrow for we ought to start for Howth unless there was an absolute gale. The excitement is almost too great as the time gets near, and I have a horrible vision of being weatherbound here. Still I know Erskine will get across if it is humanly possible to do so. It's a pity Mr Gordon is not back with us for this final venture.

FRIDAY 24TH. Bad weather still, though the barometer is rising. Molly acted as alarm bell at 4 a.m., 5 a.m. and finally 6 a.m., so one's night was rather short, but Erskine wanted to get away as early as weather permitted. We all rather dread the next two days between us and our fatal 1 p.m. on Sunday; crucial days on which so much depends. We got off about a quarter to 10— still blowing pretty hard, and cloudy and squally, but we were going ahead fairly well when suddenly Erskine saw a tear in the mainsail. Horrors! We had to put back to harbour again and found there were two or three tears. So Molly sat and I stood on deck in our oilskins and mended the sail in the pouring rain, the sail-needle sticking horribly in the thick seams. At long last it was done and at 20 past one we started again. As we stood out of the harbour the sun came out, the blue sky appeared and our spirits rose at feeling that we were really off with a clear sky to windward.

We got through the race pretty well and then the wind fell so light that we rolled about in a horrid sea for a bit. A gull followed us for a long time poised just above the mizzen. Molly declared it was Mrs Green thinking of us. Erskine prosaically declared it was the same gull that had finished the remains of the bacon after breakfast and that he was now hoping to get some tea. We began to be afraid of being becalmed. But that was not to be. At dinner time a good breeze sprang up, still n.w. and it blew harder and harder till by midnight it was a regular gale. It was an awful night. Erskine stayed on deck the whole time; the waves looked black and terrible and enormous, and though everything was reefed one wondered if we should ever get through without something giving way. For about half the night I crouched in the cockpit or the hatchway, then crawled into the cabin where Molly and I lay, half on top of one another—which seemed to make the elements less terrible, but hardly slept a wink all night.

SATURDAY 25TH. It was a relief to see the daylight, but though the sun came out, it was still blowing very hard. Cooking breakfast was bad, eating it almost impossible. The only ray of comfort was that, in all the storm, Erskine had hit off the right place with his usual genius, and we hove to about 10 miles s.e. of Howth, and gradually progressed towards it during the morning. I spent the time recovering from last night, sitting at the top of the companion, cold in spite of three jerseys and an oilskin, swept by spray and awful showers, but much cheered to think that there was Howth—the promised land—thought of and dreamt of during these three weeks, actually ahead of us, and surely the wind must go down sometime.

Lunch was rather a pretence—I managed to eat some biscuits; Molly didn't even come in. She was desperately tired, and no wonder, and Erskine looked worn out after the storm, and the anxiety (not yet over) of calculating the time of arrival. The wind calmed down a little after lunch, and I squatted at the foot of the companion and mended the Cruising Club flag, under which we were to make our entry into Howth tomorrow—it was a job with the yacht rolling so much; however, I got it done at last. Having got near Howth we sailed on up past Lambay Island and then back towards Kingstown. 'Shall we just go boldly into

Kingstown Harbour?' said Erskine, 'it's the most natural thing for a yacht to do after a storm like this and 10 to 1 against any questions being asked.' For a minute it seemed awfully tempting, tired as we were, to turn into the harbour, but, on thinking it over, we all felt we couldn't risk it—suppose the cruiser were there and we were searched—what an ending to the expedition! So Erskine decided to keep sailing. There was still a good stiff breeze but it was off-shore and the sea much calmer. Cooking quite possible again, but by some carelessness on my part, a drop or two of paraffin got into the stew, which was to have been a special chef-d'oeuvre for the last night. Fortunately, Erskine didn't notice it and ate quite a good meal which he wanted badly, but Molly and I did, and I'm afraid it made her quite ill. The fo'castle seats are generally covered with oil and it is hard not to put things down on them in a hurry when everything is tumbling about. My bed wetter than it's ever been tonight. New leaks have appeared all over the place; however, Molly angelically shared hers with me, so I was only on the edge of the wet part. Everything in the saloon is soaking since the storm—cushions, mattresses, even my favourite seat on the ammunition box at the fo'castle door. At supper Erskine looked doubtfully at the big bunk in the saloon, which was full of rifles, and his sense of duty (always abnormal) getting the better of his fatigue, he said 'I believe I ought to shift those out tonight. What about your packing, Mary?' I was also very tired and my conscience had firmly retired for the night, I'm too sleepy. I'll get up at 5 tomorrow,' I said, and crawled into the cabin half on top of Molly, who was as usual very long suffering about it, and slept the sleep of the just, dreaming that I was at home again looking over the crops with Muir.

SUNDAY 26TH. 'Six o'clock' said Molly's voice, 'time to get up.' Then Erskine— 'Hullo, Mary, how about being up at 5? I want my breakfast.' I did very little washing that morning for I was hoping for a real hot bath in the evening, and if we had to go on to the Shannon—well, Heaven help us, nothing mattered then. Hopes were high at breakfast;

we had just turned back towards Lambay Island, the wind still a fresh north-westerly breeze, and we were up to time. The question now was would the motor boat be there, and as we came along the north shore of Lambay, Molly strained her eyes to catch a glimpse of any craft coming from Kingstown, but nothing so far. I helped Erskine shift the guns out of the saloon bunk and collected my clothes as best I could, packed them up, and went on deck again. The time crept on—11 o'clock and still no sign—the motor boat was to have met us at 10—we had sailed down the eastern side of the island and back again and my spirits sank to zero. We were to sail in, so Erskine had settled, whether the motor boat came or not; it did seem a risk. We had, of course, no news from the Provisional Committee for three weeks, and perhaps no Volunteers were coming down at all. We had to get in and out of Howth Harbour with the high tide so there wasn't much time for delays. As we got nearer I went down and cleared out the guns in our bunk, thinking as I laboured at them that if we had to put out again with them still on board what a dreary job it would be stowing them all back again. We were close by when I had finished and there was Howth pier plainly visible, and Molly gazing to see if any Volunteers could be seen. We all felt very doubtful about them for we couldn't think it was too rough for the motor boat to come out, and were afraid something had happened to make them give up the whole thing. However, as my red skirt was to be the signal, I stood well up on deck. It was no easy matter with a fresh breeze to lower the sails at just the right moment to run alongside the quay, when minutes might be so precious. Molly took the helm and Erskine and the men got the sails down, and joy, oh joy! there was a group of men on the pier-head to catch the rope. Duggan was a bit late throwing the warp and we shot on past the pier-head. But the men got hold of the rope and hauled her back alongside. A quarter to one, up to time to the minute, and a long line of Volunteers were marching down the quay. There was Mr Gordon on the pier-head and, of course, the inevitable Figgis. Then things began to move. At first there was a fearful scramble among the men on shore for the rifles as they were handed up, then Erskine stopped the delivery until he got hold of someone in command and some sort of order was restored. Molly and I and Mr Gordon stood by the mizzen and looked at the scene; it still seemed like a dream, we had talked of this moment so often during the voyage.

Then something happened that we had discussed 1,000 times; the coastguards from across the harbour put off in a boat to the yacht. The Volunteers levelled revolvers at them, and I was afraid for a minute they would fire, but the coastguards, wisely seeing that four men could do nothing against 1,000, rowed off again and in a few minutes they were sending up rocket signals for help. In about half an hour the whole ship was unloaded. I got ashore with my luggage and was warmly greeted by O'Rahilly, Eoin MacNeill, Dermot Coffey and who, but Padraic Colum in uniform and looking quite martial.[36] He pressed me to lunch with them at the hotel, but I had already promised to go to the Coffeys, a plan made that night when we parted at Cowes on the *Kelpie*. Then the Volunteers formed up on the quay with their rifles and gave ringing cheers for the yacht, and her owners, and several eager Volunteers jumped on board to help hoist the mainsail. They were rather too eager over it and it tore again, this time rather badly, and Erskine decided to hoist the trysail. Luckily it was bent on to the gaff ready, and with Mr Gordon's help and one or two fishermen it did not take long. I got on board again while they were settling it and went below, got a broom and tried to clean up the cabin and saloon, which were full of straw, broken glass, etc. (the skylight had been broken), so that they could have some prospect of lunch when they got clear. Then on shore again, and this time they were really off, standing out to sea with shouts and cheers and goodbyes. We

---

36 This is a somewhat baffling entry; Padraic Colum was a Volunteer and was at Howth on 26 July, but he informs me that to the best of his memory he wore no uniform. The Fianna were the only Nationalists at Howth who, as a group, were in uniform. Some few Volunteers sported a uniform, but the official grey green dress was not decided upon until 12 August 1914, see in Martin, *Irish Volunteers*, 1913-1915, cit., pp. 132-5—*Ed.*

watched them till she was well out to sea, I feeling rather mean at having left them to cope with all the mess, and then I turned round in search of my possessions and found I had left my one respectable garment—my white sports coat—which I had cherished for landing in, on board when I went back to tidy up. I still had my dust coat, not looking its best as it had been used for covering up the guns; however, it partially concealed my white jersey and short red skirt; also one of my bags had disappeared; they had both been handed up on the quay by Volunteers, and one must have been carried off by mistake with the ammunition. I discovered it weeks afterwards at the Volunteer Headquarters. I believe they thought it contained part of a machine gun.

Dermot Coffey seized the other bag and he, Mr Gordon and I proceeded up to their house—it seemed miles—but when we got there Mrs Coffey gave us a most warm welcome, and a lunch preceded by a much needed wash.

We heard all about the *Kelpie's* doings from Dermot Coffey, and compared notes about our experiences in the big storm.

About 5, Mr Gordon and I started back to Dublin, and I took him to tea at the Arts Club. Who should I find there but Mr Craig? I was a little embarrassed what to say to him as I didn't know how much he knew of our doings, though I guessed he must know a good deal about Conor. He asked me if I had been on the *Kelpie*. 'No,' I said, 'I've been yachting with friends, in fact I've just landed." My costume certainly required some explanation. I solemnly introduced Mr Gordon as a yachting friend and we sat at tea and talked sailing shop as if no such thing as gun-running had occurred. Dublin seemed wrapped in Sunday afternoon sleepiness, and one wondered when the news would reach it, when far down the street we heard a newsboy 'Stop Press" and Mr Gordon dashed out and bought a paper. When he came back Mr Craig had vanished out of the tearoom, so further explanations were unnecessary. In all our forecasting of what would happen we never dreamt of firing on the crowd, or indeed on the Volunteers, once the guns were in their possession, as we knew the U.V.F. carried their rifles in Belfast.

I determined to go and try and find Mrs Green at her niece's house, having had a message through Figgis that she was expecting me. So after having sat some time at the Club discussing with Mr Gordon another gun-running expedition on the *Santa Cruz*—it was all fixed for September 20th, if more guns were wanted and more money could be got, and he was to come to Foynes and pretend to hire the boat—we said goodbye and he went off to catch the boat train, and I to Sandford Terrace. I found Mrs Green just arriving in a cab as I came up to the door and she was as glad to see me and hear all our doings as I was to see her. Dr Henry hospitably asked me to stay the night. Mrs Henry was away. I was beginning to feel I could hardly drag myself any longer and I accepted joyfully.

I felt rather mean as I got into a glorious hot bath and thought of Molly and Erskine tired and worn out with everything upset, tossing about on the Irish Sea.

But my bed was heavenly.

23. Letters from the Asgard, July 1914

Mrs Erskine Childers to Mrs Stopford Green
In the *Childers Papers*

I

Dear Mrs Green,

Our evil luck pursued us up to the very last minute before we made sail from Conway which did not take place until the morning of July the 3rd. Alas, that it was so for it means simply pushing right on, bad weather or good to Cowes.

In the first place my luggage got lost in spite of its being conspicuously labelled and I did not get it and go on board until the late evening of July the 1st. One of the two hands had not turned up. In his place a delightful young Greenhorn, John Dolan, from the central office of the Irish National Volunteers at Dublin, had been lent Erskine by Casement—a charming character but with no knowledge of the sea or ropes.

Mary [Spring Rice] arrived late Wed. and came on board to find me having supper which consisted of an uncertain raw egg and some tea with condensed milk!

Thursday July 2nd. Made sail at 4 a.m. Barometer falling badly, pouring rain. Sailed for an hour, wind increasing, rain torrential. Decided that as there were only two men, E [rskine] and Pat [McGinley], for crew, it was too great a risk in that weather. Turned back and decided to wait for our friend Mr Gordon S [hephard] who was to have joined us at Holyhead. Wired him to meet us Conway. Erskine almost despairing. At about five p.m. second hand turned up smiling—by name Charles Duggan—great joy. Our Greenhorn left us at once sadly, taking our hearts with him. The next morning the 3rd sailed with all hands on board, towed out over bar. (Gordon S. had turned up early that morning). Weather unpromising. Got across the bar safely. Both Mary and Molly felt very sick. Head winds. The rest of the 3rd and the whole of the 4th indescribable discomfort. Everyone sick—everything soaking above and below. Little food eaten. Mary a Spartan, helping with everything, cooking tea, wrestling with primus lamps, Rippingill stove, etc. A heroine. Molly horribly sick. I draw a veil over this day when everyone was severely tried and during which little way was made because of head winds and nasty short sea. Second night under way was so bad, E. decided that we must put in at Fishguard and allow all on board to regain their feet—when joy of joys, Sunday a.m., the 5th brought calm seas, sun, better winds and we gave up harbour comforts and stuck to our sea going—all feeling better, Mary least recovered but still cheery and a great companion. I write on deck, ship tossing gently to a swell which makes writing difficult. We had some of your delicious cake for lunch. Greatly appreciated.

The hands from Gola Island are all Bigger promised—perfect for the job. Our one anxiety now is time being so short. We must crack on sail and make all speed we may to get to Cowes the 7th. A digression. Imagine—C. O'[Brien] wrote Erskine just as we were starting that he would not do anything at all, had given it all up! ! Mary brought better tidings. All is well. He will go to get his 750. It does seem as if everyone but you and Mary had done all they could to drive Erskine distracted. I think we now deserve good luck don't you? To make up for it all. Poor Erskine was nearly broken down with it all—but is better already and beginning to sleep and eat again, thank Heaven we are beyond reach of telegrams, letters, etc. We think of you and know you wish us well. How I wish you could see us now all lying in the sun, Erskine at the wheel, gorgeous sky, sea, coast of Carnarvon —the decks and shrouds covered with blankets, pillows, jerseys, mattresses, coats, boots brought up to dry. Looks like a gipsy camp. Just had good lunch. Mary did not eat enough!

July 6th and 7th, beating all day and night. Worried because late for Cowes. Straining every nerve to get there. Better weather, but all tired. At last on the evening of the 7th passed Longships Lightship, at Land's End and turned east and had a fair wind. I can't describe the sensation—it was so heavenly. Tore along all night—I took a watch as Erskine has a very bad finger—all next day; came up Solent after dark and anchored, oh the joy, at Cowes at 2 a.m.

Thursday a.m. the 9th, all turned in and slept till 8.30. Breakfast. Connor arrived, swore dreadfully at Mary—in a rage at our keeping him waiting—absolutely brutal! Cheered up later and came back and worked hard helping us. Will go and do his share. I did not tell you that owing to Bigger s men being late, we left Conway only half prepared for sea. Result everything has been carrying away and our day at Cowes has been spent with sail makers and carpenters aboard. Lunch on shore—so good after yacht tinned food which Mary and I can't eat. Did a great deal of shopping. Think we may not have time to put in to Dover. Had letters and wires from Figgis saying meeting at rendezvous to be Sunday the

12th. Must hurry. He has been having a dreadful time it seems—working like a slave. M[agnus] of H[amburg] not up to the work.

Dramatic moment. E. told our two hands what they have in front of them. To our delight they proved willing and good. We feared they might refuse. They knew nothing till now.

Your letter is a very wonderful one. We shall keep it for the children. I have thought of you constantly, your brave untiring spirit; of all the help and inspiration you have been and are to us. I have *felt* you with us, blessing us. And your letter brings confirmation of this feeling of mine. Do you remember I said I should think the first bird that followed us was you yourself? A great white gull was with us on the wing for a long time one day and I knew it was you. Oh, if only you could have come!

I must stop to write other letters; this is a scanty account. I hoped to do better but the difficulties of writing are great. Can you read this scrawl?

We send you love and are all trying to do our best for you and the task. Your affectionate Molly Childers.

We may not be able to write again till after the 26th. Don't worry. It may be that Mary and I shall have to leave on the tug at the rendezvous if there is not room enough. We pray not. Mary is wonderful. Well.

A Titan.

We start early tomorrow.

II

Dear Mrs Green,

We left Cowes Friday July 10th after lunch and made sail for the rendezvous—head winds, slow progress, despair lest we be late. Giving up a call at Dover and keeping on relentlessly. Mary and I had our hearts in our boots—fearing that we should not be able to get in with our cargo!

On Sunday the 12th off Dover we got a fair slant of wind and shaped our course for the Roetigen Lightship. The tide was sweeping us up the North Sea and it was a difficult business to pick up a ship in the middle of the ocean, especially as the weather was very thick and one could not see far. To have passed it or missed it spelt disaster. You can see us all straining our eyes on the look out and will know our anxiety and our joy when, thanks to the skill of our two navigators we came upon the lightship! No Conor or tug in sight. We sailed about a bit and then on the horizon descried a curious looking object which as we approached turned out to be the tug and the *Kelpie* side by side!!! Immediately upon sighting us the tug came down on us—this about 7 p.m.—towering ship she looked beside us. She came alongside. Figgis leapt on board; the captain said we must tranship at once, and the work began there in the open sea. Our hearts failed when we heard that Conor had taken only 600 and had left 900 for us; they sank into despair when we saw the 90 huge bales awaiting us and looked at our small boat. There was nothing for it but to unpack every bale and unroll every gun out of its straw. The six of us and about six of the tug hands worked like galley slaves until about 2 a.m. at the job. I wish you could have seen the scene. Darkness, lamps, strange faces, the swell of the sea making the boat lurch, guns, straw, everywhere, unpacking on deck and being handed down and stowed in an endless stream; no supper, chocolate thrust into mouths of the crew and a mug of water passed round at one moment when frail nature was nearly spent—the vaseline on the guns smeared over everything; the bunks and floors of the whole yacht aft of the foc'sle filled about 2 ft. 6 high even from side to side, men sweating and panting under the weight of the 29 ammunition boxes—heavy and hard to handle. A German face peering down the hatch saying 'they will explode if you knock them or drop them.' A huge ship's oil riding light falling down through the hatch first on to my shoulder and then upside down into a heap of straw—a flare up, a cry, a quick snatch of rescue—the lamp goes out thank God, work again, some one drops two guns through, they fall on some one; no room to stand left save on guns, guns everywhere. On and on and on. I nearly slept as I stood and handed down guns. It was all like a mad dream, with a glow of joy and the feeling of accomplishing something great at the back of it to keep the brain steady and the heart unperturbed. Then a cry from the tug— 'that is all.' We look about to see the decks heaped high with ammunition boxes still unstowed, all our bedding and clothes packed in sail bags astern on deck—the task only half accomplished still. We cast off. The captain takes us in tow and gives us till daybreak to finish stowing. So we set to again and presently out of chaos order begins to appear. Gradually everything is made ship shape. Finally the last gun is stowed, the mattresses brought down and stretched over them like a floor, blankets, bags etc. The captain and Figgis had come on board before we started towing and the former offered us a tow as far as Dover whither Figgis insisted the tug should carry him. We feared disclosure. The captain urged Figgis not to land there. He was stubborn and insisted. At last the work was done. The yacht carefully and jealously trimmed by careful hands had about 11/2 less free board and seemed to me dangerously deep in the water, but that fear was quickly dispelled when we started off in the tug's wake, being towed. (This is confused. Forgive it. I forgot we stowed after towing began.)

There were still ammunition boxes on deck to stow. Everywhere was crammed, the *Asgard* very deep in the water. Terrific efforts got all but three into safe places where they couldn't shift. Those three, after earnest consultation, were thrown overboard—3,000 that was; we had 26,000. Connor 29—We could do no better. Figgis, asked for £5-0-0 for a tip to the captain, seemed short of funds. Erskine gave it to him. He was to pay each of the tug's crew £1-0-0 for helping us.

Left to ourselves we set sail for the long stretch of days and miles that lay between us and our destination. We soon grew accustomed to the yacht's strange motion, heavily freighted as she is. She is such a fine sea boat that, if anything, she sails better now than before! Below decks we sleep, crawl over, sit on, eat on guns. Guns everywhere, lying flat save in odd corners where they stick up on end. They catch us in our knees, odd bolts and butts and barrels transfix us from time to time but we are all so happy and triumphant, so proud of ourselves that we swear we are comfortable. Mary and I sleep on mattresses laid across our cabin over the guns. One can kneel anywhere but can stand only in one place about 9 inches square. Toilet has become very difficult. Our daily rub down in alcohol takes hours, one is so pitched about in the odd positions one has to take. It is all gorgeous fun and, joy of all joys, Mary and I are up to it and are not in the way. Indeed Mary is indispensable.

Our friend [Gordon Shephard] has to leave us on the 19th and he will post this. We have to get bread too. He will be put ashore at some out of the way place where we shall be safe.

I wish I could better describe life on board to you but alas! no words can portray the peculiar fascinating savour of it—the discomfort, the glory which makes up for everything. Again and again we have been in company with the fleet! We passed our tug off Dungeness—close by. She lay at anchor. Neither of us made a sign of recognition.

Were we seen at the Roetigen? Is the *Daily Mail* full of us? We dread to hear things are known. We dread that Conor may deliver his guns and talk before our date.

Pray for us and think of us. We talk often of you.

Think of our next meeting. Oh—if only it may be a success!

I write on deck. We have just raced and beaten a fishing smack and bought some fresh fish. Mary feeds us well.

Goodbye again dear, dear, Mrs Green, and love to you from us. Molly Childers.

Can you ever read this?

III

Dear Mrs Green,

Ever since we left, Erskine has been sad that you don't know the scheme, and we haven't dared to write it. But now I can tell it as this will be posted after it has happened if it does happen. It is this. At 10 a.m. Sunday the 26th we lie off Lambay Island near Kingstown and wait for a motor boat or, if that fails a rowing boat, which is to come out from Howth to tell us if all is well or not. We set sail in her company for Howth Harbour where there are vedettes watching—men who are to behave like ordinary loungers. Meanwhile the Dublin I.V. 1,000 strong are to make their weekly route march out to Howth this day: they are to arrive and stand between the harbour and the town at ease, eating their lunch. We enter the harbour at 1 p.m. precisely and lie up alongside the eastern pier. The coastguards are way round on the western pier. The second we are tied up alongside, word is passed, a command given and the volunteers fall into rank and double up the pier toward us on the run. The guns and ammunition are passed up with lightning speed. Meanwhile the coastguards will try to get to us by crossing the harbour in their boat, as they can't get at us through the Volunteers. But the motor boat will fend them off and keep them away. There is a hope that telegraph wires will be cut, but there may be a wireless and in that case the gunboat at Kingstown will probably start off for Howth. We trust to her not having steam up on Sunday, to the coastguards' laziness or absence, but we shall probably fail to get away after the guns are delivered, though we shall make a great effort to do so. If we do get away we shall sail for some English port and lay up the yacht and leave her. If we don't, they will confiscate the yacht. I don't think they will imprison us, though they may fine E. and me in which case we should have to go to prison rather than pay. But I think they will only confiscate yacht and hope that E. and I can get away Sunday by night mail and hurry back to London perhaps to pull some wires. We have never pulled any yet in our lives, but I think we will this time! So we hope for the best and are cheerful although we *want* to get away dreadfully—as you can imagine.

If it fails, if either boat brings us word that the thing is impossible—then we must go for our second string. I think you will guess what that is if you remember who is on board. We dread it for we are pretty tired and it means a long long effort. But never mind. We hope for the best. My last letter was sent from Milford. Bad weather kept us there after landing our friend, for one night. The next day—Monday, July 20th, we set sail for Holyhead—thankful we had been left unmolested. Tuesday was a fine day. Tuesday night it blew half a gale and we were glad to get into the outer refuge harbour of Holyhead Wed. at noon. The harbour master came alongside, terrifying us, and took our name, tonnage, last port of call and destination (sic!) and left little knowing what we were. After that no one came near us. We kept watch though all the time, lest anyone board us and look down the hatch below deck. E. and M. rowed ashore for shopping.

We are sad about the news—the Conference, and fear it means Exclusion.[37] What are our efforts for, if that happens?

Today, Friday, the 24th, we set sail early in bad weather but had to put back because our mainsail split a little. Mary and I mended it. Off again about 2 o'clock and now we are on our way to our destination. Our hearts are in our mouths. Yet they are in the right place at the same time. We waver between hope and fear. Will the cruiser come out and search us before we get to Howth? You can understand it all and sympathize.

---

37 This refers to the conference held at Buckingham Palace, 21-24 July 1914, between representatives of the British government, the Conservatives, the Irish Nationalists and the Ulster Unionists. The central problem was the proposed exclusion of certain Ulster counties from a Home Rule parliament in Dublin. The negotiations broke down because of Redmond's refusal to accept the principle of Exclusion (i.e. Partition), see D. Gwynn, *John Redmond* (London: 1932), pp. 335-343.

It is now fine weather—too fine, no wind, a horrible sea left over from the bad weather. Earlier in the afternoon as we sat on deck a great gull came and hovered over us, delicately poised with outstretched wings over our mizzen mast and followed us like that for an hour or more. I told them all it was you coming to wish us well. It was very uncanny the way the gull behaved. I have never seen such a thing before. Close to our mast head, against the sky, wings motionless, floating gravely and silently above us for long periods of time. Another came and joined it and I told them it was Mr Bigger. Duggan and Pat—the men— were delighted.

I send you love, a great deal of love. You have been with us I know. We feel you so close. If only you were really here and could see it all.

I am in the saloon whither I crawled over guns, for tea. The guns are packed in evenly from side to side as high as the table and filled in up to the top under it. It keeps them from shifting when we roll and toss. On two sides of the table are laid mattresses—long and narrow. On one of them lies Erskine asleep, preparing for his night's watch. On the 3rd side there is no mattress but some sail bags over the guns. That is where I am lying. The 4th side is occupied by a lamp and a door into the foc'sle. Ammunition boxes are not in here. They are forward and aft. The whole boat except foc'sle is evenly full of guns. One can't stand; one crawls on one's knees, or walks doubled up, very low down. Mary and I are covered with black bruises! They catch you anywhere and everywhere when the boat gives a great lurch and throws you over. It is all very funny and not so bad as it sounds. One just has to alter one's point of view and habits—that is all, and then it is all right. We lie, like the ancient Romans at our meals, only twisted Romans, for we are generally clinging to something to prevent tobogganing across the table which is now our floor. Everywhere the guns are protected as well as we can by canvas and waterproof but some are a little rusty to our sorrow. The damp sea air. We spend much time tucking them up again and again. Countless things, knives, a sponge, a comb, pipes etc., got lost by falling down through chinks. Irrecoverable until after Howth. Dressing is the hardest operation. It is agonizing. How you would laugh if you saw Mary and me in our cabin. All full of guns, like the saloon. She is so splendid—such a help, such a good sailor, so brave and unshrinking. And she is well. Better than when she joined us, I rejoice to say.

Of course we are all tired and longing for the strain to be over. We shall have had four and a half nights at anchor and 18 and a half nights at sea. That is a record for a yacht of our size and we are proud of it.

Goodbye dear, dear Mrs Green. I wish I could write a better letter.

If we can we will send you word how things go.

Yours affectionately,
Molly Childers.

Turn over, s.v.p.

All came true exactly as I described it, and everything went well. Our last two days were spent in a gale—a hard one. You can imagine discomfort. On Sunday, with anxiety we waited for motor boat and then for the rowing boat which never came. Weather too bad. We decided to try for it just the same. We went into Howth Harbour at exactly 1 p.m. There were anxious moments. In the end all plans worked exactly. O'Rahilly, Cathal Brugha, MacNeill, Dolan, Figgis there. Wonderful unforgettable scene. We unloaded in 3/4 hours. Mary left us. We got off safely and came here (Bangor) because of weather. Got away safely. What can I say of the sequel? Our hearts bleed. We burn at the injustice and cruelty meted out to Nationalist Ireland. We have seen only just reports which say they (soldiers) got only 25 of our [rifles] but the street fighting is terrible. We pray it may make the air clearer. We feel we have done right, thank God for that, but it is very sad and takes away some of our triumphant elation which was *tremendjus*. MacNeill like a child with joy. Said I was the greatest soldier of them all, wrung our hands. We love that man. I will write again exactly what happened. I have not time now. God bless you and all of us.

24. Conor O'Brien

Edward Conor Marshall O'Brien (1880-1952) was a son of Edward William O'Brien of Cahirmoyle, co. Limerick, and a grandson of William Smith O Brien of 1848 fame. His family was a collateral branch of the Barons of Inchiquin, and he was a cousin of Lord Monteagle (the Spring Rices of Foynes).

He was educated at Winchester, Trinity College Dublin, and Oxford, and was an architect by profession. He was an early member of Sinn Fein, spoke Irish fluently, and with his step-sister, Nelly, was a patron of the Irish college at Carrigaholt, Co. Clare. He was an outspoken Home Ruler, and became a local leader of the Irish Volunteers, more as a follower of Redmond than of MacNeill. The threat from Carson and the Orangemen urged him to action. He immediately supported Mary Spring Rice's suggestion to run guns for the Volunteers, and was one of the eleven subscribers who financed the venture. His yacht, *Kelpie*, carried 600 rifles and ammunition from the North Sea to near the Welsh coast, where they were transferred to Sir Thomas Myles's yacht, *Chotah*, which brought them to Kilcoole on the night of 1 August 1914.

During the 1914-1918 War he served with the Navy, in the R.N.V.R. After the war he had his well-known yacht, *Saoirse*, built at Baltimore, Co. Cork. She was 42 feet long over all, with a beam of 12 feet and a normal draft of about 63/4 feet; this was his home until he sold her in 1940. In June 1923 he left Dun Laoghaire on his famous yachting expedition around the world; he sailed via Madeira, Brazil, Cape Town, Melbourne, New Zealand, around the Horn, Brazil again, the Azores, and returned two years later to a tremendous welcome at Dun Laoghaire. In recognition of his achievement the British Royal Cruising Club awarded him their coveted Challenge Cup three times in succession for the three stages of his voyage. It was the first time the Irish tricolour had been carried around the world.

He was appointed an inspector of fisheries under the Second Dáil, and was particularly interested in the co-operative purchase of boats by fishermen. In 1928 he married Katherine Clausen, the artist, and they made their base at Ibiza in the Balearic Islands; she died in 1936. He was well-known as a mountaineer, and preferred to climb in his bare feet. He was the author of more than fourteen books.

During the Second World War he volunteered for the Small Vessels' Pool. In this service he sailed several small ships across the Atlantic from America to British ports when boats were in urgent need by the Allies. He died at Foynes on 18 April 1952.

25. Sir Thomas Myles

Sir Thomas Myles, C.B., M.D., F.R.C.S.I., was born at Limerick. He was educated at Trinity College, Dublin, where he received the M.D. degree in 1889. He was resident surgeon in Dr Steevens' Hospital from 1881 to 1884 and filled a similar position at Jervis Street Hospital from 1885 to 1890. From that date he was attached to the Richmond Hospital, where for many years he was in virtual control and brought the hospital to a high state of efficiency. He was President of the Royal College of Surgeons, 1900-02.

In 1900 the Corporation of Limerick elected him an Honorary Burgess of their city and in 1910 he was appointed Surgeon to the King in Ireland. In December 1914 he was made Consulting Surgeon to the Troops in Ireland, with the temporary rank of Lieutenant-Colonel. As a surgeon he bore a high reputation for skill and though busily engaged with hospital and private practice, he found time to contribute numerous papers to medical journals.

He was one of the earliest members of the Protestant Home Rule Party, which was started in the early seventies of the last century by the late Rev. Joseph Galbraith, S.F.T.C.D. and some other influential members of the Church of Ireland. Numerically, the party was not a great success but a few prominent figures attached themselves to it. He was a consistent supporter of the policy of Charles Stewart Parnell, of whose bodyguard he was a member during the famous Louth election, and he spoke occasionally on political platforms.

He had an international repute as a yachtsman, and he and his yacht were known in almost every part of the British Isles and in many Continental ports. He was on terms of personal acquaintance with many of the titled nobility of Europe and most of the prominent figures in English Society. Highly cultured, he was an authority on French literature, and was a brilliant raconteur. His interest in sport of all kinds was rivalled only by his ability in many other spheres. His love of Irish athletics brought him to the forefront in the efforts to secure Irish representation at the Olympic Games. He was himself a noted athlete in his youth. About 1887 he stood up for three rounds to John L. Sullivan, the famous prize-fighter, and John L. is reported to have said that young Myles had 'a greater punch and more science than many alleged pugilists'.

Myles and Erskine Childers were friends, having met during holidays at Clifden in Connemara and their yachting interests gave them a common Bond. When a yacht was needed at short notice, to transfer the guns from O'Brien's *Kelpie* to Kilcoole, James Creed. Meredith arranged a meeting, at his own house between Myles and Bulmer Hobson. It was there agreed that Myles's steam-yacht, *Chotah,* would be used, and that Meredith would act as one of Myles's crew.

Éamon Martin, who took part in the unloading of the rifles at both Howth and Kilcoole, recalls a quixotic incident concerning Myles. Martin was one of the Volunteers in the Four Courts' area during 1916, and when he met Myles near the Richmond Hospital during the fighting he reminded him of Kilcoole. Myles, who then held the rank of lieutenant colonel in the British Army, declared that although he was a

Home Ruler and a Nationalist he thought the Rising was a mad venture. Later, when Martin was seriously wounded in both chest and lung, Myles took him and about twenty-five other wounded Volunteers into the Richmond Hospital. After the surrender of the Volunteers Martin was under the surveillance of the police at the hospital. One day when he was sufficiently recovered he was spirited away from the hospital in Myles's car, sitting beside Myles who was wearing his British officer's uniform. Myles continued to treat Martin until he was well enough to escape to America.

26. Contraband of war

By Conor O'Brien

From *Irish Red Cross Junior Annual,* Dublin 1947, pp. 26-29.
When in 1914 a vessel was sought for to bring a cargo of rifles for the Volunteers from Germany, the searchers met at Foynes.

Mary Spring Rice owned an Arklow smack,[38] converted to trade on the Lower Shannon; Erskine Childers, who was to be in command, came to see if she was suitable. We turned her down because nothing could make her look like a craft with a legitimate business in the North Sea, Childers offered instead his 30-ton yacht *Asgard,* because nobody asks what a yacht's business is anywhere. But she might not be able to accommodate all the guns available along with himself, Mrs Childers, Mary Spring Rice, and three others, so I proposed to sail in company in my 20-ton *Kelpie* to take the overflow. She was at Foynes and wanted very little done to make her ready for sea; *Asgard,* was at Conway in North Wales, and wanted a lot; and Childers had to go to Hamburg to arrange the shipment, and could not oversee the work on his yacht.

Darrell Figgis had bought the rifles, 1,500 of them, with 45,000 rounds of ammunition, and was to bring them to a rendezvous off the

---

38 Mary Spring Rice did not own the boat—*Ed.*

Belgian coast for transhipment to us—we were the optimists, and didn't add 'weather permitting'. I was to take 600,[39] and to make room for them under the cabin floor five tons of iron ballast had to come out. To put the yacht in sailing trim for the outward voyage I shipped as many bags of gravel as would fit in. Nobody commented on this strange operation; they were all looking at the great works in progress on the rejected smack in the inner harbour. Rumour even said that she was fitting out for a gun-running trip! Meanwhile we sailed away quite unnoticed—myself, my sister Kate, Dermot Coffey, and two Foynes men, George Cahill and Tom Fitzsimons—to rendezvous with Childers at Cowes. As neither of our yachts had an engine, we could not fix a date. *Kelpie* was additionally hampered by her lack of ballast, and would not make much headway against a head wind and sea. And a head wind is a safe bet when leaving the Shannon, and the sixty miles before one turns the corner round the Blaskets is always rough. We spent two miserable days before we picked up a fair wind off Dursey Head, but on the fifth evening reached Cowes after a glorious shove up Channel from a strong north-west wind.

Next morning there was no sign of Childers, nor the next, and I was getting worried. Cowes yachts are the smartest of the smart, and boats like mine, with dingy paint and rustic crew, do not lie in that uncomfortable anchorage day after day without exciting comment; also the date for our meeting with Figgis was very near. When at last *Asgard* arrived, she looked even less smart than *Kelpie*. The Welsh riggers had delayed her and then done the work badly; the fine breeze which had brought us up Channel was a head gale to her off the coast of Anglesea; gear had carried away and various repairs were urgent. Her news was that Figgis also had been delayed and our rendezvous postponed to the 12th of July. We had two days to make it. The distance was only 150 miles, but the wind was very light and showed no signs of improving. I began to realize that this

---

39 The original understanding was that the *Kelpie* would take 750 rifles and half of the ammunition, see above, pp, 79, 99, 101—*Ed.*

was a chancy undertaking and wanted a good string of miracles to bring it through. I got under way at once, leaving Childers to follow as soon as his repairs allowed.

We had a strenuous two days; the first, trimming fancy sails to vagrant airs, the second, after passing Dover, dismantling the yacht. We lifted off the main skylight bodily, piled all the saloon furniture on deck, ripped up the floor and hoisted out the bags of gravel. A kindly fog hid the operation from any passing eye, but also left us quite uncertain of our position, for the wind was failing and the strong tidal stream took us where it liked. At noon it took us within hearing of the fog trumpet on the Sandettie lightship; our goal was the Ruytigen ship ten miles further on, and we were drifting in that direction.

We never saw the lightship. The first thing that loomed through the mist was a German tug. It just had to be Figgis or we were done; we were already two hours late. A bearded man, clearly not one of her crew, stood on deck; I assumed he was Figgis, and hailed him, luckily in Gaelic. He answered in the same, and we warped alongside the tug. Her skipper said: 'I suppose that's Mexican you're talking?' Figgis answered for me; I had not been warned that we all had to be Mexicans, owing to an embargo by the Germans on shipments of arms to European countries. But the skipper carefully avoided looking at the label on the bottle of whiskey which I swopped for an enormous loaf of black rye bread, 'enough to last you across the Atlantic,' he said with a wink. Then all hands on busy with the cargo. We had just finished stowing it when *Asgard* drifted into sight. Another miracle? We cast off and the tide swept us away, now to the westward; the homeward voyage had begun.

The first stage was to end on the night of the 24th, when I should meet Sir Thomas Myles at a rendezvous in the Irish Sea, twenty-five miles southwest of Bardsey Island. He would land my guns at Kilcoole, Co. Wicklow, on the night of the 25th; armed with them, the Volunteers would occupy Howth Harbour, into which Childers would sail at noon next day.[40] The plan seemed accident-proof; I had twelve days to reach

---

40 O'Brien's memory is here playing him tricks. It was never intended that the Kilcoole guns be used

the rendezvous, Myles's yacht *Chotah* had an engine and could guarantee the Kilcoole landing and Childers had a whole fortnight to get to Howth, where a fleet of motor-boats would be waiting if he wanted help.[41] Now began the long beat down Channel against the usual west wind, varied only by one mild panic when we found ourselves in the middle of the British Battle Fleet (but they were thinking about the review at Spithead not about us) and a more serious inconvenience in the break-down of the galley stove. It must have got shifted in stowing the cargo; it boiled a kettle with difficulty, and it would not bake bread at all, and on the sixth day the German loaf was wearing thin. Then our luck sent us into Mount's Bay under a thick veil of fog. We anchored noiselessly and sent the boat into Penzance, Cornwall, for bread. Was it a third miracle that she found her way back to the yacht again?

Once round the Land's End we had done with head winds, but also with fine weather. The month's rainfall descended in one deluge, and a southerly gale with it. The saloon skylight, like the galley stove, had got disorganized and kept nothing out. We were soaked, but that was not my chief worry. If this could happen off Cape Cornwall on Sunday, it might just as well happen off Bardsey on Friday, and we had made no plans to meet such a case. I still had four days to explore Cardigan Bay for a secluded and sheltered meeting-place if the weather prevented transhipment at sea. Those four days were fine and calm, and very clear, and I felt I might cause comment by sailing round in circles instead of using, as a proper yacht would, the anchorage in St. Tudwell's Roads, off the Welsh coast, where vessels commonly wait for a tide or a fair wind. So I concealed *Kelpie* between a ketch and a schooner well off, and went ashore, as a proper yachtsman should. But I was not received as a yachtsman. Disguises were thrown at my head; I was identified as a Breton selling onions. When they were baulked of their onions, the

to arm Volunteers guarding the unloading of the guns at Howth; to have brought armed Volunteers to Howth would have advertized that something momentous was afoot and might easily have caused an armed clash there — *Ed.*

41 There was no plan for a fleet of motor boats — *Ed.*

people showed no further curiosity. Here was a safe and unsuspicious meeting-place, if I could only get Myles into it.

On Friday evening I went out, following the schooner. The captain of the ketch hailed me as I passed, asking me to keep an eye on the schooner; she wasn't fit to be out in the weather that was coming, and he himself was staying at anchor. It was that sort of weather. Of course, I missed Myles; of course, I stayed out there looking for him till daylight; of course, he knew as much about St. Tudwell's as I, and was snugly anchored in the Roads when I got back. My foolish excursion was described by the captain of the ketch as the day's good deed, though I never saw the schooner and could have done nothing if she had foundered. With a character like that I could do anything: tranship the guns in broad daylight, if it was any use. But it was not.

Myles had split his mainsail and without it his engine was not powerful enough to face the gale, and Kilcoole was seventy miles away, dead to windward. We could only postpone the landing for a week, tranship the guns that night, and let me get across in ballast to lay what false clues I could.

By Sunday the gale had blown itself out, and I had a light-weather passage: so light that the yacht had to anchor off Bray for the turn of the tide. Immediately she was boarded by a reporter. She asked for it; she showed a foot of copper out of the water, her paint was scarred by rough contacts, and I sat on the hatch ostentatiously cleaning a rifle. He said: 'I suppose you're the yacht that landed them at Wexford on Saturday night?' It was the first that I had heard of Wexford—an eleventh hour *canard* put up by the ingenious Figgis—but I admitted I had landed them just there. Next a British destroyer steamed by, coming from the wild-goose chase in Wexford. He gave one glance at the yacht and passed on. Nobody supposed that her cargo was still afloat in St. Tudwell's Roads, and we did not expect any interference with the postponed landing on Saturday night.

However, it was no harm to suggest that it would take place on the other side of Dublin. My sister and I were now marked characters, and many speculative eyes followed us as we sailed out of Dun Laoghaire in a big open boat, very suitable for landing on a beach, and disappeared behind Howth. It was not an evening for a pleasure trip—murky and threatening rain. But darkness fell early and hid us from the shore. We had no object in sailing invisibly to the northward and no impediment to sailing south, so our boat did fulfill its mission of landing guns on the beach of Kilcoole.

27. Guns for Kilcoole
by Diarmuid Coffey[42]

A talk broadcast from Radio Éireann, 21 August 1961.

It is difficult to realise how very different the world was in 1914 from what it is today. Then there had been no major European war since 1870, and the idea of one was almost unthinkable. The important thing for most of us in Ireland was the Home Rule Bill then passing through the British Parliament, and the resistance to it of the Ulster Unionist Party and the Ulster Volunteers. Though the Ulster Volunteers were looked upon by most people as a bluff it was felt that they might be made an excuse for the British to shelve the Home Rule Bill, and many people thought that the best reply would be to form a counter-movement.

The Irish Volunteers, with Eoin MacNeill as their head, were started on 25th November 1913 and in a very short time a large body of Volunteers was formed. There were men like Pádraic Pearse and James Connolly and

---

42 Diarmuid Coffey, born in 1888, took a degree in history at Trinity College, Dublin, in 1910, and was called to the Bar in 1912. After the Howth gun-running he joined the staff of the Irish Volunteers as secretary to Colonel Cotter, and subsequently to Colonel Moore. He was on the staff of the Irish Convention, 1917-18, librarian of the Cooperative Reference Library in Plunkett House, 1917-21, and a captain in the Free State Army in charge of a river patrol on the Shannon. He was an assistant clerk of the Seanad 1923-36, Assistant Keeper of the Public Records from 1936, then head of the Public Records Office until he retired in 1956. He died on 9 July 1964.—*Ed.*

a number of I.R.B. men who did not regard the Volunteers as a political bluff but as the nucleus of an army to fight for the freedom of Ireland. But I think I am right in saying that the majority of the Irish Volunteers in 1914 did not seriously mean to rise and fight England.

The Ulster Volunteers were importing guns and it was felt that a counter-landing of arms for the Irish Volunteers should be undertaken. This was felt not only by Irishmen but by a number of English Liberals. Money was needed and a whip round was made among Irish Nationalists like Mrs Stopford Green and Erskine Childers and Liberals like Sir Alec Lawrence.[43] Enough money was raised to buy 1500 second-hand rifles of an old pattern and Darrell Figgis was sent to Antwerp to buy them from a firm of armament dealers. It was planned to have a sensational landing in broad daylight at Howth from Erskine Childers's yacht *Asgard*.

The *Asgard* was too small to take all the rifles and it was decided to have a second landing at Kilcoole by night. Conor O'Brien was to use his yacht the *Kelpie* to bring the rifles to a rendezvous off the Welsh coast where they were to be transferred to Sir Thomas Myles's yacht *Chotah*. Myles used to sail every weekend and no suspicion would be aroused by his sailing about the Irish Sea, while Conor O'Brien might well be suspected as he was not given to weekend sailing.

It was through Conor O'Brien that I came into it. He had difficulty in getting a crew and although I was not a very competent sailor I had done a good deal of yachting and had sailed with Conor O'Brien before. I met O'Brien in the United Arts Club and he asked me to go for a cruise with him. I was a briefless barrister but thought I should not leave the Law Library in term time. When however O'Brien said he was going for 'ironmongery' I threw my business, such as it was, to the winds and

---

43 Sir Alexander Waldemar Lawrence, who died 1 Sept. 1939, was an English Liberal, a nephew in law of Lady Alice Young—see above, p. 35, and a cousin of Diarmuid Coffey. For Sir Alexander see *Walford's County Families*, p. 785.—*Ed.*

agreed to meet him on Saturday 27th June at Foynes where his yacht lay. Miss Mary Spring Rice who was one of Childers's crew lived at Foynes with her father, Lord Monteagle. The *Asgard* started from a British port.

I left Dublin by the 12.20 train on Saturday but it was delayed and so missed the connection at Limerick Junction. While we were waiting at the junction the 3 o'clock train from Dublin came in. On it was Mac Giolla Bhríde (Lord Ashbourne), a Gaelic enthusiast and one of the few Irishmen to wear a kilt. He started a conversation on the sound of the letter 'm' in the Irish word lámh, but soon began to make cryptic remarks about my journey which made me a bit uneasy as to how many people knew what we were up to. I found this conversation embarrassing and was glad when he left.

There was some disagreement between Childers and O'Brien as to the methods of securing secrecy. Childers was most careful not to say a word that could possibly give away the plan. O'Brien believed in talking so much that no one would believe what he said. I don't know which was right but as far as I knew the only people in Dublin who had any details of O'Brien's part in the gun-running were Cruise O'Brien and W. E. G. Lloyd[44] both members of the Young Ireland branch of the United Irish League. That is of course apart from certain members of the Irish Volunteer executive.

When we did at last reach Limerick the last train to Foynes had gone, and as there was no train till Monday I had to hire a motor car. This was not as common in 1914 as it is now. When I reached Foynes I found Conor O'Brien and his sister Kitty on his yacht *Kelpie*. She was a ketch of about 28 tons with a saloon, a single berth cabin, a two berth cabin and two berths in the fo'c'sle. Besides Conor and Kitty O'Brien, who was as good as a man, there were two paid hands and myself. The two paid hands were George Cahill who died some years later in the Black Sea, and Tom Fitzsimons.

---

44 W. E. G. Lloyd was an English Liberal who lived in Pembroke Park, a member of the (Dublin) United Arts Club.—*Ed.*

On Monday June 29th we warped alongside the quay to take in water and some final provisions, and then set sail. When we reached the mouth of the Shannon we ran into a rough sea and my memory is a blank of seasickness which lasted until Wednesday after which I found my sea legs. I think the rest of the crew were a bit sick too. We cleared the Fastnet at 10 a.m. that morning and sighted the Longships at 4 p.m. on Thursday. My most vivid memory of that day is that O'Brien decided to take in the topsail. It was blowing fairly hard and three of us were struggling with the sail. O'Brien had a very hot temper and a fine flow of language but when curses failed he dropped the wheel and brushing us aside did the job single-handed. O'Brien had one of the hottest tempers I had ever met and was very highly strung, but under it all he had a very warm and kindly disposition. He would curse one in a ferocious manner one minute and apologize the next. This made life aboard a bit exciting.

I could describe our sail up the English Channel and the arrival at Cowes at 11.45 on Friday night, but apart from the fact that we intended to get guns, there was nothing to distinguish us from any other yacht going to the headquarters of yachting. Cowes was where we had arranged to meet Childers as the least suspicious place for any two yachts to meet. Our final rendezvous to get the guns was for Friday the 10th July off the mouth of the Scheldt.

On Saturday, Sunday and Monday there was no sign of the *Asgard*. On Monday Hervey de Montmorency arrived.[45] He was to be an extra hand on the *Kelpie*. He was a man of means who lived in Hatch St. Dublin and was interested in Irish politics. He told us he had been treasure-hunting on the Cocos Islands and had stopped fights between Dagos armed with knives and he recounted other tales of adventure. We made a bed for him in the saloon and in the morning found a note to say he had been kept awake by the noise of the clock and had gone ashore to a hotel.

Tuesday 7th July and still no sign of Childers. De Montmorency

---

45 For de Montmorency see above.

began to talk of going back to Dublin to find out what was happening. On Wednesday when we came ashore we found that de Montmorency had left. Still no sign of the *Asgard* and O'Brien was much worried and very cross, and sent telegrams and telephone messages to find out what had become of Childers and what we were to do. Childers, we found out later, was much annoyed by this as he thought it might give away the plan. In fact he had had great difficulties in getting to Cowes and had hurt his hand badly.

The *Asgard* arrived late on Wednesday 8th or early on Thursday 9th. When we made contact with Childers we learnt that the rendezvous for Friday 10th had already been postponed till Sunday 12th July — an appropriate date — but as we had not heard of this change we had had every reason to be worried.

We arranged to sail very early on Friday morning and that Childers would follow later in the day. We got away in some fuss as we stuck on a sand bank for about an hour until the tide floated us off, during which time O'Brien woke the sleeping crew of neighbouring yachts with a wonderful flow of language. Heads kept bobbing up in all directions.

We had a slow calm passage against light easterly winds, and passed through the Straits of Dover on Sunday morning 12th July. Our rendezvous for the guns was near the Ruytigen lightship off the mouth of the Scheldt, so that if the weather turned foul we should be able to find shelter for the transfer of the guns. But the wind was so light and the sea so calm that we seemed unable to get away from the East Goodwin lightship. At 3 in the afternoon squalls from the west brought us to the Sandettie Lightship off the Belgian coast and a couple of hours later we saw a small tug.

We had arranged that on coming to our rendezvous we should hoist a white jib while the other sails were red barked. The tug approached us and we hailed her, '*Kelpie* from N.Y. in ballast.' When we were replied to in Irish by Darrell Figgis we knew that we had made the journey. Figgis had come from Hamburg with the guns in the German tug *Gladiator*. She had seemed small when we first saw her but when we came close she seemed a powerful, sizable, boat. Figgis had told the captain of the *Gladiator* that what he had was 'merchandise for Mexico'. He came aboard the Kelpie and warned us on no account to mention Ireland or guns.

We then set to the most strenuous few hours I had ever spent. We first had to take off the saloon roof and haul up and throw overboard the sandbags which O' Brien had substituted for more orthodox ballast. Then we took on the rifles which I understand were the earliest bolt action rifles used by the Prussian army soon after 1870. Our consignment later became known as the 'Howth' rifles. They were long and heavy and packed in straw in bundles of ten covered with sacking. As muzzles and butts protruded here and there the nature of our secret merchandise was obvious to everyone who saw it. The bundles were heavy, but the boxes of ammunition each of 1000 rounds were far heavier, and except for one German sailor no one was able to carry them single-handed. I asked Figgis to help me with a box I was trying to stow and referred to it as ammunition. Figgis took me up and said 'don't use that word.' When I pointed out to him that the box had red and other labels saying in German 'Cartridges', 'Explosive', etc., he was a bit taken aback but said 'it's safer not to mention it.' Figgis had a strong dramatic sense and liked to keep up the feeling of mystery.

The bales of rifles were a good deal lighter than the sandbags we had thrown overboard and took up a lot more space. We had removed the saloon table but soon the saloon was several feet deep in rifles leaving barely room to crawl over the bundles and nowhere to sit. We had been extremely lucky in the weather as it was calm and hazy so that we could lie alongside the tug as if it were a pier and there was not much risk of being noticed. By 8 p.m. we had finished the job. We took 60 bundles of rifles and several thousand rounds of ammunition, leaving 90 bundles for

Childers. I heard afterwards that Childers was, not surprisingly, annoyed as he had to take the rifles out of their bundles in order to fit them in. O'Brien however felt that the *Kelpie* would not be safe with a bigger load than he had taken and was a bit doubtful as to how she would behave with the altered trim.

We swopped a bottle of whiskey with the captain of the tug for a loaf of black bread and some cigars, and set sail. Just as we got away we saw the *Asgard* appear but soon lost sight of her and the tug. We got some sort of a meal on what remained of the saloon, lying on top of the rifles. We tried to sail the *Kelpie* but there was practically no wind and we were so tired we could hardly keep awake. At last we decided to keep one man only on deck, to steer her on her course as far as possible and to see that we did not run into anything in that crowded part of the sea. We drew lots for who would take the first two hour spell and I lost.

I tried every dodge I could think of to keep awake. Everything was very quiet but as we got to the Straits of Dover there was quite a lot of traffic and it was essential to keep a watch. I tried moving about as far as I could but found myself dropping off to sleep all the time. At last I got hold of the topsail spar, laid it beside the wheel and sat on it, so that whenever I fell asleep I fell off and woke up. At the end of my watch I tumbled into my bunk. I slept like a log until routed out to be told that we had just sailed through the British fleet and that a destroyer had made for us as if to hold us up but had steamed away again. We had not paid much attention to the news from Europe and did not realize that what we had seen was the British fleet preparing for war under the guise of a review at Spithead.

All the next week we made our way slowly down the Channel against light westerly winds. We kept near the coast but would not put in anywhere as we were afraid some inquisitive person might come aboard and look into our saloon, but on Saturday July 18th we were off Penzance in such a thick mist that we could not see the harbour. We took advantage of this to land and buy some food as we were running short of various things especially bread. We found that the rye bread which we got from the *Gladiator* kept fresh far better than ordinary bread but we had finished it by then.

We had had calm seas and light winds so far, but as we came off the Longships the glass began to fall rapidly and the wind to rise. We were a bit anxious as to how the *Kelpie* would behave in rough weather as her trim was so much altered by having the rifles instead of normal ballast, but though it got pretty rough she rode the seas in good style. Our rendezvous with Sir Thomas Myles's yacht the *Chotah* was 20 miles west of Bardsey Island and we reached Bardsey on the morning of the 23rd. We hove to and later anchored in St. Tudwell's Roads off the little seaside resort of Abersoch. We anchored some way out to discourage visitors and rowed ashore where we found we were taken for Breton onion sellers who used to come to Wales in the summer.

Our rendezvous was for Friday evening and we set sail at 8 a.m. in a stiff breeze from the west. This died out to a flat calm and by 3 o'clock we were still. 18 miles from our rendezvous. The wind began to rise and soon was blowing very hard from the west, and we eventually reached our destination on Saturday morning but there was no sign of the *Chotah*. We hung about till breakfast time and then decided to run back to St. Tudwell's as it was too rough to transfer the arms even if the *Chotah* did turn up.

We had an exciting run as we had to pass through the Bardsey tide race. As we came into the race I noticed that some cartridge boxes which were stored to leave a passage to the fo'c'sle were coming adrift. I went below to see what could be done and decided the only thing to do was to prop my feet against one and my shoulders against the other to prevent them taking charge. As I looked up through the saloon skylight I saw green water. This was rather alarming but we were nearly through the race and in a few minutes were in calm water.

When we got to St Tudwell's we found that Myles had arrived there during the night. He had split his mainsail in the storm and had found it necessary to run for shelter. He himself had gone up to Port Madoc to look for a sail maker. On the *Chotah* we found de Montmorency, who had left us at Cowes, and also James Creed Meredith who afterwards became a high court judge.[46]

The *Chotah* was a much bigger boat than the *Kelpie* with several cabins and a large saloon so she would have no difficulty in taking the rifles, but with her split mainsail Myles thought he could not get over to Kilcoole in time for a landing as had been planned. Accordingly it was arranged that the landing should be postponed for a week and that I should go by the mail boat to report this to Eoin MacNeill. The *Kelpie* and the *Chotah* were to wait in St. Tudwell's and to take whatever opportunity there was to tranship the arms. This was done late one night without being observed.

I went to Bangor by train and took a late train to Holyhead. I did not see anyone I knew on the nearly-deserted pier and went straight to a cabin before any of the main line trains came in, and stayed in my cabin till all the other passengers had gone ashore. But a couple of days later I was greeted by an acquaintance with the words 'What were you doing at Holyhead on Saturday night?'

When I reached Dublin I found the streets full of Volunteers who were being marched off to Howth. It was difficult to locate MacNeill but eventually I managed to find him and give him the message about

46 James Creed Meredith, a Protestant Home Ruler. He was an outstanding student at Trinity College, Dublin, where he took his M.A. and LL.D. He was called to the Bar in 1901, to the Inner Bar in 1918, and was elected a bencher in 1924. He was one of a group — Francis Sheehy-Skeffington, Cruise O'Brien, Rory O'Connor, Tom Kettle — in the Young Ireland branch of the United Irish League. He was noted as an athlete and a student of German. He became president of the Supreme Court under Dáil Éireann in 1920. In 1924 he was appointed a judge of the High Court, and in 1934 was chosen as vice-president of the Supreme Plebiscite Tribunal in the Saar. He was appointed a judge of the Supreme Court in December 1936, and died on 14 August 1942. — *Ed.*

the change of plans. I had just time then to reach Howth, where my parents were staying for the summer, in time to see the *Asgard* sail in. I got through the cordon of Volunteers on the pier and had a few words with Childers to tell him what had happened to the *Kelpie*. The story of the landing of the arms and the shootings at Bachelor's Walk is too well known for me to repeat it. I waited at the pier until Childers sailed off leaving behind him Miss Spring Rice and 'Mr Gordon', whose real name was a mystery. They came to lunch with my parents and told us of their adventures.

A week later the arms from the *Kelpie* were landed at Kilcoole. I was not there to see it but was told that when the arms were put ashore a mysterious fleet of taxis appeared and removed a lot of the rifles and I never heard for certain who was in charge of them. There were already groups of varying opinions in the Volunteers.

Part IV
The Guns Arrive

Acknowledgements:

Thanks are due to Eoin P. Ó Caoimh for permission to re-publish the chapter on the Howth gun-running by Bulmer Hobson in *The Irish Volunteers, 1913-1915*, ed., F. X. Martin, O.S.A., Dublin 1963. Anybody who wishes to study the gun-running and its background will be indebted to Bulmer Hobson for his collection of papers in the National Library of Ireland.

The 'lost' article on the Howth gun-running by Arthur Griffith was located due to the advice of Desmond Ryan and Seán Ó Luing, and a photostat copy was kindly provided by His Excellency, M. L. Skentelbery, Minister of Ireland to the Argentine. Rev. Michael Kennedy, S.A.C., acting editor of *The Southern Cross*, supplied full information on the newspaper and its past editors.

I am grateful to the Talbot Press, Dublin, for permission to re-publish the letter of Sean MacDiarmada, and to Mrs Tom Clarke for information.

Thanks are due to Harry Nicholls and to the Irish Times for permission to re-publish the article on the gun-running.

28. Waiting in Philadelphia for a telegram

Roger Casement to Mrs Stopford Green.
In *Stopford Green Papers*, N.L.I., MS 10,464 (10)

5412 Springfield Avenue, Philadelphia, Pa., U.S.A.
26 July 1914

My dear Woman of the Ships!

If all goes well, today should be a happy day at home for the Volunteers. We are praying for it!

I am staying with a splendid character [Joe McGarrity] here, and he knows all.

This War that has come like a bombshell from the Almighty Arsenal may throw *everything* into the fire. If Germany is involved as seems most likely, John Bull will have to face the music—whether he likes it or not. And then . . . !

I am screwing the Irish here up to a high pitch. They are good men, and are keen to help.

[He goes on to discuss the Hibernian Convention which had just taken place at Norfolk, Virginia, U.S.A., and other matters of Irish interest].

Remember any more picnics must be run by only two or three caterers at outside. Bringing in others opens the door to the gang always on the watch.

If this war breaks out as seems likely—then be prepared for everything. God knows what may come from it—all I have predicted of which you know—may come or be attempted.

I am waiting hourly for a telegram today from Ireland to say the picnic has been held or prevented or broken up. Today was the day of Fate.

All thoughts of affection, Yours, R. C.

29. The plan succeeds
By Bulmer Hobson

In *The Irish Volunteers, 1913-1915*, ed. F. X. Martin, O.S.A., Dublin 1963, pp. 32-43.

When the Volunteers were started in 1913 we very rapidly got an enormous number of members, variously estimated to be between 100,000 and 150,000. It was this fact which probably impelled Mr Redmond to seek control, but, while we had this vast membership, we had very little funds, and virtually no arms.

In order to try and end this deadlock, which was endangering the whole

Volunteer position, Casement, on his own initiative, went to London in the early part of 1914 and got together a few friends who between them advanced £1,500. Mrs Alice Stopford Green was responsible for about half this amount; Erskine Childers, his wife, the Honourable Mary Spring Rice, Captain Berkeley and Casement himself subscribed the rest of the money. With the exception of Casement, none of the subscribers had had any previous connection with the Volunteers. The idea was that the money should be used to purchase arms, to bring them to Ireland, to sell the arms to the Irish Volunteers and to reimburse the subscribers. The subscribers took a very uncommercial risk, and I think they must have been very astonished when they did subsequently get their money back.

This London Committee selected Darrell Figgis to go to Antwerp to purchase rifles, and Erskine Childers and Conor O'Brien volunteered to bring the guns to Ireland in their yachts. Darrell Figgis had no previous connection with the Volunteers. Figgis purchased 1,500 rifles and 45,000 rounds of ammunition.

I think he got excellent value for the £1,500. He was also to hire a tug at Antwerp and bring the guns to meet the two yachts at an appointed time and place in the North Sea. The guns were Mauser rifles, old-fashioned and heavy, but were in perfect order. They were, I believe, the rifles with which the German Army were re-armed after the Franco-Prussian War. The first I heard of this project must have been in June, 1914, when Casement asked me if I could make arrangements for the landing of the two cargoes. He had already seen MacNeill and O'Rahilly, but so far no working scheme had been framed. I agreed with the suggestion, on condition I was not to be hampered by any committee, and I agreed to meet him and Childers in Dublin within a week and have some practicable plan ready.

On thinking the matter over I decided that 1,500 rifles would not go very far in solving our problem, but that if we could bring them in in a sufficiently spectacular manner we should probably solve our financial problem and the problem of arming the Volunteers as well.

With this in mind I decided to land the guns during daylight, in the most open manner and as near to Dublin as possible. I personally examined every harbour between Greystones and Balbriggan, cycling the whole way, and only turned down the North Wall in Dublin because I thought that we might not get time to unload before the authorities would appear.

I decided that Howth was the most suitable harbour, and that the best method was to march a large number of Volunteers to meet the yacht, to arm them on the spot and march them back. I felt that this could be done, provided the movement was executed with sufficient rapidity to enable us to get back past the narrow neck of land at Sutton before the Castle could intervene. I felt that the task of seizing so many guns from so many individual Volunteers, who would be scattered over a wide area, would be beyond the powers of either police or soldiers.

Pádraig Ó Riain was the one man with whom I discussed all these arrangements in complete confidence.

I met Casement and Childers at Buswell's Hotel, Molesworth Street, Dublin, one Sunday about the end of June, and proposed my plan, with which they both agreed. Childers and I went out to Howth next day and looked at the harbour, and settled just where he was to come in. At that meeting it was fixed that Childers should sail into Howth Harbour at twelve noon on 26th July and that I would have the Volunteers there to meet him.

Childers then went off to keep his appointment with Figgis in the North Sea, and I did not see him again until he brought his cargo of guns into Howth Harbour on 26th July. I then went to MacNeill and asked him to propose at the next meeting of the Provisional Committee that all the Volunteer Companies in Dublin should have a joint route march every Sunday morning. The first march, I think, was to Lucan, another to Dun Laoghaire, and another to Clondalkin. The police were enormously interested in the first and followed in strength. At the second they were not so active, and the third week they were indifferent. When we finally marched to Howth on the 26th July they assumed that it was just another route march and were not present at all. They did not suspect anything unusual was on hand and neither did the general body of Volunteers who marched to Howth.

In preparation for the gun-running, I got the carpenter members of the I.R.B. to make about two hundred oak batons which were to be used in case we were attacked by the police. The Volunteers, although they were being given rifles, were far too raw and undisciplined to be entrusted with ammunition on that occasion.

As the day when Childers was due to come to Howth approached, one apparently insuperable difficulty arose. There had been a lot of talk following the Carsonite gun-running at Larne as to the probability of similar gun-running exploits being carried out in other parts of the country. The British authorities as a precaution sent *H.M.S. Porpoise,* which anchored in Dublin Bay. In the last week before Childers was due to arrive, I went out and looked anxiously at the *Porpoise* every morning, but she showed no signs of going away. Eventually on the Wednesday of that week I went to see John Gore, who was an elderly solicitor, and was one of the treasurers on the Volunteer Committee. John Gore was a charming old man, but he was not noted for his reticence. I told him in strict confidence that we were bringing a cargo of guns into Waterford on the following Sunday. I expected that he would be unable to refrain from giving this news in strict confidence to every client who came to see him. Whether this calculation was correct or not, it is a fact that two days later *H.M.S. Porpoise* steamed south. When the *Porpoise* got to Wicklow, apparently doubts began to occur, and the anchor was dropped. On Sunday, when we were engaged in bringing in the guns at Howth, the *Porpoise* was immobilized at Wicklow because they had given shore leave to the crew.

About twenty members of the I.R.B. under the command of Cathal

Brugha were sent to Howth early on the morning of Sunday, 26th July, with instructions to disport themselves about the harbour, hire boats and generally look as much like tourists as possible. Their business was to receive the yacht, help to moor her, and in the event of any police interference they were sufficiently numerous to deal with it.

It was my intention to bring the ammunition away from Howth in taxis and distribute it at several points in the city. For this purpose several members of the I.R.B. were each instructed to invite a lady friend out for the day. They were to go by taxi to Howth and order lunch at the hotel, keeping a close watch on the harbour. When they saw the yacht coming in they were to abandon both the ladies and the lunch and bring their taxis up the harbour ready to carry their appointed loads to their appointed destination.

The Volunteers met on Sunday morning at Father Matthew Park in Fairview, probably about eight hundred in all, including over one hundred of the Fianna.

It was the practice on the route marches that the command was taken by one of our ex-Army paid instructors, and on this occasion a retired sergeant named Bodkin was in charge. Just before we marched off, MacNeill instructed Bodkin to carry out any instructions which I gave him throughout the day. When we got near Howth I told Bodkin what was about to happen.

It was difficult to get started in good time, with the result that we had to march at a fast pace, and without a stop, to Howth, a distance of between seven and eight miles. Protests came from various parts of the column that the pace was too fast, but we had no time to lose and paid no attention to the complaints.

Fortunately we reached Howth just as the yacht sailed into the harbour. When we got to the harbour we put a strong guard at the entrance.

In order to expedite the unloading, I had asked Childers to take the guns out of their packing while at sea and lay them in layers on the floor of the cabin, so that the moment the hatches were off the guns were passed from hand to hand down the column, and the whole unloading of nine hundred guns took, approximately, half an hour. When the last gun came ashore, the ammunition was already on its way—before the column left—the bulk by taxis, and some 2,000 rounds remained with the Fianna, who were the only body on whose discipline I could count.

As I was afraid of the authorities cutting us off before we got past Sutton, no rest was given to the men and no halt was permitted until we got to Raheny. As we were approaching that village, a special tram filled with police passed us on their way from the city. We had a number of cycle scouts scouring the country in every direction and we had not long left Howth when I was aware that the authorities were sending out, or had sent out, soldiers and police to intercept us.

I asked Laurence Kettle, who had a car, to take me down to look at them. I went to Clontarf in his car and looked at the police, and re-joined the Volunteers before they got to Raheny. They were halted there.

The question then presented itself as to how we should get past this barrier. The men had already marched from Fairview to Howth and back to Raheny without time for rest, and many of them showed signs of exhaustion. I decided that it was quite impracticable to ask them to approach Dublin by longer and indirect routes, and that the only thing was to go right on and deal with the police and soldiers when we got that far.

Just before we left Howth I had instructed the officers of each company to make a careful note of the names and addresses of the men who had rifles, and to tell them that they would have the option of either delivering them at their company meeting the following week or of retaining them and paying for them by small weekly instalments.

When we approached Clontarf we saw the soldiers drawn across the road, and, in order to avoid them and to give them an opportunity of avoiding us, we turned sharply to the right on to the Malahide Road. The police and soldiers came at the double round to the Malahide Road and confronted us again.

While I expected that the authorities in Dublin Castle would attempt to prevent the landing of rifles, I knew that the Liberal Government in England, having already remained inactive on the occasion of the Carsonite gun-running at Larne, would find it very embarrassing to take active measures against us. I rather expected, what was afterwards established as a fact, that the local police or soldiers were acting without orders from their superiors.

When we approached the opposing forces, the soldiers were drawn two-deep across the road, armed with rifle and bayonet. About eighty policemen, standing two-deep, occupied the foot-path at right angles to the soldiers.

When we came up to the police, Assistant Commissioner Harrel, who was in charge, stepped forward, and as he did so I halted the column. I was marching at the head of the column with the instructor, Bodkin. Immediately, Harrel said that we were an illegal body, illegally importing arms which he was about to seize, and before I had time to reply he turned to the police and ordered them to seize the arms. A considerable number of the police did not move and disobeyed the order, while the remainder made a rush for the front company of the Volunteers and a free fight ensued, in which clubbed rifles and batons were freely used. This fight lasted probably less than a minute, when the police withdrew to the footpath of their own accord and without orders. Meanwhile I had been standing with Mr Harrel and was a spectator of the *melée*.

At this point I told Mr Harrel that these men, although they had rifles, had no ammunition, that they were peacefully going to their homes, but that there was ammunition in the column and that if he attacked again I could not prevent the distribution, that a great many of his men and my men would be killed, packed in that narrow road, and that sole responsibility would be his. I had already suspected that he might have gone out without orders, and I rapidly saw that his nerve was now ebbing and that he realised the impossibility of taking rifles from nine hundred men with eighty reluctant policemen.

At this stage Tomás MacDonagh and Darrell Figgis came up and entered into an argument with Mr Harrel. Either of them could have talked him blind, their combined effort was overwhelming. I decided that this colloquy would last for a considerable time, so I ran to the back of the column and ordered the men to disperse across the fields and through the grounds of the Christian Brothers in Marino, to make their way home as quickly as possible and avoid any conflicts or anything which would cause them to lose their rifles. I saw company after company disappear through the hedges and did not return until all but the last company was left when I found Mr Harrel, looking rather dazed, still listening to Figgis and MacDonagh. Just as I approached, the sergeant spoke to Harrel and drew his attention to the fact that the Volunteers had nearly all gone. Mr Harrel then told the soldiers that he did not require them any further and they marched off towards Dublin, where they got into conflict with a crowd of civilians at Bachelor's Walk. This episode had no connection whatever with the Volunteers or with the gun-running.

Captain Michael Judge, who was wounded at Howth Road, left his company without orders and went and abused some of the soldiers. One of them gave him a poke with his bayonet, which grazed his arm. Much publicity was given to this supposedly dangerous wound of Mr Judge, but none was given to several men who, in the *melée* with the police, received considerable injuries.

Mr Harrel then hastened along Fairview Strand to Philipsburg Avenue in the hope of intercepting some of the Volunteers who had gone across the fields. Several of us, seeing his object, went ahead and meeting a few of the Volunteers warned them not to go down to Fairview.

We took our stand on the roadway outside Father Matthew Park, and

Mr Harrel and his policemen halted on the footpath opposite.

The cycle scouts, of course, followed me throughout the day, and I told them, one after another, to ride at top speed out of sight and to come back in a minute or two and pretend to whisper a message. They went off in all directions and a scene of great activity ensued, which was further enlivened by the arrival of a gentleman, locally known as 'the Pope Flanagan', on horseback. Mr Flanagan, at my request, galloped his horse off at a furious pace and added to the noise. Mr Harrel stood for a considerable time before it happened to dawn on him that the object of this activity was to keep him standing there while the Volunteers got safely home with the guns.

It subsequently transpired in evidence at the Royal Commission on the Howth gun-running that Mr Harrel had gone out without orders.

The police captured nineteen of our rifles, all of which were broken in the struggle, but the authorities were in such consternation at the turn events had taken that Colonel Moore went up to the Castle the following day and succeeded in securing the remnants of the nineteen rifles.

While we were facing the soldiers at Howth Road, several of our men who had small arms fired at the soldiers and would have precipitated a catastrophe for us had the officer in charge of the soldiers not thought that the shots came from a hostile crowd assembled in a side street. I suppressed the firing as quickly as possible. Éamonn Ceannt was one of those who fired.

Some of the Volunteers made repeated attempts to rush the Fianna trek carts to get some of the ammunition with which to fire at the police and soldiers, but the Fianna, under the command of Pádraig Ó Riain, carried out their orders and no ammunition was distributed or used.

A fortnight previously Figgis had handed over the guns to the two yachts in the North Sea, then hurried across to Dublin, apparently with the intention of taking charge of operations at our end. None of us had ever met him before, and I had to tell him firmly that the arrangements were made, and were not going to be disclosed to anybody, unless such disclosure was essential to enable him to play his part in the plan. As a concession I allowed him to accompany Cathal Brugha down to Howth early on the Sunday morning, and he was with the men who were there to receive the yacht when it came in. Further than that he had no part in planning or carrying out this operation.

Of the 900 guns and 26,000 rounds of ammunition landed at Howth, none were lost except the nineteen captured by the police and some which were abandoned by some of the Volunteers on their way across the fields and which fell into the hands of members of the Citizen Army, whose premises at Croydon Park were close by.

The Citizen Army did not take part in the Howth gun-running and knew nothing about it. The only two organizations which took part in the Howth gun-running were the Irish Volunteers and the Fianna.

With the Howth gun-running, we not only succeeded in landing a considerable number of arms but I also succeeded in my second objective of getting something done in a sufficiently spectacular manner to make people subscribe to our funds. We got £1,000 from America the day after, and thereafter we received help from different organizations in America at the rate of about £1,000 a month.

Money also came in from various parts of Ireland, and after the gun-running we never had any serious financial worries.

Of the 1,500 guns purchased by Figgis in Antwerp, Childers brought 900 to Howth. The other 600 guns and portion of the ammunition were placed on Conor O'Brien's yacht. Both yachts were loaded from a tug which Figgis hired in Antwerp, and which met them in the North Sea.

Childers and O'Brien were both first-rate seamen, but in other respects they differed. Childers was secretive and efficient. O'Brien was talkative to a degree that made him a dangerous colleague for anybody engaged on an enterprise of this sort. For this reason Childers flatly refused to have

O'Brien come in to Howth with him as he felt that O'Brien's lack of reasonable precautions would endanger the whole enterprise.

Childers told me that O'Brien wanted to bring his guns into his native County Limerick, so we agreed that we could tell him to go and make his own arrangements and to bring them in where he could. In the event O'Brien made no arrangements, and when it became time for him to leave Dublin to keep his appointment in the North Sea he went to Lloyd, a solicitor, and Cruise O'Brien, a journalist, neither of whom had any connection with the Volunteers, and both of whom were active members of Mr Redmond's organization. They were not the sort of people likely to be mixed up in gun-running. Fortunately they went and told James Creed Meredith, later a judge of the Supreme Court, what had happened. Meredith was one of Redmond's nominees on our committee and one of the very few who co-operated with us and did not behave like a mere partisan on the committee.

Meredith realized that this must be some project of the Irish Volunteers that had got into strange hands, so he came at once to MacNeill, who sent for me and said: 'Here is the cargo you refused at Howth come back again.' I was much too busy with the arrangements for Howth, and with other work, to take on this additional responsibility, and besides there was the possibility that both yachts might come in at the same time. In fact, the Howth yacht came in on the 26th July and the yacht at Kilcoole on Saturday, 1st August. It was agreed, therefore, that Sean Fitzgibbon should take charge of that landing.

Before he left Ireland, Conor O'Brien's reckless talk had roused the suspicion of the authorities and they started searching fishing and other boats all round the Irish coast, and it was felt that it was not safe to permit him to bring the cargo to Ireland. It was arranged, therefore, that he should lie off Bardsey Island, off the Welsh coast, and tranship his cargo to the yacht of Sir Thomas Myles, a prominent Dublin surgeon.

Before I retired from the scene, I went to Meredith's house at his invitation and met Sir Thomas Myles to discuss where the guns were to be brought in. I suggested Kilcoole, County Wicklow, and as the water was too shallow there to enable the yacht to come close in, that the unloading should be done by a couple of motor boats.

Childers's crew, as far as I can remember, consisted of himself, his wife, the Honourable Mary Spring Rice, a Captain Shephard, who was afterwards killed in France, and two fishermen from Cola [sic] Island off Donegal.

Sir Thomas Myles's crew consisted of Sir Thomas, James Creed Meredith, Dermot Coffey, Captain Hervey de Montmorency of the British Army, and two sailors, George Cahill and Thomas Fitzsimons, from Foynes, County Limerick.

At Fitzgibbons's request, I went to Kilcoole on the night of the landing of the guns. As he was not a member of the I.R.B. he thought that perhaps his orders might not be readily accepted by some of them. There was, however, no danger of this.

We arrived at Kilcoole about midnight, and the unloading was completed by 4 or 5 a.m.

The only policemen we met were two individuals who were patrolling the railway line. We put them under arrest and when we left they had several miles to walk to barracks before they could give the alarm. There was no other interference of any kind from the authorities.

I came back to Dublin on a large motor charabanc, which was so overloaded with men, guns and ammunition that it broke a back axle in the middle of the town of Bray, about 5 a.m. on Sunday, 2nd August. We sent a motor cyclist to Dublin, and in a surprisingly short time we had a number of taxis and a couple of lorries, and the guns and ammunition were safely taken to Dublin.

On Childers's way from the North Sea, he sailed right through the great naval review at Spithead, where the king of England was reviewing his navy.

After the outbreak of war, I heard that Childers had been asked by the British naval authorities to join because he had a more intimate knowledge than anybody they had of the islands and channels off the German coast, which figured in his novel *The Riddle of the Sands*.

Conor O'Brien in one of his books complains of the ridiculous secrecy with which the Volunteers shrouded their operations, and we had cause to complain of his reckless talking. He stated that when he tried to get any information he was always referred to a mysterious John Dolan, but that he never could find out who Dolan was. In fact, John Dolan had no existence except as a name to which letters could be addressed to an office in College Street to enable Childers to communicate with me.

Although I make this criticism of Conor O'Brien he was a wonderful seaman, a charming person, and he rendered us very great service.

30. Challenge from police and soldiers

By Darrell Figgis.[47]
From *Recollections of the Irish War*, pp. 43-58.
After the guns had been transhipped from the *Gladiator* to the *Asgard* and *Kelpie* I went on to London, and waited a week there, in an attempt to pull up arrears of my own work, before going on to Dublin for the final act. For my trust would not be discharged until the munitions had actually been put into the hands of the Volunteers.

In Dublin, Bulmer Hobson was in charge. Eoin MacNeill told me that O'Rahilly knew nothing of the new plans, and I therefore avoided him guiltily. The plans, as I heard them, were complete and elaborate. It had been agreed that Childers should lie up on the far side of Lambay Island, off Howth, on Saturday night; and I was to go out to him there

---

47 It is particularly in this chapter that Figgis gives himself a position of importance which does not accord with the facts as we know them from other sources—*Ed.*

that night on a motor-boat from Howth, with a small staff that would be told off to accompany me. In the meantime two other motor-boats were to come up the coast from Kingstown (now Dun Laoghaire) and from Bray. While the yacht bore in towards the harbour, the three motor-boats, full of armed men, were to cruise about the narrowing waters, lest any attempt were made from the coastguard station at Howth to intercept her.

In the meantime the Volunteers were to march out from Dublin. On the previous two Sundays they had been taken on route marches, and had on each occasion been accompanied by a posse of police—much stronger on the first than on the second occasion. It was expected that on this third occasion custom would have staled the adventure, and the expectation proved correct, for the posse on the critical day was but small. The Volunteers were to be timed to arrive a few minutes ahead of the yacht, to hold the port, receive and make away with the munitions, while the telephone and telegraph wires were cut so as to dislocate Howth from official headquarters.

The only matter that caused us concern was that a gunboat was posted in Dublin Bay, which could very quickly arrive on the scene to disconcert us. But in the end this gunboat was lured out of the way by a very simple ruse. For at this time Joseph Devlin and the political leaders were also attempting to land rifles; Italian rifles, as they proved, of an old pattern, without ammunition. An attempt had already been made somewhere in Wexford, but it had been foiled, and the boat bearing the guns had not come in from neutral waters. On the Saturday evening, therefore, as I went to Howth, I sent a clumsily coded telegram to a certain political leader making an appointment for 12 o'clock that night at Wexford, and later that night my comrade and I had the satisfaction of seeing the gunboat making southward under full steam, well out of the way of the events of the morrow.

It was as well, for our plans that night fell to pieces, and the least interference from sea the next day would have brought the entire enterprise to disaster. That Saturday evening a fresh wind sprang up from the north-west, and the sea was bestrewn with 'the white blossoms of the ocean'. At Howth the owner of the motor-boat said that no arrangements had been made, and refused to take out his boat on such a night for any madcap fishing-party. No persuasion could change him, so we had to dismiss our party and make our way back to Dublin.

Seán McGarry had been in charge of the party, and he was my companion for that night's disappointments. At Dublin he and I took a motor to Kingstown, in the hope to catch the party there. There we saw the gunboat making south, but we found no party there, and met the same experience as at Howth. At about four that morning, tired and disheartened, we turned into the Marine Hotel for a few hours sleep, and by the first train the next morning we made our way back to Howth. There we met the party that had come from Bray, but the boat had been so battered on her voyage that morning that the skipper would not venture to sea again in her. So Seán McGarry posted her crew, who were all armed, at the base of the north pier, to head off any attempt of the coastguards to make their way round by land.

This was about 9.30 a.m., and already the yacht could occasionally be seen, as she cruised to and fro on the yonder side of Lambay Island. I wondered what Childers was thinking of our failure to keep our appointment, and we made every effort to get even a fishing-boat out to sea, but without success.[48] So we confined ourselves within our arrangements on shore, expecting Childers to hold to his time schedule whatever happened. We found a place for the yacht to berth, near the end of the south pier,[49] so that, when her cargo was clear, she might easily ship to sea again, and we disposed our arrangements accordingly.

---

48 Gordon Shephard, who was with Figgis on the pier, has a different story, see below, p. 163-4—Ed.

49 It was the east pier. Among the Childers Papers is the detailed map of Howth Harbour, drawn by Childers, showing where the guns were to be landed—Ed.

Then a little man, with a back like a ramrod, flowing moustache, and steel-grey eyes as clear and relentless as a sword-stroke, stepped up to me, spoke my name, and said he was instructed to report to me and put himself under my orders. He nodded to Seán McGarry at my side, and said he had fifty men with him, armed. I asked him to send couriers up the road to bring me word of the coming of the Volunteers, so to detail his men that at a sign every person on the pier and on boats in the harbour (the pier was full of holiday-makers) might be put under temporary arrest, and tell off others to keep close watch on the coastguard station on the opposite pier.

This was Cathal Brugha. I have often thought how characteristic was that first meeting. I might have dropped from the clouds (and, in truth, very largely did) for all he knew of me; but his orders were to put himself at my disposal, and he would have leapt into the sea and swam to the yacht if required to do so. No one could look on that man without perceiving his consuming, terrific, relentless courage. He was a born fighter, without a crooked patch in him; a sword in other people's hands, that would be shattered before it would bend; bonny in battle, and the greater the odds the bonnier; and unquestioning where he accepted and whom he accepted. One felt contented to know that he and his fifty men were on the pier; contented, though it were the first time one's eyes rested on him, or took the challenge of his own.

The yacht was now cruising between Lambay and the mainland, tacking to the north, obviously, so as to make straight into the harbour under the north-westerly wind on one long south-westerly course. It was now towards 12.30, and still there was not a sign of the Volunteers and no news from our couriers. The minutes passed on, and the strain on everyone was manifest on their faces. The coastguards on the opposite pier-head had their glasses trained on the incoming yacht, at the helm of which, for our accepted sign that all was well, Mrs Childers sat in a red jersey; and it is probable that the lady at the helm deceived the coastguards. So 12.35 came, and then 12.40, and still there was no sign from or of the Volunteers. The yacht was now heaving slowly towards us with her sails shipped, slapping the seas, a few cables' length from the pier-head, and our men were taking their places to receive her.

Then, just as the yacht was off the pier-head, I heard Seán McGarry beside me say: 'Here they are; look at 'em; aren't they a beautiful sight?' And they were a beautiful sight as they filed out of the town and marched company by company, across the road at the base of the harbour. There was beauty in their movement, and there was amazing beauty in their extreme punctuality. I told off an orderly to ask their commandant to send them up the pier, company by company, at the double, and signed to Cathal Brugha to make his arrests, when a hawser from the yacht fell across our feet, and a number of our men, running forward, lashed it to the pier. As we drew the yacht to the pier-side we heard, behind and beyond us, the solid tramp of hundreds of feet, as the Volunteers came up the pier at the double, and sharp words of command as they were halted and lined in two ranks down the long length of the pier.

It was not long till the rifles were brought out and passed to the Volunteers. Then a strange sight was seen, revealing to every doubter, and even to us who never doubted, what ancient national hopes were in the nurture of each man's blood. Seasoned men broke into tears when the first rifle was handed up out of the hold, and the ranks were broken by the rush towards the yacht. When order was restored, the command was given that each rifle should be handed down to the end of the column, but as each man received his rifle he put his foot upon it and passed the next down.

While this was being done the cry was suddenly raised that a boat-load of coastguards had crept round beneath the lee of the yachts in the harbour, and had just reached the open space of water that lay around our own yacht. Instantly a number of men lined along the yacht, with their rifles trained on the approaching boat. Challenged to stop and return, the coastguards did so. In none of these rifles, however, was there a cartridge—though there were revolvers ready for action if the need arose.

That was the only attempt to interfere, for, after this, the coastguards were content to signal, by rocket, for a gunboat that was no longer there. The boxes of ammunition were at once taken away by motor; and the yacht unloaded, the Volunteers took the road, rifle over shoulder, for a public march into Dublin.

My task was done, and I went into the hotel at Howth with Eoin MacNeill to render account. Before I went, however, O'Rahilly came to me eager and enthusiastic, and I explained to him the shabby trick necessity had compelled us to play on him. But he would not hear of apology. Clean, generous man that he was always, all that had been done had been rightly done, he said, for it had come to a right conclusion.

Unhappily, as it proved, we had not yet made a conclusion. After we had lunched, Eoin MacNeill took me with him in his car to pick up the column as it made its way to Dublin. We found them on the road resting, and there we met Sean MacDiarmada, anxious at the critical time being wasted. He started the column again in motion, and we joined him in his car, moving continuously between the head of the column and Nelson's Pillar as the column approached Dublin and our journey to and fro continually shortened. We were troubled lest troops should be called out.

On our last journey Eoin MacNeill stepped off at the Pillar, for the head of the column was now within a quarter of a mile, or thereabouts, and all seemed clear. But as we turned back through Earl Street a man ran up to me, where I sat beside the driver, and said that two tram-loads of troops with police had just passed down Abbey Street to meet the advancing column. We raced back to the head of the column, and as we reached the Howth Road, down which the column was advancing, we overtook the troops that had just dismounted there. Actually our car made its way through them, and they, not knowing who we were, stood aside for us to let us through.

So behind us the troops (the King's Own Scottish Borderers, with accompanying Dublin Metropolitan Police) blocked the end of the road, while in the distance we could see the Volunteers marching towards us as we raced towards them. A conflict seemed unavoidable. When we reached the head of the column the military commandant for the day could not be found, and in the general indecision the column continued on its way. Those at the head of the column, seeing the end of Howth Road barred by a double rank of bayonets, turned to the right down Marino Crescent into the Malahide Road that runs parallel with the Howth Road. At once we saw the military break and turn at the double down the tram road so as to confront the column again. Directly this happened several urged that the rest of the column should continue down the Howth Road, in order to surround the military on both sides, hoping thus to hem them in while the main body of the men made their way into the city. Had this been done the situation would have been entirely changed. The military would have been confined and restricted instead of, as happened, the Volunteers. But in the absence of any kind of direction or command all was confusion; the situation was left to itself, and no clear decision seemed possible just when it was most needed.

So a small knot of us, including Sean MacDiarmada, Bulmer Hobson, and myself, hurried after the head of the column, that was already confronted by the military, again barring the road. Then, after a time of deadlock and indecision someone in civilian attire (whom I afterwards learned to be David Harrel, the Assistant Commissioner of Police) stepped forward into the open road between the two forces and asked to know who was in command of the Volunteers. Twice he asked the question and no one answered. The others were, of course, preserving order in the ranks; but the situation was a little tense—a little awkward— when finally I stepped out to meet him and assumed authority.

My authority had ended at Howth Pier, but it was necessary that someone should answer. So, not knowing who might come to dispute my assumption with me, I endeavoured to keep within my expired authority.

I told him that to march with rifles through an Irish city was not illegal, seeing that such a march had been permitted the Sunday before in Belfast City with the Ulster Volunteers. The only offence of the day had been the illegal landing and for that I took entire responsibility. I offered myself for arrest, on condition that the men should proceed on their way, since the right that had been allowed in one Irish city clearly could not, a week later, become an offence in another Irish city.

During this conversation Bulmer Hobson joined me, but, as I remember, left before it was over. Mr Harrel peremptorily demanded the surrender of our rifles. I would not move from my point of legality and allowance, and after we had each thrown warnings at each other, the conversation was ended by his stating that he intended to seize the rifles and by his ordering the police to that task. I stepped back and stood with the first company in the tussle that followed.

Our men were without ammunition and used their new rifles as clubs, some, including myself, being armed with heavy ashen truncheons as well. It was thus truncheon and helmet against truncheon and club, deft duckings and lusty layings-on. In an effort to come to the rescue of one of our men (a little fellow who was being swung like a pendulum by a huge policeman at the end of his rifle, to which he manfully clung) I was borne to the ground by two policemen, who belaboured my head with their truncheons. Half dazed for the moment, I was captured—when I found myself seized by one of the police themselves and pushed back to my place beside the head of the column, with a whispered adjuration (to my sore head) to 'keep to the thinking and leave the fighting alone'.

The first attack failed. The police were thrown back in confusion. But our first company was also thrown into confusion, and it was necessary to clear their confused ranks out of the way in order to meet the new attack with the second company. For now the Borderers were ordered to a bayonet attack, and I have no doubt many another of our line beside me experienced ugly qualms and desperate promptings at the sight of a line of steel borne towards us, not with fine abandon, but at a thoughtful thought-begetting slow march. Little wonder that some of our men pulled out revolvers and began to fire and that the ranks broke. Yet the fight was held. Give the Borderers their due, they fought with no enthusiasm, and when they heard the firing, and when some of their men fell with bullet wounds,[50] their ranks broke also. If the steel was unpleasant, so was the sound of shooting. In the encounter that followed men fell on each side— the commandant of the company, standing beside me, receiving, without an effort to move or defend himself, bayonet lunges between the arm and body that were not nice to see. The fighting was broken, desperate and confused, but in the end the Borderers also were thrown back.

Then Mr Harrel came forward again, desiring further parley. Swiftly a plan came into my head. I pointed to the ugly sights on the road and refused to parley there. If he would go to one of the gardens of the houses near which we stood, I would follow him. In the meantime I would restrain our men if he would restrain his. When he was gone I turned to the commandant of the third company, a resolute steady man, told him to extend his men across the road, so as to mask all that passed behind him, and to send runners down the column at once, telling the men, while I held Harrel in conversation, to disperse from the rear as rapidly as possible, taking their rifles with them.

At any other time there would have been humour in the conversation that followed in the secluded garden. Mr Harrel was excusably surprised at hearing the entire controversy between North and South entered upon from the beginning, but he was resigned to silence when he found that each of his interruptions caused the amazing argument to return upon those beginnings. In the middle of our argument Thomas MacDonagh joined us, and he, too, protested against its curious irrelevancy. But I was

50 Only two soldiers were wounded slightly by revolver shots. There is much information on the affray at Howth Road and the shootings at Bachelor's Walk in the Royal Commission into the circumstances connected with the landing of arms at Howth on July 26th, 1914, London 1914—
Ed.

playing desperately for time to complete the manoeuvre that had been put in motion, and all the more desperately because I saw Chief Inspector Dunne seeking by a kind of mime-show to attract Mr Harrel's attention. Finally the inspector gave up his signals and drew his chief's attention to the remarkable circumstance that while we had been discussing the Volunteers had gone, rifles and all.

Yet they were not all gone. The faithful third company stood awaiting orders, and while Mr Harrel began to complain of a 'discreditable manoeuvre', I ran to its commandant and told him to dismiss and disperse his men as quickly as possible.[51]

Instantly his command rang out, calling his faithful company to attention. It was apparent on every face that his men knew what was coming, and almost within seconds of their dismissal they had melted miraculously away, leaping over the wall of the park beside which we stood, and running quickly down the turning through which we had come. For a few moments there was a noise of the scurry of their going, and then all was still in their absence.

So, of all our Howth Company, I was left alone on the road, with the Borderers and the police still indomitably holding the pass against me. Less from a reasoned policy than from intuition I did not go my way, however, as I could quite easily have done, but continued walking to and fro across the road. It seemed to me that while I remained the military and police would also remain, and that they were better occupied standing there in idleness than in searching the neighbourhood. Behind them, in the distance, across the main road, stood the large crowd that had collected. I had been too occupied to notice them before then, but no one could help noticing them now, for they had seen all that had passed, and they were shouting with challenge and exultation at the

---

51 Two years after this, in Reading gaol, I learned from Arthur Griffith, that he was in the ranks of this third company. He told me that the commandant's name was Kerrigan, and that he had been an old soldier. We agreed that his coolness and steadiness were the feature, as they were the salvation, of that day—*Darrell Figgis*.

armed forces that stretched between them and me. It was through them that the military would have to pass on their way back, and it was patent that the passage would not be happy, though no one could foresee how fatally it would end.

My intuition proved correct, for as I walked to and fro, Mr Harrel and his officers, military and police, walked opposite me, manifestly determined that they would not be the first to leave. Then a rider on a horse came to me. He was in Volunteer uniform, and he asked for further orders, saying that the rifles that had been flung into the bushes of the park were being collected and stowed away in the houses round about. I urged him to phone to Dublin, and to order every available taxi-cab and motor, so as to get the rifles without delay to safer places. I did not know that the others were already busy at this task, and, indeed, that all the undertakers also were being requisitioned for hearses and coffins, in which rifles were removed to Dublin during the better part of that evening and night. I suppose everybody knew the cause of the extraordinary number of funerals that night, but all the people had, in a manner we were yet in later years to learn so well, become confederates in the secret work, and in the upshot not more than nineteen rifles were found to be missing. In recompense for these, six rifles had been captured from the Scottish Borderers—a more than sufficient exchange.

Thomas MacDonagh and Bulmer Hobson then appeared on the scene from the work on which they had been engaged. By this time a number of couriers had been engaged, and they came to and fro with whispered messages, some pretended, some real; and while we remained there the military and police also remained, until at last we heard the Borderers called to attention, and saw them marched through the crowd that swarmed about them crying imprecations upon them.

The excitement had now passed, and I was sick and dizzy with the thwacking my head had received. So, leaving the others, I made my way back to my hotel. There I lay in bed, when, at ten that night, Colonel Moore, Inspector-General of the Irish Volunteers, and Colonel Cotter, Chief of Staff, came saying that they had inquired concerning the day's proceedings, and had had some difficulty in finding me. They insisted on the necessity of my going with them to the papers to give an authoritative account of all that had occurred. Particularly was this necessary, they urged, because of the later events of the day, and for the first time, then, I learned from them that the Borderers, followed on their way back to barracks by a hostile crowd, had turned and fired upon them, with loss of life.

Indeed, the necessity of such an account had already been apparent to me; but what had also been apparent to me was that the prominence into which I had so strangely been flung that day would (human nature being what it is) probably be the cause of bitterness in some bones. I had already felt this before I had left the others. It was intelligible enough, for I had come that day into the midst of action from an outer desert, but I was certainly not disposed to invite more bitterness than I had already earned. Colonel Moore, however, characteristically put all this down to a sick head, and the two of them took me out with them, putting me under their orders.

It was as well they did so. Our statement that night displaced an official account which, with scattered and fragmentary stories pieced together, would not have proved comforting to us. To be sure, there are as many parts to a tale as there are tellers to tell it, and the philosopher has said that truth lies at the bottom of a well. Our statement merely recorded what I had seen exactly as I remembered to have seen it. I have not seen it since I read it the following morning as I returned to London. Yet, as I was the only person at the head of our column from beginning to end of the action, and as the other side attacked and argued by different numbers, I certainly was the only person who could see it all of a piece and tell the different parts of it together.

31. Bringing in the guns
by Arthur Griffith[52]

From *The Southern Cross* of Buenos Aires, 28 August 1914, pp. 3-4.

Dublin, July 29th, 1914.

Seven years after the Act of Union became law, the British Parliament, against the opposition of Irish members of all shades, passed a Disarming Act for Ireland. The Act made it a crime punishable with transportation (and later with penal servitude), for any Irishman to possess a pistol, gun, pike, sword or other military weapon, unless he possessed a licence from the magistrates appointed and paid by the Government who were required to investigate and assure themselves of his loyalty to the existing regime.

Practically speaking that has been uninterruptedly the law in Ireland from 1807 until the advent of the present Government to office. During the hundred years' interval some thousands of men, particularly in connection with the Young Ireland and Fenian movements, have been imprisoned for long periods for being found in possession of arms.

The present Government did not renew the Arms Act. For the first time, therefore, it became possible for the average Irishman to possess arms without running the risk of seven years' penal servitude.

But for a year or two no movement towards arming was made. Then the Ulster Volunteers began to form, drill, and arm. For a year the Government looked on, and it would have continued to look on had the Nationalists not roused themselves up and decided to form Volunteer corps also. This was a horse of another colour. Immediately by proclamation, not by the ordinary procedure in Parliament, the Disarming Act was revived, making it a criminal offence to import arms into Ireland.

---

52 Arthur Griffith was a regular contributor to *The Southern Cross* which had been founded by Dean Dillon at Buenos Aires in 1875 as a newspaper for the Irish Catholics in the Argentine. Its best known editor was William Bulfin who was also its sole proprietor, 1896-1910. Griffith was among the Volunteers who brought the guns from Howth to Dublin—*Ed.*

As no arms are manufactured in Ireland this, of course, was equivalent to nullifying the National Volunteer movement. The Ulster Unionists who were only partly armed ignored the proclamation and landed at Larne 35,000 rifles and a large store of ammunition. The Government instituted no proceedings against them, but placed warships around the coast to prevent a recurrence. The officers—or many officers—of the ships along the Ulster coast supplied the Ulster Unionist leaders with information and rendered them assistance in procuring further supplies of the munitions of war. The Government became aware of this, but it did not interfere with the officers or substitute the ships by others. It, however, vigorously kept up the blockade around the south, west and east coasts of Ireland.

Nevertheless a fair number of rifles were smuggled in by the Nationalists but at a very high cost. The Dublin Volunteers were almost wholly unarmed. On last Sunday they dramatically changed their situation and brought about a state of public feeling in Ireland which has every young and middle-aged man in Ireland of average health and strength who has not hitherto joined the Volunteers excitedly beseeching enrolment.

On Sunday morning last the city of Dublin Volunteers were ordered to assemble for a route-march at Fairview. About a thousand men answered the call, and at 25 minutes past ten they set out unknowing their destination but variously speculating that it was Portmarnock, Baldoyle, Sutton or Howth—all places from 6 to 8 miles distant. At Raheny the column was joined by about 250 North County Dublin Volunteers and marched forward without pausing. At 25 minutes to 1 precisely it reached Howth town—about 71/2 miles from the starting-point. As the head of the column reached the entrance to the East Pier a white yacht glided into the harbour and moored at the little quay seven or eight hundred yards away. The officers of the leading companies immediately gave the order: 'Left Wheel—double march', and in a moment about 500 men were running rhythmically in fours down the pier. The remaining companies at the same time were formed at the pier-entrances with orders to let none but Volunteers pass in or out.

Even as the men ran up the pier few of them realised that they were engaged in anything but a manoeuvre to test their stamina—and a run of half-a-mile along a rough-stone pavement immediately after a two-hours' quick march is a good test. Yet I observed only two of my comrades fall out, and none of us were sorry to hear the commands to halt when the leading files got abreast of the yacht. It was only then the men realised what was about to happen. Oak truncheons were served out to a number of them to guard against any possible interference while the yacht was being unloaded, and a line of men two deep fell in from the vessel's side to the end of the pier. Along the line the rifles were rapidly passed from hand to hand, thus ensuring that the last men of the column would be first armed. The police looked on helplessly while the coast-guards who attempted to approach the yacht in boats were warned off at the guns' muzzles. They returned and attempted to get into telephonic communication with Dublin, but the wires had been attended to. They then sent up signals for a warship. But there was none in the bay. The one stationed the previous day six miles away from Kingstown had been decoyed by a suspicious-looking motor-boat to Wicklow town twenty miles further away.

The ammunition and surplus rifles were rapidly packed into motor-cars and driven off. Then the column formed up, each man carrying his rifle, and marched rapidly out of Howth at 1.40—just one hour from the entry. The rain was falling heavily and the wind blowing half-a-gale, but no rain and no wind could subdue the surging enthusiasm of the men as they swung along to Dublin—the first time in over a century 1200 disciplined men with rifles on their shoulders to serve Ireland had marched to Dublin.

What might be before them was uncertain. The news of what had happened would be in Dublin long before they could reach the city. But this, was the feeling of almost all: That no matter whether it meant life or death to them, now that they had secured rifles in defiance of the Government, they would not yield them on any demand. But few anticipated interference. In Belfast the previous day 5,000 Ulster Volunteers, each man armed with a rifle had publicly paraded. Some who realised that in Ireland there is no law for the Nationalist, during a brief halt of twenty minutes at Raheny urged that ammunition should be served out to a selected portion of the men who understood the rifle and had cool heads. It was decided otherwise, and the decision, although as events turned out, did no harm, might have been disastrous. At ten minutes past four the head of the column had come in sight of Fairview and at that moment it was seen that the road was held by the military with fixed bayonets while supporting them could be seen dark masses of the constabulary with carbines and, on the flanks of the military, bodies of the Dublin Metropolitan police.

The column swung aside through Charlemont Road in order to reach the Malahide Road which on its west side affords cover for a fight. The enemy moved at the same time and the two forces came face to face on the Malahide Road. The Volunteers marched steadily on, until a command rang out from the other side to lay down their guns. They ignored the command and the military levelled their pieces. Two volleys of blank cartridge were fired and then the police were ordered to move forward to seize the arms. Some of the police refused to obey. Two constables cheered for the Volunteers. The remainder charged with their batons and were met by the Volunteers with clubbed rifles. In a few minutes the police were beaten back. The military then charged with fixed bayonets. They, too, were met with clubbed rifles, and a few revolver shots. In a minute they fell back to their line carrying with them three of their number while three of the Volunteers— one of them Mr M. J. Judge, a member of the governing body, lay on the ground. In the *melée* a few of the Volunteers lost or smashed their rifles while two rifles with bayonets attached were wrested from the soldiers.

Then for a few minutes there came a lull. The front companies of the Volunteers sent back to the rear a demand for ammunition. The officers, hastily consulting, decided on another plan. The rear-guard formed across the road and the Volunteers' column fell back slowly behind it, when they received orders to disperse in small parties carrying their rifles and to store them singly or in twos and threes in places where they could be rapidly collected. Some were stored in the houses of the neighbourhood, including the houses of many Unionists who freely and honourably assisted in preserving the weapons. Others were carried across the fields towards Glasnevin and Drumcondra. All were collected again within 24 hours.

While this manoeuvre was being carried out, the Volunteer rear-guard and the military were lined across the road face-to-face at a distance of about 50 yards. One volley from either side would have slain half the front line. None was fired. The guns of the Volunteer rear-guard were empty. But the other side did not know that. They evidently believed that this covering guard at least had bullets in their guns, else they would have advanced to prevent the departure of the main body of the Volunteers they had been called out to seize. In a few minutes the Volunteers had melted away—each with his gun. And when the rear-guard was dismissed to secure its guns, the forces of the English Crown were outwitted. They made no attempt to advance along the road, but turning marched back towards town.

When the present writer had secured his rifle safely he returned to inspect the military at close quarters as they returned to town. They were a poor-looking lot of men, and many of them were trembling with nervous excitement. Obviously these men should never have been allowed to march back through the city without a civilian magistrate in control. I did not anticipate what actually occurred, but I did anticipate trouble from the panicky condition in which so many of them seemed to be. As they marched through the town they were jeered by the people and the remnant of their nerves gave way. They turned and fired straight into the crowded pathways and men, women, and children fell dead and wounded along the street. But of this tragedy you have already read.

If I were asked what impressed me most in the day, I would answer: The profound truth of the saying, that every Irishman is born a soldier. In the ranks of the Volunteers that day nearly every class and certainly every creed was represented. There were men of leisure, professional men, clerks, artisans, farmers and unskilled workers. I saw near me lawyers, professors, teachers, civil servants, carpenters, railwaymen, printers, shopkeepers, and agricultural labourers. The man on my left-hand in the rear-guard was a Belfast Protestant, and I saw a prominent Dublin Church of Ireland man wielding a clubbed rifle with success. Not 10 per cent of the men who faced the soldiery had any military training six months ago. Individually courageous enough, they would not have stood a moment before the levelled guns and bayonets if the discipline of six months' drill had not in that critical moment developed the latent soldier in them all. I am told and I have no doubt it is true that a score of the men lost nerve. But what I saw was one man only running to the rear and one very young man faltering and half-turning in the ranks. That his nervousness was not cowardice was proved a little later. For the stern voices of his comrades turned him again to face the soldiers and he faltered no more.

We have got the guns, but better still, we have got back some of our respect and confidence in ourselves. The Volunteer movement is making men by the thousand, out of the doubting and vacillating.

32. Sealed orders

The Part the Fianna Played at Howth

by Corporal Willie Nelson [i.e., Pádraig Ó Riain].[53]

From *Nodlaig na bhFiann,* December 1914.

I was awakened by a loud knocking at the hall door. I awoke slowly, and wondered who the disturber of the Sabbath morn was. I yawned, stretched myself, and finally looked at the clock. It was five minutes to seven. I then began debating with myself, for, being a member of the Sluagh committee, I have an aptitude for debate, as to whether the disturber was the post, a seller of the *Sunday Freeman,* or an early rising milk-man. I pride myself for having a logical mind—a gift which Madame [Markievicz] was the first person to discover I possessed. I reasoned like this. It cannot be the post for he only gives two short raps and departs; neither can it be a milk-man, for every sane milk-man supplements his knocking by melodiously rattling his can on the curb. I was about to turn over and leave the honour with the seller of newspapers when the knocking grew louder and more persistent. Curiosity impelled me to get up, and on looking out of the window, to my astonishment, I saw my leader, Paddy Holohan, renewing

---

53 Pádraig Ó Riain was a member of the I.R.B., and according to Bulmer Hobson, From the foundation of the Fianna in 1909 to the Rising of 1916 he was the dominating personality in the Fianna. He had a natural capacity for leadership and did an enormous amount of work.' Ó Riain's father was caretaker of the Irish National Foresters' Hall, 41 Parnell Square, and the secret drilling of the I.R.B. took place there before the formation of the Irish Volunteers in November 1913. Ó Riain went North in 1916 to help the rising in county Tyrone; when the rising mis-fired he went on to Belfast, and lived there until his death some years ago. Ó Riain contributed the weekly notes on the Fianna to *The Irish Volunteer,* and to the Nodlaig na bhFiann the organ of the Fianna, under the nom-de-plume of 'Willie Nelson.' For another account of the part played by the Fianna at Howth see Gearóid Ó hUallachain, 'Teacht na nArm go Beann Éadair i 1914,' in *An Gaedheal,* i Meitheamh 1935, p. 2.

his attacks on the knocker with great vigour.

'Hello, Paddy,' said I, 'what's the row about?'

'You lazy beggar,' he shouted back, 'I have been knocking here for the last half hour and I might as well have been knocking at the Morgue for all the notice was taken of it.'

Then in sterner tones he commanded: 'You are to parade in the Hardwicke Street Hall at half-past nine, and bring rations for a day's march with you'; and, muttering something about sealed orders from the military council he bolted off.

When I arrived in Hardwicke Street, I found nearly all the older members of the Sluagh present; also members from An Chéud Sluagh and the Sluagh in Inchicore. They were all speculating about the march. Some argued that we were going to Lucan to start a new Sluagh, whilst others asserted we were going on a day's manoeuvres with the Volunteers. This view was generally accepted when we subsequently joined the Volunteers at Fairview.

Pádraig Ó Riain, who was in command of the Fianna, in a few words gave us to understand that strict discipline was to be maintained throughout the day. Seán Heuston had charge of the transport section. The trek-cart was heavily loaded and closely covered. I was in this section and understood Seán to say that the cart contained minerals and refreshments for the Volunteers.

We were allotted a position in the centre of the column, which we held until we were very near Howth, when we proceeded to the head of the column. We entered the village at the head of the Volunteers, and halted at the pier near the foot of the hill.

We went up the pier at the double and outran the Volunteers. Some men were already unloading a yacht. The Fianna were ordered to assist. Our section, under Sean Heuston, at once unpacked the trek-cart, which disgorged not minerals or sandwiches, but large wooden batons. These were rushed down and distributed to the companies which blocked the entrance to the pier. The object of our march was now obvious. Rifles had at last arrived. The coastguards sent up rockets for help; and the Volunteers sent up great triumphant cheers which re-echoed from the Hill of Howth to Dublin Castle, and soured the champagne of the Kildare Street Club.

When I returned to the top of the pier the Volunteers and Fianna were feverishly unpacking the rifles. There was an intense and silent activity. We quickly loaded our trekcart with rifles and transferred them to the companies at the other end of the pier. I was engaged in this work until all the Volunteers were supplied.

The Volunteers and Fianna now carried rifles on their shoulders. Ammunition and rifles were also packed in our trek-cart and the remainder were dispatched in motor cars. We were ready to depart and awaited orders.

The long lines of armed men stretching the whole length of the pier was the most entrancing sight I have ever witnessed. We were filled with great joy, and our souls were thrilled with the spirit of freedom.

As we left the pier the people of Howth came out in great crowds to greet us. A priest from top of a tram blessed the rifles as we passed, and we cheered response to his benediction.

I was beginning to feel tired as we neared Dublin. The long march to Howth and back; the pulling of our heavily-laden trek-cart; the running and exertion on the pier now began to tell against me. But the thought of a triumphal march through the streets of Dublin, with a rifle on my shoulder buoyed me up and made me feel extremely happy. I had not taken Dublin Castle into consideration, and did not believe our friendly Government would permit her to play her last stroke in as villainous a manner as events afterwards proved.

On the Howth Road, a few hundred yards from Clontarf, I saw a company of soldiers with fixed bayonets blocking our way to the city. As if to avoid the military we turned to our right along Charlemont Road, and on to the Malahide Road.

Before we were a hundred yards on the Malahide Road we knew that the first companies of Volunteers were in conflict with the military. The sounds of rifles clashing, revolver shots and shouting, made a terrific din. We got the order to "halt!' and were told we had got to defend the ammunition at all costs. The captain of Céud Sluagh drew an automatic pistol, and with some of our fellows dashed off to join in the fray. It was with difficulty Seán Heuston and Pádraig Ó Riain restrained others. We clustered around the cart with our rifles gripped tightly in our hands. Suddenly we saw the Volunteers scatter and run. Some of the men were bleeding from the head, but most of them seemed uninjured and still clung to their rifles. As they passed us we appealed to them to stand. We shouted and called them cowards. Our commander, not knowing that they had received orders to retire and get off with their rifles, shouted: 'By God! We won't run away.'

Before I had time to realize what had happened the road in front of us was almost clear, and I saw the police with batons and rifles rushing in upon us. Then Pádraig rushed out in front and shouted to us to come on. His voice was harsh and he shouted and cursed most horribly. We dashed out to meet the police. I was near Paddy Holohan and O'Connor. They, too, were cursing and shouting defiantly. Everything was confusion. I saw the police and the soldiers and the glitter of their bayonets as in a maze. A huge policeman with a rifle swooped towards me. I was seized with a sort of frenzy, and putting forth all my strength, I made a deadly blow at his head.

I think my last ounce of strength went into that blow, for I do not remember what happened after till I heard Seán Heuston calling me to lend a hand to pull the trek-cart. I distinctly remember his shrill voice when he gave the order. 'Take strain— Quick march.'

We were now retreating back along the Malahide Road. Joe Robinson was clinging to the back of the trek-cart, in which the ammunition and rifles were still safely packed. There were only ten or twelve of us. Éamon Martin, Garry Holohan, and some others were left behind. They were enjoying the sport too much to leave till all was over.

We wheeled to our left off the main road, and were soon clear of immediate danger. We passed a couple of old men chatting near a pump. They seemed to be enjoying the summer's evening, and apparently knew nothing of the bloody episodes that were being enacted only a mile away.

We turned up a country lane near a big house, and concealed ourselves in a bit of a wood on our right. It was now dusk, so we decided to make a pretence of camping out and to conceal the rifles and ammunition until we could have them safely removed after dark. Our commander went up to the house and got permission to camp near the wood. We buried the treasure, which was removed after dark in a taxi, and is now safe.

33. Watching from Howth Pier

Gordon Shephard to his father, Sir Horatio Hale Shephard. From *Memoirs of Brigadier-General Gordon Shephard*, pp. 174-5.

Eastchurch, 1 August 1914.

(He begins by referring to the mobilization of the armed forces, on the eve of World War I)

We were suddenly ordered here yesterday and had to come without any luggage, etc. The authorities, I have often remarked before, invariably lose their heads at any crisis. It was absurd to send us off without any stores, mechanics, etc. In my opinion, the chances of our having a war are small, as we have no interests at stake. The Howth business is rather losing importance now, but it should stimulate the Nationalists. I will give you a proper description when I see you. The events of Sunday were, briefly: I rode out to Howth on a tram from Dublin, and at 10.30 a.m. saw the yacht a long way off behind Lambay Island. On arrival at Howth I went down the pier and found a knot of men at the head crouching behind the parapet. They were most amusing to look at, and their leader was Figgis, whom I knew before. He told me the motor-boat had not left owing to the weather. I tried to persuade him to lend me a hand and I would have gone out in a sailing-boat. However, he would not rise. I then arranged where the yacht should lie and told off men to catch the warps.[54] Nobody there knew anything about such matters. At 12.45 p.m. punctual to the minute the yacht arrived. Childers had luckily decided to chance it without the signal from the motor-boat. We moored the yacht and took off the cargo in about an hour. The whole was carried out in a most orderly manner, though there was some scrimmaging at the start. The Volunteers marched off when all was over. I then helped to set a trysail and saw him off. I believe they might have stayed otherwise. Miss Spring Rice and I then lunched with some friends at Howth and went into Dublin by train. I did not hear that anything serious had happened till on the steamer. The Childers' are now in town. The military seem to have behaved very badly.

34. An eye-witness at Howth

The Lady of the Yawl.
From *The Times,* London, 27 July 1914, p. 10.

A Dublin lady who is staying at Howth for a holiday gave a vivid story of the unloading of the yawl, which she witnessed from beginning to end.

'I was on the head of the East Pier about noon,' said this lady, 'when I noticed a white-painted yawl of at least 50 tons, smartly kept, and steered by a lady. The yawl at first took up moorings in the mouth of the harbour. She had on board an unusual number of men, many of whom were obviously not professional sailors.[55] A stiff westerly wind was

---

54 Mrs Erskine Childers has a marginal note in her copy of Gordon Shephard's Memoirs, 'He was the only one present who provided help in our mooring alongside the high quay.'

55 There were three men and two women on board—*Ed.*

blowing, and surprise was occasioned among the few people on the pier when the yawl was loosed from her moorings at about twenty minutes to one and approached the head of the pier. Someone on the yawl asked the few men on the pier-head to make fast a cable, and the yawl was hauled up, with her broadside next the end of the pier.

Turning round at that moment I saw at least a couple of hundred men running for all they were worth towards the pier from the direction of the railway station, while three or four hundred ran to the head of the pier. Some of them formed a solid phalanx at the bottom of the pier. Some of the men were in uniform, some had only badges, but all of them carried long oak life-preservers, and their officers carried revolvers in their hands. The majority of the men seemed to have come from Dublin. While they were running up the pier the hatches of the yawl were opened. Some of the men from the pier jumped down, and handed up to their comrades Lee-Enfield rifles of recent pattern, wrapped in straw.[56] As each man received a rifle he stripped off the straw. There were many more rifles than men, and a large number of rifles and boxes of ammunition were taken away in taxi-cabs and private motor 'cars. About fifty boy Sea Scouts were helping in the work, and took away boxes of ammunition on their patrol carts.[57]

A small machine gun, with wheels, was also taken off the yawl, but it was so well wrapped up that I could not see what it was like.[58] About twenty minutes after the hatches had been lifted three coastguards in a boat approached the yawl, but went away in response to a warning from the men on board.

Very few people realised what was happening under their very eyes. It was evident that every man knew exactly what he had to do, and all

56 The rifles were old-fashioned Mausers—*Ed.*

57 These were Fianna Boy Scouts—*Ed.*

58 There was no machine gun; but see above, p. 96—*Ed.*

the operations were carried out with marvellous rapidity and precision. A very remarkable feature was that the whole affair was conducted almost in silence, very few orders being given. There was no hesitation or delay, but there was no hurry or confusion. When the yawl was unloaded the men were addressed by an officer and gave cheers, holding up their headgear on the muzzles of the rifles. All the men then marched off in the direction of the station. Twenty minutes afterwards—that is to say about ten minutes past two—an attempt was made to raise the mainsail of the yawl, but it was found to be unfit for use, owing to a rent in one corner. The men took off the sail and bent on a try-sail, which they hoisted, and the yawl sailed off between the Kish Lightship and Lambay Island.

During the whole proceedings I was, with another lady and our escort, kept "under arrest" by two men, who treated us courteously and apologized for the necessity of detaining us, while the officers also expressed apologies for the course they had taken. We were about to get into a motor boat when the men appeared, and they kept us in the boat as long as they were there.

The yawl was exceptionally well-found in every way and very smartly kept. There was nothing to suggest that she was of foreign or American ownership, or that those on board were foreigners. The lady at the wheel, who took the yawl out again, was young rather than old, of fresh complexion and pleasant expression. She wore yellow oilskins and a sou'-wester, as it was blowing fresh, with heavy showers, and she handled the boat well. There was no hurry about the departure at all. At the present moment I imagine that I must have dreamt it all.

35. The guns are safe
Seán Mac Diarmada to John Daly of Limerick.[59]

59 John Daly was the well-known Fenian, who in 1882 swore Tom Clarke into the I.R.B. Daly and Clarke were later fellow-prisoners in Chatham Jail, England. Daly was released in 1896 after twelve and a half years' imprisonment, and was elected mayor of Limerick. Tom Clarke after his release married Kathleen Daly, niece of John. Daly died on 30 June 1916. Ned Daly was nephew of John Daly, and brother in law of Tom Clarke. During the Rising he was in charge of the Volunteers in the Four Courts' area, and was executed on 4 May 1916—*Ed*.

From Le Roux, *Life of Tom Clarke* (Dublin: 1936), pp. 141-2.

77 Amiens Street, Dublin. 26 July 1914

Here I am at above address. Mrs C[larke] is getting tea for Tom and myself, so I give you a line on things up to the present. Just a very rough outline—that's all I can give you yet.

About 1,600 rifles were landed all right at Howth. The men marched into Clontarf, but the authorities prepared in the meantime and special trams were chartered to bring out military and police.

Tom and myself were down on scout duty, so we got our taxi out and met them. Some of them felt all was safe, that no attack would be made, but it was clear to us that they would not be allowed to march on to town. The military and police had taken up their position, and our men had no chance, so we got on the job later, with the result that practically all the rifles have been saved. There was very little real fight so far as I know at present. There were only a few shots fired. We are only just getting the news ourselves, and this is just to let you know that the principal part of the cargo is safe, as probably the papers to-morrow will say that all have been seized. We have a good deal of work before us to-night, yet—getting some of them removed to safer places, etc.

The crowds in the streets have been charged several times by the military. It will do good and all is well. This ought to open the eyes of the fools as to what Liberal Government is.

Pardon this line, the tea is ready, and here it is.

Your friend,

Seán Mac Diarmada.

P.S.—All this is safe. A pretty good supply. Our friend Fahy had charge of that.

I am glad to say that Ned [Daly] acted all the part of a man all day.

36. With the I.R.B. at Howth and Kilcoole

By Harry Nicholls[60]

From *The Irish Times,* Saturday, July 29, 1961, p. 5.

THE FIRST SUMMONS TO KILCOOLE

One afternoon in July, 1914, when I called in to Seán MacDiarmada's office in D'Olier street, he asked me if I would be available on the Saturday. When I said I would, he told me that he wanted me to attend at the Catholic Club, Great Brunswick (now Pearse) street on Saturday afternoon, 25th, at three, and that the job would take most of the night. Having ascertained that it was not essential to know more, I duly turned up on Saturday afternoon and found that about 20 or 30 had gathered there, nearly all of whom I knew. When the number had been checked, we drove away in a charabanc and finally pulled up in the Rocky Valley. We were then told that there had been a hitch in the plans and the operation was off. To avoid rousing any suspicion, we spent two or three hours around the valley and then drove back and got off at the corner of Leeson street and St. Stephen's Green at nearly seven o'clock.

This was rather awkward for me because when I was leaving home, knowing there was a Volunteer mobilisation for Sunday, I had told my people I would not be back until late on Sunday. To return on Saturday evening would have involved explanations which might be troublesome. I asked Tom Hunter for his advice, he invited me to spend the night at his place in Dollymount and I gladly accepted.

SUNDAY MORNING AT HOWTH

On the Sunday morning, Tom told me to take the first tram out to Howth and go down the East Pier, where I would see some men I knew. He was going to his battalion at Fairview and he felt it would be hard for me to get across the city to Kimmage, where the 4th Battalion were mobilising.

---

60 For a similar account by another I.R.B. member, Peadar Kearney, see in Séamus de Búrca, *The Soldier's Song: the story of Peadar Kearney,* Dublin 1957, pp. 97-102.

When I got to the East Pier, there was some time to wait before most of the others arrived and then a couple of hours before things began to move. The yacht was sighted making for the mouth of the harbour and almost at the time she entered the harbour, the marching Volunteers appeared along the quay. Our group got busy helping to tie up the boat and to get ready to unload. By the time we were ready to unload, the first company of Volunteers had arrived and we started passing out the rifles to the Volunteers and as each company was armed, it was moved back and gave way to the next. The whole operation worked very smoothly and in a short time all the Volunteers were armed. Boxes of ammunition were carried in hand-carts manned by the Fianna. I fell in with my battalion and we started the march back to Dublin. Near Raheny we passed Tom Clarke, who stood and watched the armed men pass. It was a great day for him after his years of work for Irish freedom.

As we came down the Howth Road, we saw the British military drawn up across the road and our column turned right to reach the Malahide Road. However, here again our way was barred and having halted, orders were passed back for the men gradually to get away across the wall into what was then the ground attached to Croydon Park House. The house then belonged to the Transport Workers' Union. Rifles were gathered together and large numbers of the men were sent off by Philipsburgh Avenue.

After discussing things with some others, I suggested that I would take a tram into the city and try to get a taxi to help to get the arms away in safety. This was agreed to and I got a tram to Amiens street, where I went into the North Star Hotel and asked if I might telephone for a taxi to go out to Clontarf. I was told that there wasn't much chance of getting one, as there had been a clash between Volunteers and military out that way. I expressed amazement, but made two or three calls without any result and then returned to Philipsburgh Avenue, where I found that some taxis had been secured, and I helped carrying down the rifles and loading them into the cars. This went on until long after dark and three or four of us, with a couple of rifles each, went home in a taxi. My rifles were kept safely in my bedroom. The next two days were occupied in moving guns and ammunition into places regarded as safe. Many had been left on the Sunday evening in the hands of people who were supporters of the Parliamentary Party, and it was felt risky to leave them there. Monday and Tuesday afternoon and evening, a few of us got orders from the Volunteer offices near the Queen's Theatre and went with them in taxis supplied by Thompson's, whose garage was nearly opposite. These orders, mostly signed by L. J. Kettle, Hon. Sec., were presented to the householders and the rifles or ammunition were taken away to some safe place.

LANDING THE GUNS AT KILCOOLE

The following Saturday, 1 August, I had the same orders as on the other occasion and this time when we got to the Rocky Valley in the charabanc, we wasted a couple of hours and then, in small groups, had tea at one or other of the tea houses near Kilmacanogue and afterwards played cards until dark when we paid our bills and departed, ostensibly for home. However, our destination was Kilcoole and we got off at a gate lodge where there was a long avenue. It was very dark, and we had strict orders to keep quiet and show no lights.

After a wait, which seemed very long, we got word to move down to the beach. Then the work started down on the shingly beach, helping to haul up boats, into the water up to our knees, and then carrying batches of rifles up to the road, where they were loaded into the charabanc. This was quite a strenuous job, on account of the nature of the beach, and we were all glad when it was finished. The charabanc and, I believe, some cars went off and we started to march back, having been told that a lorry would be sent to pick us up. However, we were near Kilmacanogue and it was fully light when a lorry arrived on which we packed and started for town.

As we passed through Little Bray, we saw the charabanc which had broken down and many of the inhabitants of the houses were out and cheered us as we went past. Another step towards arming the Volunteers had been taken.

37. What the Howth gun-running means

Pádraig Pearse to Joe McGarrity, 28 July 1914. Authenticated copy in *Bulmer Hobson Papers*, N.L.I., MS 13162.

Turlough, Rosmuck, Co. Galway.
28th July, 1914.

A Chara Chroídhe,

The successful landing of over 2000 rifles at Howth on Sunday last has to a certain extent changed the situation for the better since I last wrote you. Most of the Dublin Volunteers have now guns; and a large proportion are necessarily in the hands of our friends. There is therefore not quite the same urgent need for haste on your part as there was when I wrote over a week ago.[61] You can do things on a larger scale than I then contemplated, forming your plans carefully, and working to send us as large a consignment as you can of serviceable rifles and ammunition. When our followers in the city are armed we have Dublin County to attend to; and then there is the whole country. The essential thing (and this remains as essential as when I wrote before) is that arms in large quantities should reach us, so that our men are armed. Strong efforts will be made here to prevent arms from getting into the hands of any men who cannot be relied on to obey Redmond: this is what we have to fight against.

The stirring events of Sunday will resound enormously to the advantage

---

61 Pearse was not at Howth for the gun-running and did not know of the scheme in advance. He seems to have learned something of it at a late stage. During that week he had been staying at Rosmuck, with his brother, Willie, and Colm Ó Lochlainn. On Saturday he left unexpectedly for Dublin, with the cryptic remark that 'something big' was on in the city—see Desmond Ryan in *Sunday Press*, 26 July 1964, p. 7.

of the movement. The discipline of the Volunteers was splendid. The soldiers ran before them. There has been nothing like it since 1798. The brutal murders of the unarmed crowd by the soldiers who an hour previously had run from the Volunteers have given public sentiment just that turn that was desirable. The army is an object of odium and derision and the Volunteers are the heroes of the hour. The whole movement, the whole country, has been re-baptized by blood shed for Ireland.

In the meantime, the Redmondites are fastening their grip on the central government. Last Friday's meeting of the Provisional Committee was perfectly disgusting. Two of Redmond's nominees were drunk. We succeeded in getting Seán MacDiarmada and Col. Moore added to the Standing Committee, but to balance that the aim of the movement was to back up Redmond and the Parliamentary Party. I replied by saying that the aim of the movement was to secure and maintain the freedom of Ireland, and that it must be kept open to all who were willing to work and fight for that end whether followers of Redmond or not. There was a good deal of plain talking, and the two parties stand clearly defined. It will be a fight all the way. They have officially decided to send all arms to Ulster—which means to Devlin's followers. We are determined not to acquiesce in this: independently of the Provisional Committee, we must arm our men in every part of Ireland and bid them never to part with their arms. The need, therefore, for you on your side to send arms to us, and not to the Provisional Committee, is evident and urgent. I beg of you to see to it that the arms are sent to the right people.

I write in haste. I am sending Devoy a similar letter. My letters go under cover to a friend in New York. Remember the address that gets me if you have anything confidential to say: 'Miss O'Hara, c/o Miss Byrne, Cullenswood House, Oakley Road, Rathmines, Co. Dublin.'

Praying for successful efforts on your side,

Sincerely yours,

P. H. Pearse.

P.S. I will have a copy of Monday's *Irish Independent* sent you direct, as it has the best account of Sunday's events. Read the description by a Volunteer, and Darrell Figgis's account.[62]

---

62 The reports by a Volunteer and Darrell Figgis in *Irish Independent*, 27 July 1914, p. 6, are inaccurate on several points.

Part V
The Aftermath

Acknowledgements:
I am grateful to the MacNeill family for permission to publish Eoin MacNeill's letter to Roger Casement; to Mrs Joan Fitz Hardinge Berkeley for permission to publish chapter X of her husband's memoirs; and to the *Irish Times* for permission to re-publish a leading article of 27 July 1914.

38. Bloodshed at Bachelor's Walk

SHOT BY TROOPS IN DUBLIN
TERRIBLE SCENES IN THE STREETS
4 DEAD AND MANY WOUNDED
GUN-RUNNING SEQUEL
BAYONET CHARGE AND BULLETS
WOMEN AND CHILDREN VICTIMS

From *The Daily Chronicle* 27 July 1914, p. 1.

Serious trouble has broken out in Dublin.

Four persons have been killed, several others—including a child—are said to be dying, and about 30 others are lying in hospital wounded, as a result of a collision of troops and police with the Irish National Volunteers and a crowd.

There were two conflicts. Both were the outcome of a gun-running exploit by the Irish Volunteers at Howth yesterday morning.

From a private yacht the Nationalists landed, it is said, over 2,500 rifles and 170,000 rounds of ammunition. They cut the telegraph wires and stopped communication with Dublin, which is nine miles away.

Motor-cars awaited the arrival of the yacht in the little harbour, and conveyed the rifles and ammunition to Dublin. They were stopped at Clontarf by the King's Own Scottish Borderers and the police, and some firing occurred. The troops seized a few of the rifles.

When the soldiers and police marched back into Dublin last evening they were followed by a crowd, mostly lads and women, who cheered for Mr Redmond and Home Rule.

Some stones were thrown, and at Bachelor's Walk, near the O'Connell Bridge, the troops turned and fired on the crowd. Three women were among those who fell at the first volley. In Liffey Street the pavement was covered with blood.

In Jervis Street Hospital there are 30 patients suffering from bullet wounds and bayonet thrusts. Many others were slightly injured.

A great many rifles were safely got away by the National Volunteers, and last night many Volunteers and others were carrying rifles in the streets of Dublin.

In Ulster all is quiet.

39. 'The greatest deed in Ireland for 100 years'

Roger Casement to Mrs Stopford Green, 29 July 1914.
In *Stopford Green Papers*, N.L.I., MS 10, 464 (10).

Dear Woman of the Ships!
How can I tell you all I have felt since Sunday! I can never tell you. I was in anguish first—then filled with joy—and now with a resolute pride in you all. We have done what we set out to do! And done it well.

The Irish here are mad with anger but filled with pride, joy and hope. All else is swept aside in these feelings—old J[ohn] D[evoy] says with a glow of joy 'the greatest deed done in Ireland for 100 years'—and keeps on repeating it.

Well, Woman of Three Cows, Agra, you see our plot did not fail, and all we planned went well—and 'Napoleon' too planned well. We have struck a blow for Ireland [which] will echo round the world.

Were it not for the stupendous war cloud, the Press here would be filled [with news of Howth]—as it is, they give much— altho' they are a bad press. A real bad press, uninstructed, fumbling, stupid, and unenlightened on everything but baseball, American finance and politics. Their 'interviews' are ineptitude condensed.

The Irish here would make me into a demi-god if I let them. In Philadelphia they have christened me, a deputation told me, 'Robert Emmet'! They are mad for a Protestant leader. At the Hibernian Convention when I opened the ball and said I was a Protestant they cheered and cheered and cheered until I had to beg them to hear me. And after I had done, a man sprang into the stage box and called for cheers again and again. Then 'priests and people' came round to 'shake' and pledge their support. Redmondism has no real support here at all. It is all bunkum. The 'promises' and money to him are fakes, and the only subscribers who materialize are Shoneen Irish who have made a million or two and want to fit into English Society and find Redmond respectable and 'loyal'.

Oh! Woman of the Stern Unbending Purpose, Autocrat of all Armadas, may your knee never be bowed—may it be strengthened and may the God of Erin put rifles into the arms of Irishmen and teach them to shoot straight. My grief is that I was here, and not on the Howth Road last Sunday—and my blood is hot with wrath when I think of that bayoneting arid bulleting. But God bless you and Mary of the Yacht, and all who helped the noble gift of arms, and those two Irish lads who shipped as hands aboard.

May this bring a new day to Ireland. I see it coming—new hope, new courage on the old old manhood.

Yours devotedly and always,

The Fugitive Knight.

40. What happened at Howth and Bachelor's Walk

Eoin MacNeill to Casement, 15 August 1914.
In *Bulmer Hobson Papers*, N.L.I., MS. 13174(3)

19 Herbert Park, Dublin.15 August 1914.

A Rúaidhrí chroídhe—I got your letter this morning. Pardon my not writing sooner, but I was hoping that friends were keeping you well up in the news, and my hands have been full. Let me supplement what you are likely to have heard about the Howth-Clontarf affair.

In the first place, I feel that our plans had leaked out beforehand, not through any playing false but through the mere leakiness of certain individuals who knew too much. Secondly, I believe that the leakage was so unguarded that the authorities took it for a deliberate game to set them on a wrong tack. The authorities felt all the more foolish when at the last moment they found that the thing was actually coming off in broad daylight in the 'Royal Harbour' of Howth. It was too simple and audacious to be credible till it was known to be true. The chiefs of police thought they would be disgraced if the Volunteer coup came off. I say 'they'. Harrel's action did not stand alone. Sir John Ross 'of Bladensburg', Harrel's chief, resigned immediately when the affair became public. At the sham inquiry recently held by a Royal Commission, Sir John was not implicated in any way. Why then did he resign? Not because he was Harrel's superior. The Under Secretary, Sir James Dougherty, was Ross's superior, and did not resign, though he was implicated. Why did Ross resign? The answer is that the Government is still concealing something and have concealed something very material from their own Royal Commission. The leopard does not change his spots. The Castle is still what we know it to have been.

Harrel formed his plans rapidly in the old Castle spirit. He would teach these Nationalists a lesson. Lest the glory should be shared, he cut himself off from all communication with the Castle authorities, and went straight to the Kildare Street Club. There, in conjunction with General Cuthbert, he planned his great stroke. Harrel was to collect every available policeman. He swept the city of its unduly large police force, and added a contingent of the R.I.C. from the Depot. Cuthbert provided 200 of the King's Own Scottish Borderers. Not knowing where to deliver the attack with all this formidable force, Harrel stationed the military and a strong force of police at the approaches to the city. The rest of the police were sent forward by train and tramway to Howth. The idea clearly was that the main body of police were to take the Volunteers in rear and flank, while the remainder, including the military with fixed bayonets and, as the inquiry showed, with rifles already loaded, were to meet them in front. The plan was murderous enough, and it failed for two reasons: 1, The police for once remembered they were Irishmen. 2, The movement by rail and tramway was late.

Except for the presence of counsel, who watched the case in silence, the I[rish] V[olunteers] took no part in the inquiry. We did not put in a single witness. There were witnesses, including Judge and Figgis, who could have brought the police and military commanders to shame. I absolutely vetoed it. The shame belonged to the whole Castle regime, to the old abomination, the English government of Ireland, and I was determined to let them have it all, and not to help them in their game of making scapegoats (who would be duly compensated later on for their temporary disgrace).

I remained in Howth in great anxiety until the yacht and its gallant crew got safe away. They were delayed for nearly an hour by an accident to the rigging, but such a paralysis had fallen upon British aplomb and presence of mind that during all this time the Royal Harbour Master and the brave old tars who formed the Howth coastguard force, after their first repulse, which took place without a blow, never stirred an inch to interfere with the yacht, though every man of the Volunteers had marched away. If they had tried to interfere, however, I firmly believe that the Howth fishermen, who alone remained in a crowd on the pier, would have been equal to the occasion. An instance of presence of mind did happen, not in the case of any hired defender of the satrapy. The coastguard commander, when he had sufficiently assured himself that he was not dreaming all that went on, rushed to his telephone. The telephone was not working. Now I have inquired and ascertained that there was no interference with the telephone on the part of the Volunteers, and I conclude that some onlooker saw his chance and was not idle. That is not all. The baffled commander ran up the harbour to the Saint Lawrence hotel, which stands at the head of the west pier. Remember that the coastguard station occupies the whole end of this pier, and that between it and the spot where the guns were discharged at the end of the east pier is only a short stonethrow. The 'boots' at the hotel door calmly informed the coastguard that telephone communication at the hotel was cut off, and that the only other telephone in the place was also cut off. The coastguard had to walk all the way to Baldoyle to wake up John Bull by telephone. Meanwhile, the hotel telephone was in perfect order. The 'boots' did his part for Ireland. He told a lie that will not come against him when 'around Patrick on the day of doom the Men of Ireland will come to judgment'.

An acquaintance of mine met the Royal Harbour Master that afternoon. The poor man was in great distress, said Howth was a Royal Harbour, his commission was direct from the Viceroy, it was his duty to collect for the Crown the dues on every cargo that came into Howth. He detailed how he was ordered off his own pier by the Volunteers, and how the police whom he brought to his aid were likewise told to go away. Never never had such things been done in his time before. He never thought it possible, and could not think what the country was coming to.

It seemed hours till the yacht got clear. At last she cast off, and I sent a blessing with her as she flew before a stiff half-gale off into the unknown. Then I mounted a tramcar to follow the Volunteers. Just before I left, the first detachment of Harrel's expeditionary force arrived by train and marched to Howth harbour, to find there only the excited and elated residents and visitors telling each other all they had seen. I overtook the Volunteers at Raheny where they were halted for refreshments. Several detachments of the police passed us going out by tram. Their orders apparently were to go to Howth, and they took care to fulfill these orders, even when they saw the Volunteers marching past them on the way to Dublin. In fact, one detachment of the police, as their car swept past the Volunteer force who were carrying their new rifles, burst out into a cheer. We know what the police have been. They have not been Irishmen because Irishmen have not been Men. As Irishmen recover their manhood, Irish policemen and soldiers recover their nationality.

At Raheny, I found the Volunteers halted on the road. I thought they were inviting trouble by spending their time at the halt and Hobson, at my request, sent them off once more on the march. Still another detachment of police was drawn up at Raheny, and these were chatting amicably with the Volunteers and looking at the rifles. I half anticipated some massing of police, with a view to break up our array. Our one object was to secure the arms, and I felt that a rapid march into Dublin would effect this. As a matter of fact, it was the halt for over half an hour at Raheny that enabled Harrel to intercept the Volunteers outside of the city. Once among the houses he would hardly have dared to do anything to them.

From Raheny I marched with the Volunteers most of the way to Clontarf. The police marched beside us.[63]

Most of the ammunition had already been sent by cars into the city. A small supply however was loaded into a small trek-wagon belonging to

---

63 One incident occurred at this point which, illustrates MacNeill's belief that at least some of the policemen were in sympathy with the Volunteers. Mr John Haughey, now chairman of Córas Tráchtála, then a young civil servant and a Volunteer in C Company of the First Battalion, was marching back in column to Dublin with the unfamiliar Mauser rifle awkwardly on his shoulder. One of the policemen who was marching alongside leaned over to him and said, 'If you hold it this way, sonny, it'll be easier.'—Ed.

the Fianna Scouts, and was guarded by the young lads under Pádraic Ó Riain. They were in the middle of the column. It occurred to me that at some point the police might rush this wagon and capture it, or force us to extremes to defend it. My instructions, both for Howth and a week later for Kilcoole, were to avoid bloodshed, only to use violence if violence of a dangerous kind were offered, to spare life, and as far as possible to meet opposition by enveloping the attacking party closely and smothering any attack with a solid crowd: above all to keep the arms and get them safe. I would not have even one policeman killed if we could gain that object otherwise.

Pádraic's lads were formed up before and behind their wagon. I told him to change the formation and place them on each side of the wagon, so as to guard it from a possible flank attack, the front and rear being sufficiently protected by the Volunteers before and behind. Padraic made this change immediately. It was lucky he did so. The wagon was attacked at Clontarf, not by the enemy, but by the Volunteers rushing for ammunition. The boys defended it, and not a cartridge was loaded up in the rifles that day.

As we neared Clontarf, I came upon Tom Clarke and Seán MacDiarmada in a taxi-cab. I asked them to take me up and go ahead of the Volunteers right into the centre of the city to see if there was any sign of a hostile movement. All the way to Nelson's Pillar there was not a sign. It was then about 4 p.m. I believed that the enterprise was secure. I had an engagement to go North by the 6 p.m. train, so I determined to rush home, spread the good news, get a bite to eat, and return to the train. Tom and Sean went back in their car to report all clear.

At home I sat down to tea, and just then Col. Moore called. I told him all my story. My sister and a cousin reproached me with having kept them in the dark. I told them to go out and take a tram and they might yet see the finish. They went, and the Colonel and I soon followed, he coming with me to discuss business till we neared Amiens Street. The streets were now unusually crowded, and I inferred that the Volunteers had marched through. At Amiens Street we both got down, and parted, I going to the terminus, Col. Moore back towards the Pillar. Just then a lad with bandoleer and belt rushed up to me breathless. I asked him had the Volunteers passed through. He said no, that they had gone into town by a roundabout. 'Run and tell Col. Moore,' said I, 'there he goes up the street.' The lad ran after him. As I went up the steps of the railway station, another Volunteer overtook me. He was excited. 'An tú Eoin Mac Néill?' he said. 'Is mé,' said I. 'What are we to do with the stuff that was left behind?' he said. 'What stuff was left behind?" said I. Then I got what he knew of the story. They had been attacked by soldiers and police at Clontarf. Some were wounded on both sides. Judge was badly wounded. The rifles were saved. "Where are your lot?' I said. "We stored them in Croydon Park." 'Did you leave a guard on them?' He was not certain. 'Get back there at once,' I said, 'and get your rifles under guard. Allow nobody to take them.' Off he went. Croydon Park is the parade ground of the Transport Union.

I had still a few minutes before the train started. For a while, I considered whether I could stay and be of any assistance. I concluded that by that time whatever had happened was decisive one way or another, and I took the train. Next day I was back in Dublin and learned what was not in the papers.

Harrel's forces occupied the Dublin end of the Howth Road. They must have arrived there just after Tom Clarke returned to report all clear. The Volunteers, reaching the opposing force, were ordered to cross to the Malahide Road. Harrel marched his forces across to intercept them. The leading companies demanded ammunition, and there was some disorder. Seeing this, Judge, who was some way distant, ordered his men to march forward and halted them within a few paces of the military who held the road in a solid mass with loaded rifles and fixed bayonets. Judge demanded the name of their commander. Harrel stood forward. Judge said they must be allowed to pass, they were orderly and peaceful and had a right to take the road. Harrel replied 'I must have those rifles.' Judge said 'The rifles are our property and no one has a right to take them from us. We will not give them up.'

Harrel then ordered the military to advance and told his police, who were in great force on each side of the military and behind them, to seize the rifles. The officer in charge of the military asked Harrel's leave to fire. Meanwhile a number of the police absolutely refused to obey Harrel's order. This was a new element in Castle experience, and Harrel's decision failed him. He refused to sanction the order to fire. The police revolt prevented a scene of murder and carnage. The soldiers pressed forward a few paces with the bayonet. The Volunteers clubbed their rifles and stood firm. The soldiers flinched. A few of them, upon a word of encouragement from an officer, began to use their bayonets. Our men went at them with the butts of the rifles. Two or three Volunteers were slightly wounded. Two soldiers were knocked down. Judge got two bayonet thrusts, one in the arm and one in the thigh. He was just about to receive another bayonet in the breast, and would have been killed, when a Volunteer named Spencer, who was beside him, came down on the bayonet with clubbed rifle and smashed it. During this *melée*, about 20 of our rifles were seized. That was the extent of Harrel's battle of Clontarf.

The Volunteers at the front continuing to hold the road, Hobson ordered those behind them to get away with their rifles, which they quickly did. Their movement was screened by two or three ranks of Volunteers across the road, who were probably not one to ten against Harrel's forces, the 'forces of the Crown'. I imagine that the few rifles lost were probably taken by the police force who marched beside the Volunteers from Raheny. Having given his orders, Hobson pressed on to the front and at once challenged Harrel's conduct. Figgis joined in the battle of words. The police and soldiers stood inactive. Hobson and Figgis deliberately prolonged the argument. At last Harrel's wits recovered. He looked around and saw that Volunteers and rifles had got clear away. 'I call that a very mean manoeuvre', was his chagrined remark.

The police and military, under their noble commander who didn't like mean manoeuvres, lingered on at Clontarf not knowing what to do with themselves. They were still there when Col. Moore arrived on the scene at 6 o'clock, and had to stand a fresh lecture from the Colonel. Meanwhile our lads were as resourceful as ever. The first of them who met me at Amiens Street said he was looking for a taxi and could not find one. The reason was, as I learned afterwards, that his comrades had got all the taxis in the town to assist the 'mean manoeuvre', their cycle scouts acting with promptness when the need was seen.

Here we had on the one side a man trained in the military traditions of the Irish police, with an army of police at his command, and 200 British regulars under their officers who had seen active service—all fresh and ready for action, all equipped with deadly weapons. On the other side, 1200 city lads who had been on foot for more than seven hours, under great strain, and had marched 18 miles in that time, besides the work of getting in the rifles, and had not tasted a solid meal that day, who had never before faced a hostile force, and whose leaders and officers were novices in their craft. And between the two, wherever it was a question of courage or coolness or resource, the weary Volunteers, without a cartridge in gun or belt, with the knowledge that a settled government was behind their enemies and the British Empire behind that government, the Volunteers proved themselves superior in every point.

The news from Howth and Clontarf soon got all over Dublin. The King's Own Borderers had to bear the brunt of the disgrace of Chief Harrel and General Cuthbert and the Castle regime. Even at Clontarf, a young girl cried out upon them for cowards and asked the women to line up before their bayonets. Half a mile further towards the city, at the North Strand, a jeering mob collected round them and reminded them of their prowess in South Africa. In Talbot Street they thrice charged the unarmed populace with the bayonet, and still the cry of 'cowards' followed them, all along O'Connell Street to Bachelor's Walk. When they reached the Metal Bridge, they could stand it no longer. Women and children were following them with taunts and jeers. The evidence shows that there was no crowd in front to bar their way. At Liffey Street, their commander halted them. An order was given to 'get ready to fire', this the commander admits. But none of their officers dared to admit the actual order to fire, though it was proved to have been given. The two rear ranks knelt down and fired into the unarmed crowd, several soldiers firing three or four times. Three persons fell dead and about fifty were wounded. The excuse for this was that the soldiers were under a fusilade of stones. For about a mile of the way before the firing began, the streets are paved with setts, and there is not a pebble to be seen anywhere. All the adjoining houses are business houses, and it was a Sunday evening after five when all these houses were closed. From Amiens Street to Liffey Street you could not find a missile of any kind, except orange or banana skins, and these dangerous weapons of contempt were proved to have been flung at the soldiers by children. Not a single soldier was in danger of life or limb. No missile of any kind was afterwards found on the street. An automobile with large glass screen in front and rear passed through the crowd and through the military force just before the firing began. The chauffeur gave evidence. No missile touched the car. An officer and several soldiers testified to blows of stones *on their rifles*, and one soldier exhibited a cut scalp. But those rifles and that scalp had been at the abortive battle of Clontarf the same afternoon, where blows were freely given. Disgrace, then murderous revenge, then perjury organised, were the achievements of the King's Own Borderers on Sunday, July 26th.

Harrel achieved something more. Till then, Dublin Castle was hated. Since then it is openly despised. Of the policemen who refused to attack the Volunteers, two were dismissed.[64] There is no denial that they and many others openly disobeyed orders. Yet the Government has been forced to reinstate the two constables, and Ross of Bladensburg who dismissed them and Harrel who commanded them have been sacked. No such thing ever happened before in the history of the foreign regime in Ireland. For the moment that regime is almost paralysed, and if certain persons can be got to see the real state of affairs, all the king's horses and all the king's men will not set Humpty Dumpty up again. We could have effective self-government in a week without waiting for any enactment.

Last week a Royal Commission sat in Dublin to inquire into the Howth-Clontarf affair. Lord Shaw, an eminent judge, presided. Mrs Green told me that she held him in the highest esteem, but I somewhat astonished her by producing on the spot the clearest documentary proof that Lord Shaw's Commission was a prearranged 'hypocritical sham'. I will give you another proof. Not a word was said at Lord Shaw's inquiry to incriminate Ross of Bladensburg. If Ross was not incriminated, why in the name of the British Providence was he forced to resign? He was not even allowed to give evidence at an inquiry by Royal Commission into the events which had led to his resignation. The whole object of the Royal Commission was to assuage the Irish people and save the face of the British regime.

During the sitting of the Royal Commission the second consignment of arms was landed at Kilcoole, a little south of Bray, and removed safely to Dublin. This time Fitzgibbon was in charge, and the whole plan was carried through with precision. One large motor lorry broke down, at Little Bray, and to remove its contents several cars had to be sent for to

---

64 One of the dismissed policemen, Andrew O'Neill, is still alive and resides at Chapelizod, county Dublin. See his statement in *Irish Press,* 29 July 1961, p.3, and 2 August 1961, p.9. For official evidence on the dismissals see *Royal Commission into the circumstances connected with the landing of arms at Howth,* cit., nos. 1717-1752.

Dublin. Such of the police as came in sight were treated with prolonged and attentive courtesy until the operation was complete.

These arms, as you know, are a mere stopgap, and their importation served mainly to show that the men who built up the Volunteer movement were men of the right sort, possessed of ability and courage and resource sufficient to handle bigger enterprises. They have been subjected to a continuous fire of childish petty jealousy ever since, and not one word has ever been said by their detractors in acknowledgement of their merits. God send Ireland soon the fresh air of freedom. We are stifled and our blood is corrupted in the foul air of this prison, we are reduced to an ignobility that we can hardly bear with or excuse, the worst of all our wrongs. Until we got the arms, our enlarged committee was working fairly together, since then there has been a gradual increase of tension— and no progress made except outside of the committee.

We had warning of the European war, precise and exact, from Berlin about a week before the Austrian ultimatum to Serbia, which was expressly made known to us as the contemplated beginning, [The Home Rule conference was then in sitting, and care was taken to convey the warning to Redmond. Whether this helped to stiffen him and prevent his hand being forced further, I have no information. At all events, the conference broke up almost immediately.]^65

Redmond's statement after the declaration of war from Britain has been a good deal criticised. Still I must say that Grattan at his best would not have gone beyond what Redmond said, had he been faced with a similar situation. In fairness to Redmond it should be remembered (1) that he asserted the free action of Ireland as a national factor, (2) that he made no pretence of an Irish quarrel with Germany, (3) that he spoke of defending Ireland only, and (4) that he invited the Ulster Volunteers to join in common action with the Irish Volunteers. [Our committee at its

---

65 The section in square brackets is marked *Confidential* in MacNeill's letter—*Ed.*

next meeting adopted a carefully worded declaration, for which I take full personal responsibility, inviting the U.V. to join with us in the defence of Ireland. This was passed unanimously.][66]

I followed up the Committee's declaration immediately by offering to establish communications between the I.V. and the U.V., without at that stage committing either side to a definite programme. I went to Belfast where Carson was announced to attend a meeting, to receive the honours of the city. The day before the meeting I wired to Carson, who was still in London, asking him for an appointment. At the same time I wrote him a letter which he was to receive when he was to arrive in Belfast, stating fully the purpose of the interview. The following morning, Carson's visit to Belfast, for which great preparations had been made and loud heraldings in the press, was cancelled on the pretext of important political engagements in London, which engagements were in no way specified and remain a mystery. Carson was to have had a triumphal reception from the Lord Mayor, Corporation, and citizens, in Belfast City Hall at two o'clock that day! Now I fear that Carson is a coward after all, a loud crowing cock on a safe dunghill, a mere politician and unworthy to lead the Orangemen. I will never couple his name with Volunteers again at the risk of the peace. He sent a bare and belated acknowledgement of my telegram, none of my letter. There is great uneasiness among the Volunteers now lest an attempt should be made to hand them over to Government control as an Imperial force. The basis for this suspicion is a conference held between the parliamentary leaders and Lord Kitchener C-in-C, and announced in the Press, and a further Press statement about a plan proposed by the 'Irish Command'. I am reliably informed that Kitchener has no ideas about the I.V. except to tap them for recruits. Carson, by the way, in the Empire's extreme need, has counselled the U.V.F. to stay where they are. I don't think many of the I.V. will desert.

---

66 The section in square brackets is marked *Published* in MacNeill's letter —*Ed.*

Kitchener sent General Sir Brian Mahon to Dublin two days ago.[67]

As I gather, Mahon has no authority to treat with us, and take it that his business is to get recruits. He made no stay in Dublin but went on to Cork where, I hear, the Irish Volunteer committee are refusing to allow a parade to be inspected by him. There is similar news from Killarney. I trust that the I.V. Committee will shortly declare that any effort to induce our men to desert will be regarded as an unfriendly act, and that they endorse an appeal made yesterday by Col. Moore to the men to stay in the I.V.

41. When the news reached Belfast
By George Fitz Hardinge Berkeley.[68]

Chapter X of Berkeley's 'Memoirs', in *Childers Papers*.

In July 1914 I was busy in Belfast, training the Irish Volunteers. My difficulty was that our people had no rifles for their own defence, and that many of them did not know how to use a rifle; in fact as yet they had no striking power; even if arms were supplied to them a good many people would be handling them for the first time. It was then that an event occurred that gave a great stimulus to my Musketry and in fact to the Volunteers in general. I mean the landing of arms at Howth. I

---

67 For General Mahon in Ireland, see Colonel Lewis Comyn and Eoin P. Ó Caoimh in *The Irish Volunteers, 1913-1915*, ed. F. X. Martin, O.S.A., pp. 146-152.

68 George Fitz Hardinge Berkeley (1879-1955), a collateral descendant of the famous Bishop Berkeley, bishop of Cloyne (1734-53); educated at Wellington and Keble College, Oxford. He read history for his degree and played cricket for Oxford University, 1890-3. After some years in business he served with the 3rd battalion of the Worcestershire Regiment, 1898-1901. He was a Liberal in politics, and went to Belfast to act as military instructor to the Irish Volunteers. During the 1914-18 war he served as brigade musketry officer with the cavalry reserve. He was an historian of distinction, best known for his three volume history of the *Risorgimento*, and his history of the Irish battalion in the papal army of 1860. Some of his papers concerning Ireland during the period, 1914-22, are in the National Library of Ireland. He died on 14 November 1955 at Hanwell Castle, Banbury, Oxford—*Ed.*

well remember how the news of that landing reached me. It was the evening on which we were to hold a public meeting of all our supporters in order to raise funds for the Volunteers. I had been preparing my speech and came down at about 7 p.m. for dinner. In the doorway of the hotel were several journalists, and I was just exchanging a few words with them when the representative of the *Daily Chronicle* came running in with an evening paper in his hand, saying in his usual rather melodramatic way: 'It has begun; the troops have fired on the people; it has begun.' Knowing that he was always rather given to heroics, I remained somewhat sceptical until I had actually seen the news. But it seemed to be true enough. The telegrams said that arms had been landed at Howth, that the troops had fired on the people landing them, and that some people had been killed. I forget the exact number of deaths reported, but I remember that the first two telegrams were a good deal exaggerated. The journalists of course were delighted; but to me it came as rather a shock. In the first place it seemed evident that our arms had been seized during their landing; that a fight had ensued, and that some of my friends, at all events, had been killed; and it might of course mean civil strife all over Ireland. It was a very sad evening for me. When I went to the meeting all the other speakers were in great excitement, but I asked them to let me forego my speech. Violent death at that time was an unfamiliar spectre. We looked upon it in an absolutely and entirely different light from that in which we regard it now, since the German War has dulled our sense of the value of life. I was wondering most of that evening whether I had done right in subscribing money to the enterprise. Moreover I was wondering, should the conflagration become general, what in the world I was to do. Here we were, several thousands strong of course, but as yet only very slightly trained, and hardly able to raise a single rifle between us; no bayonets and no ammunition. We had no possible chance of success. In case of emergency it seemed useless even ordering the men to fall-in, seeing that I had no arms to give them. To resist would be waste of time and waste of life; yet I knew that for the sake of honour we should have to make some sort of defence if occasion arose.

While the speeches were in progress I racked my brains to try to provide for every possible outcome of the event. Then I was called upon to speak. So I spoke as shortly, and as sanely as I could. I told them that if occasion arose for our battalions to fight, they would certainly not hang back; but that they would be acting as military units, and that there must be no unauthorized movements; that it was our duty to view the new incident calmly, and turn it to the account of our cause as we should any other incident that occurred. Considering the electric condition of the atmosphere, my rather uninspiring remarks were very kindly received.

Next morning the papers were more cheering: and, oddly enough in Belfast the Orangemen, so far as I could gather, seemed to have taken rather a sympathetic view of the landing. One or two of my people who worked on the Island told me that when they arrived there, they were well received by their Orange work-mates who merely grinned and said: Ye're more in earnest than we thought ye were.' The Ulster Volunteers certainly had no cause for complaint, because on the very day on which people were bayoneted for landing rifles near Dublin, the Orangemen in Belfast were marching down the street, fully armed, in broad daylight, without the slightest let or hindrance— which fact was made plain in the *Daily Mail*, with a view presumably to stirring up anger in Ireland against the British Government.

And now, as the days wore on, I began to receive news of the little white yacht that was steered by the lady. I was so much excited during the first two days, wondering whether my friends would escape, that Mr Campbell actually enquired whether there were some romance in the matter, and whether the lady was my affianced bride. He even offered to pay for a signaller's lamp for the Volunteers, if I would tell him the whole story, and it struck me as ludicrous that the Tories should offer to buy signallers' lamps for the National Volunteers. After the third day I felt that we could safely assume that 'the little white yacht' had got safely away.

At our Volunteer Headquarters they were keenly interested to hear that the arms had been run by friends of mine; and that we could expect at least a portion of the rifles shortly, and perhaps have a chance of making some attempt at defence: and although inwardly I felt that a weak defence was worse than none, I also knew that until we had some arms on parade we should always be regarded as a negligible quantity. Above all, I felt it would be a proud day for the Volunteers when our battalions marched through the streets with rifles over their shoulders, and bayonets by their side; the movement would then have some definite weight in the scale.

'And where is the little boat gone now?' one of our people asked me.

'Oh,' I said, 'the little yacht has slipped away across the waves, and they'll never see her again.'

I suppose the news spread of my entirely vicarious success, for I sprang into immense popularity. On the following Saturday evening when I rode at the head of my battalions, on my noble black steed after our drill, the main street of the Catholic quarter was absolutely crammed with people who had come to see us. Not only were the pavements packed with people, so close that they could not pass each other, but the crowd bulged right out into the roadway, so that there was barely room for our men, marching in fours, to get through; and the windows were full of enthusiastic waving handkerchiefs. For a mile we passed through these thousands who were cheering us deliriously; there certainly must have been thirty or forty thousand people there. I have never seen such enthusiasm. At one point a woman rushed forward and presented me with a bunch of flowers. It seemed profoundly pathetic to see the joy of these poor folk at thinking they were to receive arms. It made me feel how deeply they had felt the shame of being separated from the rest of their native land, without even striking a blow.

These were 'the hewers of wood and drawers of water'; and they had seen a momentary gleam of hope.

From that day out, matters began to move faster. So many recruits came in that it was nearly impossible to keep pace with them: the parade ground and the drill halls would hardly hold them. For about a week we could scarcely cope with the movement, and were obliged to enlarge our organization.

42. Danger and duty

Leading article in *The Irish Times,* 27 July 1914, p. 4.

It is not for us to criticise the conduct of the Nationalist Volunteers in landing a cargo of rifles at Howth yesterday. We cannot fairly blame their almost exact imitation of deeds which we have not condemned in Ulster. The coup was cleverly and boldly made, and the result is that a large number of rifles— estimated variously at 1,200 and 2,500—are now in the hands of the Dublin Volunteers.

The state of our country is desperately critical. The administration is helpless and discredited. Everywhere men are taking the law into their own hands. The nation is divided into two rival armies. Passion runs stern and high. British statesmanship is distracted between the menace of the Irish problem and the imminent fear of European complications. None of us knows what the morrow may bring forth. Anything may happen in Ulster, and yesterday's incidents prove that even the welfare and safety of the capital city of Ireland are trembling in the balance. We hear much of the ideal of self-government. For all intents and purposes Ireland is governing herself today. Her peace and good name are in the hands of her own citizens. On their patriotism, good temper, and common sense depends the question whether the country is, or is not, to emerge from the present terrible crisis without much sorrow and many deep and shameful sufferings.

43. How matters now stand with the Volunteers

Pádraig Pearse to Joe McGarrity, 12 August 1914.
Authenticated copy in *Bulmer Hobson Papers,* N.L.I., MS 13162.

Turlough, Rosmuck, Co. Galway.12th Aug. 1914.

A Chara Chroídhe,

I have come back here after a few busy days in Dublin, and send you the following chronicle of events.

First, to remove some misimpressions which I and others may have given you. I think I told you that the number of guns landed at Howth was 2,500, and Tom Clarke in his cable to 'G. A.' says 2,000. We have both exaggerated, relying on rumour. The actual number was only 900. The number landed at Kilcoole was only 600. This gives 1500 in all. They are 11 mm. Mausers of a rather antiquated pattern, without magazines, and are much inferior to the British service rifle and even to those which Carson's men have. Moreover, the ammunition landed is useless. It consists of *explosive* bullets, which are against the rules of civilized war, and which therefore, we are not serving out to the men.[69]

As to these 1500 rifles, the Provisional Committee insists on sending as many as many as possible to Ulster—which means to Devlin's Hibernians—and unheard of efforts will be made to keep guns out of the hands of men not known to be loyal to Redmond. In fact, the last meeting of the Provisional Committee was largely devoted to a squabble as to who is to get the guns. Redmond's men roundly charged us with attempting to steal them and a sub-Committee was appointed to ascertain the whereabouts of all the guns and send as many as possible north.

Well, the European crisis finds the Irish Volunteers with 1500

---

69 The bullets were not explosive; they were the standard leaden issue, predecessors of the nickel cased bullets which were then coming into vogue—*Ed.*

or (allowing for other small quantities landed) 2000 rifles, and no ammunition. It is obvious that before we can intervene, or even pretend to intervene, in the crisis to any purpose we must have arms. Hence the one great duty of the hour, the duty which overshadows every other duty, is to get guns and ammunition into the country. It is up to the American Committee to act *at once* and on a *large scale*. You are as much alive to the need as I am. Every penny you can command must be expended now and the goods sent to us with as little delay as possible. A supreme moment for Ireland may be at hand. We shall go down to our graves beaten and disgraced men if we are not ready for it.

Publicly, the movement has been committed to loyal support of England: not officially, so far, but by implication. To everyone in Ireland that has any brains it seems either madness or treachery on Redmond's part. His followers on the Provisional Committee passionately resent any suggestion that all is not well. The Provisional Committee at its last meeting took no action either way, but simply leaves it to Redmond to speak and act for the whole movement in this grave crisis, and squelches any attempt even to discuss his action.

Last week the Dublin County Board of the Volunteers made an effort to set things straight. They drew up a resolution for adoption by the battalions expressing readiness to co-operate with Ulster for the defence of Ireland but unwillingness to support the British Government against foreign nations with which Ireland has no quarrel. Three out of five Dublin battalions adopted this unanimously and paraded in front of the Provisional Committee's office during a meeting and sent in spokesmen to convey the resolution to the Committee. The reply of the Provisional Committee was to order the Dublin County Board and all concerned to apologize and promise not to adopt resolutions dealing with matters of policy again, on pain 'of suspension!' In the meantime companies everywhere are adopting resolutions *approving* of Redmond's offer 'of loyal help. In other words, Volunteer bodies are free to pass resolutions supporting Redmond, but not free to pass resolutions or take any action even indirectly disassociating themselves from his offer of loyal help. Redmond's capture of the government of the Volunteers is absolute and complete.

I had hoped that the original members would act together and save the movement from complete capture. That hope has proved vain. All Hibernians and Redmondites (with the honorable exception of Judge) vote with the new members, and steadily vote us down. I personally have ceased to be any use on the Committee. I can never carry a single point. I am now scarcely allowed to speak. The moment I stand up there are cries of 'Put the question', etc.—after the last meeting I had half determined to resign, but have decided to stick on a little longer in the hope of being useful at a later stage.

I blame MacNeill more than anyone. He has the reputation of being 'tactful', but his 'tact' consists in bowing to the will of the Redmondites every time. He never makes a fight except when they assail his personal honour, when he bridles up at once. Perhaps I am wronging him, as I am smarting under the remembrance of what I regard as very unfair treatment of me personally and of all who agreed with me at the last meeting. He is in a very delicate position, and he is weak, hopelessly weak. I knew that all along.

Now it is perfectly clear that whatever is to be done for Ireland in this crisis must be done outside the Provisional Committee. The men are sound, especially in Dublin. We could at any moment, rally the best of them to our support by a *coup d'etat;* and rally the whole country if the *coup d'etat* were successful. But a *coup d'etat* while the men are still unarmed is unthinkable.

The British Government will arm and train us if we come under the War Office and accept the Commander-in-Chief in Ireland as our generalissimo. Detailed plans are already drawn up and have been tentatively submitted. So far, the Provisional Committee is unanimous against it. But if Redmond directs them to submit? Then, I think, the split will come.

I am sending a letter in similar terms to Devoy. Do not use any of this for publication.

Sincerely yours, P. H. Pearse.

My Old Howth Gun

(Air: *Sean Bhean Bhocht*) by Seamus McGallogly[70]

There is sorrow in my heart,
O, my old Howth Gun!
Since we lately had to part,
O, my old Howth Gun!
For in Ireland's day of need
Well you proved a friend indeed,
When you made the bullets speed,
O, my old Howth Gun!

How glorious was your feel,
O, my old Howth Gun!
When you made the Saxon reel,
O, my old Howth Gun!
When the Lancers, trim and neat,
Charging down O'Connell Street,
Had to beat a quick retreat,
O, my old Howth Gun!

But a day will come again,
O, my old Howth Gun!
When I'll join the fighting men,
O, my old Howth Gun!
With some brave, determined band,
Proudly there I'll take my stand
For the freedom of our land,
O, my old Howth Gun!

---

70 Séamus McGallogly (i.e. James Doherty) was one of the Irish in Scotland who came to Dublin for the Rising in 1916.

Index